raphic Information published by the Deutsche albibliothek

eutsche Nationalbibliothek lists this publication in eutsche Nationalbibliografie; detailed bibliographic s available online at http://dnb.d-nb.de.

ary of Congress Cataloging-in-Publication Data

IP catalog record for this book has been applied for at the Library of gress.

Studies on Balkan and Near Eastern Social Sciences
Volume 2

C000027403

Cover image: iStock.com/Zffoto
Cover Design: © Olaf Glöckler, Atelier Platen, Friedberg

ISBN 978-3-631-74727-8 (Print) · E-ISBN 978-3-631-75333-0 (E-PDF)
E-ISBN 978-3-631-75334-7 (EPUB) · E-ISBN 978-3-631-75335-4 (MOBI)
DOI 10.3726/b13866

© Peter Lang GmbH
Internationaler Verlag der Wissenschaften
Berlin 2018
All rights reserved.

Peter Lang – Berlin · Bern · Bruxelles · New York ·
Oxford · Warszawa · Wien

Rasim Yilmaz / Günther

Bibliog
Nation
The D
the D
data i

Libr
A C
Co

Studies on Balkan a
Near Eastern Social Sci

Volume 2

PETER LANG

Foreword

The book *Studies on Balkan and Near Eastern Social Sciences – Volume II* is a collection of research papers on a wide range of social science issues written by researchers from several different universities and institutions.

Mucan Özcan reviews the literature on the relationship between country of origin and country image. İzmir conducts a research regarding the effect of the image of the country of origin on the product evaluation and also the direct and indirect effects of the image of the country of origin on the purchase intention by using Structured Equation Modelling. Topal, Bölükbaş and Bostan scrutinize the relationship between public debt and unemployment growth for the sample including Portugal, Ireland, Italy, Greece and Spain. The study by Yaşar and Yaşar focuses on wealth distribution and its relation to demographic differences.

Beken reviews conceptual and theoretical discussions on the middle-income trap. Kaya and Kutval inspect the reserve option mechanism and the reserve option coefficient. The study of Akyazi and Al aims to investigate the impacts of globalization on monetary policy and central banking. Kaya, Çelenk Kaya and Kaya aim to conduct a situation analysis of public hospitals in the Eastern Black Sea region of Turkey in terms of disaster management. The main focus of Özyurt Kaptanoğlu's study is the marketing of health tourism in Turkey and the world. Oral and Kaya attempt to conceptually study disaster and disaster waste management. Varol Kiliçaslan examines innovation in the health sector. Çelenk Kaya and Ölmezoğlu evaluate the knowledge level of miners regarding occupational health and safety.

The panel study by Koyuncu and Okşak scrutinizes the relationship between religion and female labor force participation. Özen and Saritaş attempt to empirically analyze the impact of religion on corruption. Yalçinkaya Koyuncu and Ünver empirically examine the impact of corruption on labor productivity by using 13 different productivity indicators. Özcan aims to determine the state of renewable energy potential of Turkey. Birinci and Genç evaluate the relationship between fiscal devaluation and foreign trade in Turkey for the period 1985–2014 by Toda and Yamamoto's causality test. Benli empirically studies the asymmetric effect of exchange rates on exports from Turkey to the United States. The study of Akinci empirically examines the relationship between public investment expenditures and private investment expenditures in Turkey. Tuncer, Sağdiç and Yildiz aim to analyze the public expenditure of the central government on the social security and social solidarity services in Turkey from the point of view of the geography of public finance.

The study of Benhür Aktürk conceptually analyzes the concept of ethical leadership. Akdöl attempts to conceptually study leaders as ethical role models for the 21-century business environment. The study of Benhür Aktürk focuses on corporate governance. The study of Topak analyzes sustainability reporting of the chemical industry firms in Turkey.

The study by Özçelik and Sunay focuses on the Sabri F. Ülgener's views on the Ottoman economic mentality and the relationship between the Ottoman economic mentality and the Ottoman economic crises. Boynukara and Karagöz attempt to offer an insight into the primary assumptions and tendencies of postcolonial literature by centering on its preeminent scholars and their theoretical convictions as regards the impacts of colonialism on the colonized people. Uncu and Çalişir investigate the gender of color and the history of color representation of gender.

Contents

Burcu Mucan Özcan

The Relationship between Country of Origin, Consumer Ethnocentrism and Country Image: Literature Review

1 Introduction

Effects of country of origin (COO) on consumers' product choices become a popular topic as international trade grows and the consumers are increasingly faced with a choice between local and non-local (or foreign) brands (Akram et al., 2011: 292; Batra et al., 2000). As a result of the rapid globalisation of production, the definition of COO has become blurred in recent years (Ahmed et al., 2002). Some researchers define COO as the country where corporate headquarters of a company or brand is located (Al-Sulaiti and Baker, 1998: 150). According to Nagashima (1970, 1977) the term "made in …" refers to the product's COO.

Globalisation causes consumers to develop similar tastes across countries, improves consumer desire for global image products and increases similarity in lifestyles across the world (Punyatoya, 2013: 193). The growth of multinational companies and the evaluation of hybrid products with components from many source countries have in many cases blurred the accuracy or validity of "made in …" labels (Al-Sulaiti and Baker, 1998: 150; Baker and Michie, 1995). For example, Samsung Electronics is currently manufacturing 50% of its mobile phones in Vietnam and only 8% of them in Korea (Jin-young, 2015). Another example is Zara fashion retailer, about half its clothes are made in Spain or nearby countries (Berfield and Baigorri, 2013). Thus, consumers have been unable to evaluate the relative importance of the source country and other relevant cues such as brand names in affecting consumer evaluations of products (Han and Terpstra, 1988).

Many researchers have attempted to evaluate how COO affects behaviours of consumers. The COO of a product on its label can influence consumers' perceptions regarding quality of the product (Chryssochoidis et al., 2007: 1519; Bilkey and Nes, 1982) and their purchase decisions (Roth and Diamantopoulos, 2009; Haubl, 1996). The purpose of this study is to examine relationships among COO, consumer ethnocentrism (CE) and country image perceptions by reviewing the literature on COO.

2 Literature review

2.1 Country of origin

The manufacturing location of products and its effect on consumer preferences have long been discussed in the marketing and international business literature under the concept of "country affiliation" (Elliott and Cameron, 1994: 50; Chao, 1989). Several researchers have examined the effect of COO on purchase intentions of consumers (Berry et al., 2015; Wang et al., 2012;Wel et al., 2015; Heslop et al., 2004; Acharya and Elliott, 2001; Lin and Chen, 2006), consumers' overall evaluation of product quality and attitude towards brand (Agrawal and Kamakura, 1999: 55), product evaluation (Ahmed et al., 2002; Kaynak et al., 2000; Katsumata and Song, 2016; Josiassen et al., 2008; Karunaratna and Quester, 2007) and brand perception (Koubaa, 2008; Fetscherin and Toncar, 2009; Magnusson et al., 2011).

According to Bilkey and Nes (1982: 89), both empirical observations and experiments indicate that COO has a considerable influence on the quality perceptions of a product. Most of COO effect studies have focused on high-involvement products (e.g. automobiles and electronics) for which consumers usually look beyond cues such as price or design in making their purchase decision (Ahmed et al., 2004: 103). The study of Kaynak et al. (2000: 1238) reveals that the products that originated from advanced developed countries were perceived to be associated with similar attributes such as good or very good quality, reliability, performance and good workmanship, and the products originating from developing countries of the South were perceived to be less desirable in quality. Kaynak and Kara (2002) found that Turkish consumers had significantly different perceptions of products coming from countries with different levels of socio-economic and technological development. Maheswaran (1994: 362) found that consumers' level of expertise and the strength of attribute information determine influences of COO on product evaluations. Consumers' knowledge about a product's COO has an impact on their subsequent product evaluations (Kaynak and Kara, 2002). Study of Cilingir and Basfirinci (2014) reveals that COO cues have a significant effect on the product evaluation process.

2.2 Consumer ethnocentrism

In 1906, the concept of consumer ethnocentrism was introduced by William G. Sumner (Chryssochoidis et al., 2007: 1519). Several studies have attempted to evaluate CE (Jiménez and Martín, 2014; Zolfagharian and Sun, 2010; Chryssochoidis et al., 2007; Balabanis and Diamantopoulos, 2004; Zolfagharian et al., 2014; Watson and Wright, 2000). CE focuses the loyalty of consumers to products manufactured in their home country (Shimp and Sharma, 1987). Zolfagharian et al. (2014) examined how the COO and CE affect first-generation immigrants. Results indicate that non-ethnocentric immigrants favour the products of economically advanced countries. Ethnocentric immigrants prefer the products of their home and host countries to foreign products, regardless of the economic standing of the foreign country. Chryssochoidis et al. (2007) evaluated the CE and its implications on their evaluation of food products. They found that CE and COO effect are linked together. Cilingir and Basfirinci (2014) suggested some important points regarding the relationship between COO and CE. Their study points out that consumers consider the COO as an indicator of risk reduction and quality. COO also serves as an indicator of one's group identity which is the link between COO and CE concepts.

2.3 Country image and product attributes

Some of the COO studies have examined the link between country images and products. Country images are considered as mental representations of a country's people, products, culture and national symbols (Verlegh and Steenkamp, 1999: 525). The image of countries as origins of products is one of many extrinsic cues, such as price and brand name, that may become part of a product's total image (Laroche et al., 2005). According to Nagashima (1970: 68), the "made in" image is the picture, the reputation, the stereotype that businesspersons and consumers attach to products of a specific country. This image is created by representative products, national characteristics, economic and political background, history and traditions. Souiden et al. (2011) found that compared to country of origin, country's image is a more effective tool in reducing consumers' uncertainty and increasing their aspiration to purchase high-technology products.

Consumers' perceptions of the COO of a product comprise three components: a cognitive component (include consumers' beliefs about the country's industrial development and technological advancement), an affective component (consumers' affective response to the country's people) and a conative component (consumers' desired level of interaction with the manufacturing country) (Laroche et al., 2005). When consumers are unfamiliar with a product, country image may serve as a "halo effect", through which consumers infer product attributes (Ahmed et al., 2002: 282). The halo hypothesis has two theoretical implications. First, consumers make inferences about product quality from country image. Second, country image affects consumer rating of product attributes (Han, 1989: 223). Researchers have revealed that country images have considerable effect on consumers' product evaluations (Wang et al., 2012; Laroche et al., 2005; Han, 1989;

Kaynak and Kara, 2002; Agarwal and Sikri, 1996; Roth and Diamantopoulos, 2009). Laroche et al. (2005: 96) found that when a country's image has a strong affective component, its direct influence on product evaluations is stronger than its influence on product beliefs. Alternatively, when a country's image has a strong cognitive component, its direct influence on product evaluations is smaller than its influence on product beliefs.

Many researchers studied the relationship between COO and product evaluations (Bilkey and Nes, 1982; Maheswaran, 1994; Elliott and Cameron, 1994; Wang et al., 2012; Nagashima, 1970, 1977; Ahmed et al., 2004; Lin and Chen, 2006). These studies suggest that consumers evaluate a product according to information cues (Han and Terpstra, 1988; Elliott and Cameron, 1994; Bilkey and Nes, 1982). Such cues can be analysed under two categories, namely, intrinsic (e.g. taste, design, performance) and extrinsic (e.g. price, brand name, warranties) (Han and Terpstra, 1988: 236). This information is used by consumers to form their preferences and purchase decisions, but it also elicits emotions, feelings, imagery and fantasies (Verlegh and Steenkamp, 1999: 522). COO has considerable effect on product evaluations. For example, consumers recognise that the production of high-quality technical products requires a highly trained and educated workforce. Hence, they perceive that such products are of better quality when produced in developed countries (Verlegh and Steenkamp, 1999: 525). The findings of a study by Maheswaran (1994: 362) suggest that consumers' level of expertise and the strength of attribute information determine the extent to which COO influences product evaluations.

3 Conclusion

The effects of COO on consumers' product choices become a popular topic as international trade grows and the consumers are increasingly faced with a choice between local and non-local (or foreign) brands. COO can affect behaviours of consumers. The COO of a product on its label may influence consumers' perceptions regarding the quality of product they intend to purchase and eventually their purchase decisions. Thus, COO provides consumers with additional information that has both direct and indirect effects on purchase intentions of consumers. Empirical studies indicate that COO of a product affects product evaluations of consumers. COO also affects the product and purchase perceptions. In the literature, the link between COO and country image and the link between COO and country ethnocentrism are also analysed.

References

Acharya, C. and Elliott, G. (2001). "An examination of the effects of 'country-of-design' and 'country-of-assembly' on quality perceptions and purchase intentions". Australasian Marketing Journal, Vol. 9, No. 1, pp. 61–75.

Agarwal, S. and Sikri, S. (1996). "Country image: consumer evaluation of product category extensions". International Marketing Review, Vol. 13, No. 4, pp. 23–39.

Agrawal, J. and Kamakura, W.A. (1999). "Country of origin: a competitive advantage?". International Journal of Research in Marketing, Vol. 16, No. 4, pp. 255–267.

Ahmed, Z.U., Johnson, J.P., Ling, C.P., Fang, T.W. and Hui, A.K. (2002). "Country-of-origin and brand effects on consumers' evaluations of cruise lines". International Marketing Review, Vol. 19, No. 3, pp. 279–302. DOI: 10.1108/02651330210430703.

Ahmed, Z.U., Johnson, J.P., Yang, X., Fatt, C.K., Teng, H.S. and Boon, L.C. (2004). "Does country of origin matter for low-involvement products?". International Marketing Review, Vol. 21, No. 1, pp. 102–120.

Akram, A., Merunka, D. and Akram, M.S. (2011). "Perceived brand globalness in emerging markets and the moderating role of consumer ethnocentrism". International Journal of Emerging Markets, Vol. 6, No. 4, pp. 291–303.

Al-Sulaiti, K.I. and Baker, M.J. (1998). "Country of origin effects: a literature review". Marketing Intelligence & Planning, Vol. 16, No. 3, pp. 150–199.

Balabanis, G. and Diamantopoulos, A. (2004). "Domestic country bias, country of origin effects, and consumer ethnocentrism: a multidimensional unfolding approach". Journal of the Academy of Marketing Science, Vol. 32, No. 1, pp. 80–95.

Baker, M.J. and Michie, J. (1995). "Product country images: perceptions of Asian cars". Working Paper Series No. 95/3, Department of Marketing, University of Strathclyde.

Batra, R., Ramaswamy, V., Alden, D.L., Steenkamp, J.E. and Ramach, S. (2000). "Effects of brand local and nonlocal origin on consumer attitudes in developing countries". Journal of Consumer Psychology, Vol. 9, No. 2, pp. 83–95.

Berfield, S. and Baigorri (2013). Zara's Fast Fashion Edge. www.bloomberg.com http://www.bloomberg.com/bw/articles/2013-11-14/2014-outlook-zaras-fashion-supply-chain-edge (accessed on 17.11.2015).

Berry, C., Mukherjee, A., Burton, S. and Howlett, E. (2015). "A cool effect: the direct and indirect impact of country of origin disclosures on purchase intentions for retail food products". Journal of Retailing, Vol. 19, No. 3, pp. 533–545. http://dx.doi.org/10.1016/j.jretai.2015.04.004.

Bilkey, W.J. and Nes, E. (1982). "Country-of-origin effects on product evaluations". Journal of International Business Studies, Vol. 13, No. 1, pp. 88–89.

Chao, P. (1989). "Impact of country-of-origin dimensions on product quality and design quality perceptions". Journal of Business Research, Vol. 42, No. 1, pp. 1–6.

Chryssochoidis, G., Krystallis, A. and Perreas, P. (2007). "Ethnocentric beliefs and country-of-origin (COO) effect: impact of country, product and product attributes on Greek consumers' evaluation of food products". European Journal of Marketing, Vol. 41, No. 11/12, pp. 1518–1544.

Cilingir, Z. and Basfirinci, C. (2014). "The impact of consumer ethnocentrism, product involvement, and product knowledge on country of origin effects: an empirical analysis on Turkish consumers' product evaluation". Journal of International Consumer Marketing, Vol. 26, No. 4, pp. 284–310. DOI: 10.1080/08961530.2014.916189.

Elliott, G.R. and Cameron, R.C. (1994). "Consumer perception of product quality and the country-of-origin effect". Journal of International Marketing, Vol. 2, No. 2, pp. 49–62.

Fetscherin, M. and Toncar, M. (2009). "Country of origin effect on U.S. consumers' brand personality perception of automobiles from China and India". Multinational Business Review, Vol. 17, No. 2, pp. 111–128.

Han, M. and Terpstra, V. (1988). "Country-of-origin effects for uni-national and bi-national products". Journal of International Business Studies, Vol. 19, No. 2, pp. 235–255.

Han, C.M. (1989, May). "Country image: halo or summary construct?". Journal of Marketing Research, Vol. 26, No. 2, pp. 222–229.

Haubl, G. (1996). "A cross-national investigation of the effects of country of origin and brand name on the evaluation of a new car". International Marketing Review, Vol. 13, No. 5, pp. 76–97. http://dx.doi.org/10.1108/02651339610131405.

Heslop, L.A., Papadopoulos, N., Dowdles, M., Wall, M. and Compeau, D. (2004). "Who controls the purse strings: a study of consumers' and retail buyers' reactions in an America's FTA environment". Journal of Business Research, Vol. 57, No. 10, pp. 1177–1188.

Jiménez, N. and Martín, S.S. (2014). "The mediation of trust in country-of-origin effects across countries". Cross Cultural Management, Vol. 21, No. 2, pp. 150–171.

Jin-young, C. (2015). Samsung Made in Vietnam. www.businesskorea.co.kr http://www.businesskorea.co.kr/news/industry/8785-samsung-made-vietnam-50-samsung-mobile-phones-made-vietnam#sthash.Z4p9yu7J.dpuf (accessed on 21.10.2015).

Josiassen, A., Lukas, B.A. and Whitwell, G.J. (2008). "Country-of-origin contingencies: competing perspectives on product familiarity and product involvement". International Marketing Review, Vol. 25, No. 4, pp. 423–440.

Karunaratna, A.R. and Quester, P.G. (2007). "Influence of cognition on product component country of origin evaluation". Asia Pacific Journal of Marketing and Logistics, Vol. 19, No. 4, pp. 349–362.

Kaynak, E. and Kara, A. (2002). "Consumer perceptions of foreign products: an analysis of product-country images and ethnocentrism". European Journal of Marketing, Vol. 36, No. 7/8, pp. 928–949.

Kaynak, E., Küçükkerimoğlu, O. and Hyder, A.S. (2000). "Consumers' country-of-origin (COO) perceptions of imported products in a homogenous less-developed country". European Journal of Marketing, Vol. 34, No. 9/10, pp. 1221–1241.

Katsumata, S. and Song, J. (2016). "The reciprocal effects of country-of-origin on product evaluation: an empirical examination of four countries". Asia Pacific Journal of Marketing and Logistics, Vol. 28, No. 1, pp. 92–106.

Koubaa, Y. (2008). "Country of origin, brand image perception, and brand image structure". Asia Pacific Journal of Marketing and Logistics, Vol. 20, No. 2, pp. 139–155.

Laroche, M., Papadopoulos, N., Heslop, L.A. and Mourali, M. (2005). "The influence of country image structure on consumer evaluations of foreign products". International Marketing Review, Vol. 22, No. 1, pp. 96–115.

Lin, L-Y. and Chen, C-S. (2006). "The influence of the country-of-origin image, product knowledge and product involvement on consumer purchase decisions: an empirical study of insurance and catering services in Taiwan". Journal of Consumer Marketing, Vol. 23, No. 5, pp. 248–265.

Magnusson, P., Westjohn, S.A. and Zdravkovic, S. (2011). "'What? I thought Samsung was Japanese': accurate or not, perceived country of origin matters". International Marketing Review, Vol. 28, No. 5, pp. 454–472.

Maheswaran, D. (1994, Sep.). "Country of origin as a stereotype: effects of consumer expertise and attribute strength on product evaluations". Journal of Consumer Research, Vol. 21, No. 2, pp. 354–365.

Nagashima, A. (1970). "Comparison of Japanese and US attitudes toward foreign products". Journal of Marketing, Vol. 34, No. 1, pp. 68–74.

Nagashima, A. (1977). "A comparative 'Made in' product image survey among Japanese businessmen". Journal of Marketing, Vol. 41, No. 3, pp. 95–100.

Punyatoya, P. (2013). "Consumer evaluation of brand extension for global and local brands: the moderating role of product similarity". Journal of

International Consumer Marketing, Vol. 25, No. 3, pp. 198–215. DOI: 10.1080/08961530.2013.780857.

Roth, K.P. and Diamantopoulos, A. (2009). "Advancing the country image construct". Journal of Business Research, Vol. 62, No. 7, pp. 726–740. DOI: 10.1016/j.jbusres.2008.05.014.

Shimp, T.A. and Sharma, S. (1987). "Consumer ethnocentrism: construction and validation of the CETSCALE". Journal of Marketing Research, Vol. 24, No. 3, pp. 280–289.

Souiden, N., Pons, F. and Mayrand, E-M. (2011). "Marketing high-tech products in emerging markets: the differential impacts of country image and country-of-origin's image". Journal of Product & Brand Management, Vol. 20, No. 5, pp. 356–367.

Verlegh, P.W.J. and Steenkamp, J.E.M. (1999). "A review and meta-analysis of country-of-origin research". Journal of Economic Psychology, Vol. 20, No. 5, pp. 521–546.

Wang, C.L., Li, D., Barnes, B.R. and Ahn, J. (2012). "Country image, product image and consumer purchase intention: evidence from an emerging economy". International Business Review, Vol. 21, No. 6, pp. 1041–1501.

Watson, J.J. and Wright, K. (2000). "Consumer ethnocentrism and attitudes toward domestic and foreign products". European Journal of Marketing, Vol. 34, No. 9/10, pp. 1149–1166.

Wel, C.A.C., Alam, S.S. and Omar, N.A. (2015). "The effect of ethnocentrism and patriotism on consumer buying intention". Int'l Conference on Business, Marketing & Information System Management (BMISM'15), Nov. 25–26, Paris (France).

Zolfagharian, M., Saldivar, R. and Sun, Q. (2014). "Ethnocentrism and country of origin effects among immigrant consumers". Journal of Consumer Marketing, Vol. 31, No. 1, pp. 68–84.

Zolfagharian, M. and Sun, Q. (2010). "Country of origin, ethnocentrism and bicultural consumers: the case of Mexican Americans". Journal of Consumer Marketing, Vol. 27, No. 4, pp. 345–357.

Onur İzmir

Country of Origin Image and Consumer Knowledge Effects on Product Evaluation and Purchase Intention

1 Introduction

Consumers daily face lots of purchase decisions when they are buying products and services (Baş, Mert and Altunişik, 2016). They rely on some certain elements of the products to make the right decision about which product to buy. Some rely on extrinsic cues such as brand, country of origin (COO), store name, and price, while others take into account intrinsic cues of the intended product such as taste, smell, design, and durability (Wall, Liefeld and Heslop, 1991; Chao, 1998). Consumers are inclined to make inferences regarding a given product depending on the information and experience level that they have with it (Johansson, Douglas and Nonaka, 1985; Han, 1989 and 1990).

There is a well-known positive relationship between price and the quality (Zeithaml Valarie, 1988). COO information also provides consumers with some insight about the quality of the product (Li and Wyer, 1994) as such consumers attribute some certain features to certain countries (Ahmed and d'Astous, 1993; Verlegh and Steenkamp, 1999). Consumers develop stereotypes concerning "made in" labels of the products (Han, 1990 and Ahmed et al., 2004). For instance, Germany is famous for its high-quality and -durability automobiles; Japan is a well-known country in terms of its high-technology products especially in electronics; Italy and France are good at design and fashion and so on. There is also a negative association between some countries and consumer's perception. For example, Chinese products are perceived negatively in terms of quality (Verlegh and Steenkamp, 1999; Kinra, 2006; Kerbouche, Adouka and Belminoun, 2012). As a consequence, consumers' perception about the image of the COO matters in terms of product evaluation and purchase intention to some extent.

According to Verlegh and Steenkamp (1999), COO affects consumers' evaluations by three ways. Consumers are affected by cognitive, affective, and normative elements in product evaluation by relying on the inferences related to COO image. Moreover, Johansson, Douglas and Nonaka (1985) and Han (1989) state that familiarity and expertise are important factors for product evaluation in COO studies.

This study aims to conduct a research regarding the effect of the image of the COO on the product evaluation and also the direct and indirect effects of the image of the COO on the purchase intention by using Structured Equation Modelling (SEM) by Analysis of Moment Structures (AMOS) 20.0. The COO effects on high product involvement categories are examined by analyzing Renault and Peugeot brands in the French automobile industry.

2 Literature analysis and hypotheses

Nagashima (1970) asserts that the COO is a set of features attributed to a certain country. Consumers have a tendency to place positive or negative reputations and stereotypes to a given country based on their belief and perception. In the literature, the COO is addressed at three levels; namely, the production of origin (Hamzaoui Essoussi and Merunka, 2007 and Ahmed and d'Astous, 1993), the design of origin (Chao, 2001), and the brand origin (Verlegh and Steenkamp, 1999).

COO affects consumers' evaluations at three levels, which are cognitive, affective, and normative. Quality perception is a cognitive process of COO (Verlegh and Steenkamp, 1999). Consumers infer quality of the products relying on the COO information whereby the consumer has an ingrained notion that if the imported country is developed and technically advanced, so shall be the products (Li and Wyer, 1994; Li and Monroe, 1992). Consumers might also have emotional connections and symbolic associations with the origin of the products. French or Italian cloths preference of an individual who desires to be perceived as fashionable might be an example of this (Fournier, 1998; Askegaard and Ger, 1998; Verlegh and Steenkamp, 1999). Sometimes, relevant to the ethnocentrism level, consumers would like to purchase domestic product owing to the reasons like pride, patriotism, or willingness to support the state economy, which is called as a normative behavior (Shimp and Sharma, 1987; Han, 1989).

Country or origin is an extrinsic cue of a product such as brand, price, and warranty (Parvin and Chowdhury, 2006). In accordance with the suggestions of Johansson, Douglas and Nonaka (1985); Wall, Liefeld and Heslop (1991), and Chao (1998), COO, as an extrinsic cue, should be dealt with other extrinsic cues like brand and price, and also intrinsic cues like product properties. By this token, knowledge level of consumers is of great importance in terms of product evaluation and purchase intention (Jamal and Goode, 2001).

Familiarity and expertise affect COO image (Johansson, Douglas and Nonaka, 1985; Han, 1989). In this regard, the level of consumers' knowledge is an agent that determines both consumer evaluations and purchase intention (Han 1990; Ahmed et al., 2004).

H1: Consumer knowledge positively and significantly affects the COO image.

H2: Consumer knowledge positively and significantly affects the product evaluation.

H3: Consumer knowledge positively and significantly affects purchase intention.

Consumers' perceived image of COO affects consumers' product evaluations and purchase intention (Verlegh and Steenkamp, 1999). Consumers' evaluations and purchase intention are affected by information level on brand, price, and product specifications. Procurement of information, hence, determines consumers' evaluations and develops behaviors toward products (Johansson, Douglas and Nonaka, 1985; Dodds Monroe and Grewal, 1991; Kotler and Armstrong, 2001:193–201). COO image, showing halo effect, leads to indirect effect on purchase intention (attitudes) mediated by product evaluation (beliefs) (Han, 1989).

H4: COO image positively and significantly affects product evaluations.

H5: COO image positively and significantly affects purchase intention.

H6: Product evaluation positively and significantly affects purchase intention.

H7: Through the mediating effect of product evaluations, COO image indirectly, positively, and significantly affects purchase intention.

3 Methodological approach

Two models of each brand (Peugeot 308 and Renault Megane), which are assumed to be representative of French automobile industry, have been selected for the research. Single-cue studies mainly based on quality perception often cause to a vicious circle that leads to an exaggerated emphasis on the significance of COO (Paswan and Sharma, 2004; Watson and Wright, 2000). Therefore, to successfully identify the real effect of COO, multi-cue studies comprising extrinsic and intrinsic features of a given product must be conducted (Verlegh and Steenkamp, 1999; Peterson and Jolibert, 1995).

3.1 Purpose of the study

The main purpose of this study is to examine the real effect of COO image on product evaluation and purchase intention by a multi-cue approach and also to investigate the effect of consumer knowledge on COO image.

3.2 Research method and sampling procedure

In this research, a high-involvement product like automobiles is selected. Therefore, the level of consumer knowledge in high-involvement studies becomes a determinant factor for both product evaluations and purchase intention. As mentioned in the literature, consumer knowledge is also rendered an essential element for COO image studies (Schaefer, 1997).

Product selection criterion is based on model specifications of the French car brands serving in the Turkish market. In terms of real price information and model specifications such as max speed, horsepower, and average gas consumption, closest models from different French brands in Turkish market were determined. The main reason for selecting Peugeot 308 and Renault Megane is based on click-through rate (CTR) obtained from Google Trends from where the closest CTRs in Turkey among French automobile brands were selected.

In the process of determination of the sample size of the research within the universe, representativeness of the population along with the fact that SEM is to be used in the model test should be considered. According to Hair et al. (2006), in the event that sample size goes higher than 400, model fit indices get weaker, or sample size goes lower than 150, error in the prediction of parameters occurs. Sample size, therefore, is advised to be in an interval between 150 and 400.

In accordance with the calculations of the year 2015 in Turkish Statistical Institution (TUIK) records, the population of Turkey is 78,741,053. Approximately 54 million population is at the age over 18, which consists of the population of the research. Considering a margin of error of 5%, the sample size is to consist of 384 respondents. By this token, considering the difficulties of reaching the data and the use of SEM, the sample size reached to 386 respondents using convenience sampling method.

The research has been conducted in Turkey. Data are gathered through both personal interview and internet survey methods. Questionnaire has been conducted separately for both Peugeot 308 and Renault Megane. Then, the average of the variables derived from both the results of Peugeot 308 and Renault Megane has been used in the structured regression model. Data are improved through SPSS (Statistical Package for Social Science), version 21.0; confirmatory factor analyses (CFA) of latent variables and SEM of the proposed model are conducted through AMOS, version 20.0.

3.3 Research model

The model of the research described in the hypotheses is as follows:

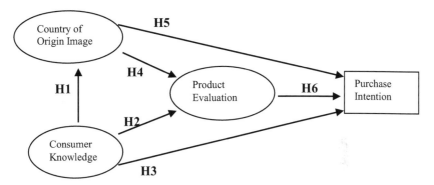

3.4 Scales used in the study

The scales used in the study, which are valid and reliable, have been obtained from the literature. Familiarity scale consists of consumers' experience and information levels, which is obtained from Diamantopoulos, Smith and Grime (2005); consumer knowledge is formed by familiarity and expertise, and the scale is obtained from Mishra, Umesh and Stem (1993); COO image is measured with COISCALE (Knight, Spreng and Yaprak, 2003); product evaluation is measured at three levels, which are cognitive (quality), affective (value), and normative (total utility to both country and the consumer) (Verlegh and Steenkamp, 1999); and purchase intention scale is obtained from Kotler (2003: 135).

COISCALE items used in this model are coded as "People are well-educated (I1); Technical skills of work force are high (I2); Products are unreasonably expensive (3); Country produces highly technical products (I4); Products are made with meticulous workmanship (I5); Products are innovations (I6); Products are distributed worldwide (I7); Advertising of products is informative (I8); Friendly toward the Turkey in international affairs (I9)."

4 Results

Owing to the space limitations, CFA of each latent variable in the model have not been provided separately, yet in Figure 1 all the latent variables are put to CFA under a unified model, instead.

Figure 1: CFA of the latent variables in the model

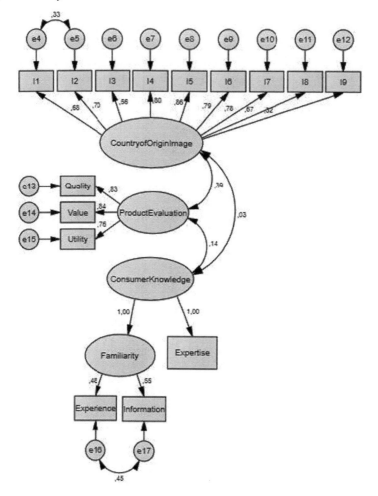

Standardized estimates, and *p* values of latent variables in the model are presented in Table 1.

Table 1: Values of the Latent Variables in the Model

Relationships in the Model			Standardized Estimate Values	*p*
I1	<---	COI	0.684	0.001
I2	<---	COI	0.694	0.001
I3	<---	COI	0.558	0.001
I4	<---	COI	0.803	0.001
I5	<---	COI	0.856	0.001
I6	<---	COI	0.792	0.001
I7	<---	COI	0.785	0.001
I8	<---	COI	0.674	0.001
I9	<---	COI	0.319	0.001
Quality	<---	Product Evaluation	0.831	0.001
Value	<---	Product Evaluation	0.841	0.001
Utility	<---	Product Evaluation	0.764	0.001
Experience	<---	Consumer Knowledge	0.726	0.001
Information	<---	Consumer Knowledge	0.820	0.001
Expertise	<---	Consumer Knowledge	0.671	0.001

Although the estimate, which is also known as factor loading, between COO image scale and item I9 (Friendliness) seems a little low; it is not lower than the suggested minimum value. Other estimate values in the table seem good and significant.

Model fit indices and reliability of the latent variable model are provided in Table 2.

Table 2: Model Fit Indices of Latent Variables

Model Fit Indices	Values	Suggested Values
χ^2/sd	2.336	≤ 5
GFI (Goodness of Fit Index)	0.931	≥ 0.85
AGFI (Adjusted Goodness of Fit Index)	0.903	≥ 0.85
NFI (Normed Fit Index)	0.927	≥ 0.90
IFI (Incremental Fit Index)	0.957	≥ 0.90
CFI (Comparative Fit Index)	0.957	≥ 0.95
RMSEA (Root Mean Square Error of Approximation)	0.059	≤ 0.08
Reliability	$\alpha = 0.868$	

Model fit index values of the latent as well as the reliability (Cronbach α) value of the scale are high. Along with the model fit indices and Cronbach α, there is a great need to mention about Average Variance Extracted (AVE), Composite Reliability (CR), convergent validity, and discriminant validity of the latent variable model before testing the structured regression model.

AVE measures the variance-extracted estimate, which is the outcome of the relationship between the variance derived from a construct (the latent variable model in this study), and the variance based on random measurement errors. Critical value for AVE is determined as 0.50 and over (AVE ≥ 0.50). To meet the convergent validity criterion, CR should be bigger than AVE (CR ≥ AVE) (Hair et al., 2006). In the model where the latent variables are presented is identified that AVE is 0.538 and CR is 0.944, so both the criteria (AVE ≥ 0.50 and CR ≥ AVE) have been met. Therefore, it can be said that convergent validity of the model has been assured.

When it comes to discriminant validity, AVE should be greater than the greatest squared correlation value among the variables in the model. The greatest correlation value in the model is determined between COO image and product evaluation, which is 0.385. The squared correlation value is 0.148 in which case AVE ≥ squared correlation value (0.538 ≥ 0.148) condition is met. Hence, discriminant validity criterion is also met.

Having met the prerequisites of the structured equation modeling, which are discriminant validity, convergent validity, and reliability, the model is presented in Figure 2.

Figure 2: Structured regression test of the proposed model

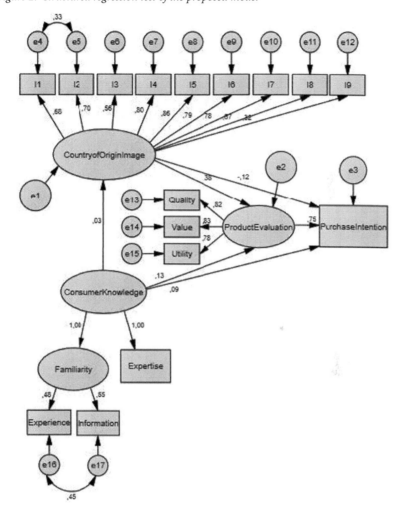

Model fit indices of the structured regression model are presented in Table 3.

Table 3: Model Fit Indices of the Structured Regression Model

Model Fit Indices	Values	Suggested Values
χ^2/sd	2.263	≤5
GFI	0.929	≥0.85
AGFI	0.902	≥0.85
NFI	0.927	≥0.90
IFI	0.958	≥0.90
CFI	0.957	≥0.95
RMSEA	0.057	≤0.08

Hypotheses put forward are tested and standardized estimates, and p values of the structured regression model are presented in Table 4.

Table 4: Hypotheses Test of the Proposed Model

Relationships in the Model			Standardized Estimates	p	Hypothesis
COI	<---	Consumer Knowledge	0.136	0.024	H1-Accept
Product Evaluation	<---	Consumer Knowledge	0.131	0.026	H2-Accept
Purchase Intention	<---	Consumer Knowledge	0.122	0.006	H3-Accept
Product Evaluation	<---	COI	0.369	0.001	H4-Accept
Purchase Intention	<---	COI	−0.130	0.004	H5-Reject
Purchase Intention	<---	Product Evaluation	0.746	0.001	H6-Accept

H1, **H2**, **H3**, **H4**, and **H6** are all accepted, except H5 because although the effect of COO image on purchase intention is significant on 0.01 level, hypothesis 5 suggests positive effect. To check the indirect effect of COI on purchase intention mediated by product evaluation, tests for mediation effect should be conducted. In **Table 5**, standardized total, direct, and indirect effects are presented.

Table 5: Mediation Effect of Product Evaluation on the Relationship Between COI and Purchase Intention

Relationships in the Model			St. Total Effects	St. Direct Effects	St. Indirect Effects
Purchase Intention	<---	COI	0.146*	−0.130*	0.275**

Note: * $p < 0.05$; ** $p < 0.01$

H7 is also accepted, so there is a significant relationship between COO image and purchase intention mediated by product evaluation. Therefore, based on the results of the tests conducted, the proposed model is accepted.

5 Discussion and conclusion

Product evaluation is found to be the strongest predictive variable in the model. This variable also indicates mediation effect between COO image and purchase intention. The effect of COO image on purchase intention is found to be negative and statistically significant, which is contrary to the literature (for example, Ahmed et al., 2004). However, when we use these two variables together in models, the effect of COO image on purchase intention turns to be a positive value. The possible reason of this result is the method used in the study whereby the parameters interact with and affect each other in structured equation modeling, hence sometimes confounding effect may come out due to this interaction among variables.

Product evaluation variable displays greater effect on purchase intention than COO image. Product evaluation variable is also the mediator variable in the model. Thus, product evaluation variable that affects purchase intention both directly and also as a mediator variable might have suppressed the effect of COO image. This is why the positive effect of COO image on purchase intention in the binary analysis is changed to a negative value in the analysis of structured model. Verlegh and Steenkamp (1999) stated that the negative perception of COO image is expected to lead to a negative effect on both product evaluation and purchase intention. However, in this study, the mean value is 4.23 on 7-point Likert scale, so the perception of COO image is not negative but moderate for French products.

The most probable reason why COO effect on purchase intention is negative is thought to be the suppression effect (inconsistent mediation) of product evaluation. Negative direct effect of COO image on purchase intention becomes positive through the mediation of product evaluation. Quality, value, and total utility perceptions of consumers play crucially important role in COO studies. Therefore, to develop purchase intention and to eliminate the negative effects of other possible variables to be used in the further studies, quality, value, and total utility variables should be utilized.

In this study, COO image is determined as the strongest variable in terms of its effect on product evaluation, while product evaluation is determined as the strongest variable in terms of its effect on purchase intention. To have consumers make a positive product evaluation, the emphasis should be made on COO as well as other vital informational cues such as brand, price, and product properties.

The main purpose of all marketing efforts is to establish profitable relationships with consumers and to increase sales. If consumers positively perceive quality, value, and utility of the product, they are expected to be more prone to develop purchase intention. Although the importance of the effect of the COO image on product evaluation is supported (Chao, 2001), the effect of COO image on purchase intention is not always supported by studies in the literature. In light of the findings of this study, firms are advised to use the positive COO image to shape product evaluation; however, firms should also be able to form positive product perceptions of quality, value, and utility to develop purchase intention of consumers.

References

Ahmed, Z. U., Johnson, J. P., Yang, X., Kheng Fatt, C., Sack Teng, H., and Chee Boon, L. (2004). Does country of origin matter for low-involvement products?. *International Marketing Review, 21*(1), 102–120.

Ahmed, A.S. and d'Astous, A. (1993). "Evaluation of Country-Of-Design and Country-Of-Assemble in a Multi-Cue/Multi-National Context", in E – European Advances in Consumer Research Volume 1, eds. W. Fred Van Raaij and Gary J. Bamossy, Provo, UT: Association for Consumer Research, 214–221.

Askegaard, S., and Ger, G. (1998). Product-country images: towards a contextualized approach. In *E-European Advances in Consumer Research, Volume 3*, eds. Basil G. Englis and Anna Olofsson, Provo, UT: Association for Consumer Research, 50–58.

Baş, Y., Mert, K., and Altunışık, R. (2016). Tüketicilerin Farklı Ürün ve Hizmet Kategorilerindeki Bilgi Arama Davranışlarında Etkili Ensurlar ve bir Model Önerisi. *Uluslararası Yönetim İktisat ve İşletme Dergisi, 12*(27), 43–66.

Batra, R., Ramaswamy, V., Alden, D. L., Steenkamp, J.-B. E. M., and Ramachander, S. (2000). Effects of brand local/non-local origin on consumer attitudes in developing countries. *Journal of Consumer Psychology, 9*, 83–95.

Chao, P. (1998). Impact of country-of-origin dimensions on product quality and design quality perceptions. *Journal of Business Research, 42*(1), 1–6.

Chao, P. (2001). The moderating effects of country of assembly, country of parts, and country of design on hybrid product evaluations. *Journal of Advertising*, 30(4), 67–81.

Diamantopoulos, A., Smith, G., and Grime, I. (2005). The impact of brand extensions on brand personality: experimental evidence. *European Journal of Marketing*, 39(1/2), 129–149.

Fournier, S. (1998). Consumers and their brands: developing relationship theory in consumer research. *Journal of Consumer Research*, 24(4), 343–353.

Hair, J. F., Black, W. C., Babin, B. J., Anderson, R. E., and Tatham, R. L. (2006). *Multivariate Data Analysis*. Upper Saddle River, NJ: Pearson Prentice Hall.

Hamzaoui Essoussi, L., and Merunka, D. (2007). Consumers' product evaluations in emerging markets: does country of design, country of manufacture, or brand image matter?. *International Marketing Review*, 24(4), 409–426.

Han, C. M. (1989). Country image: halo or summary construct?. *Journal of Marketing Research*, 26(2), 222.

Han, C. M. (1990). Testing the role of country image in consumer choice behaviour. *European Journal of Marketing*, 24(6), 24–40.

Jamal, A., and Goode, M. (2001). Consumers' product evaluation: a study of the primary evaluative criteria in the precious jewellery market in the UK. *Journal of Consumer Behaviour*, 1(2), 140–155.

Johansson, J. K., Douglas, S. P., and Nonaka, I. (1985). Assessing the impact of country of origin on product evaluations: a new methodological perspective. *Journal of Marketing Research*, 22(4), 388–396.

Kerbouche, M., Adouka, L., Belminoun, A., and Guenouni, H. (2012). The country of origin and the consumer behavior: how to improve Chinese products brands?. *Mediterranean Journal of Social Sciences*, 3, 551–552.

Kinra, N. (2006). The effect of country-of-origin on foreign brand names in the Indian market. *Marketing Intelligence and Planning*, 24(1), 15–30.

Knight, G.A., Spreng, R.A. and Yaprak, A. (2003). Cross-national development and validation of an international business measurement scale: The COISCALE. *International Business Review*, 12(5), 581–599.

Kotler, P. 2003. Marketing Management. Eleventh edition. Upper Saddle River, Pearson Education International, New Jersey.

Kotler, P., and Armstrong, G. (2001). *Principles of Marketing*. Pearson Education Asia. Low price edition, Hong Kong.

Li, W. K., and Monroe, K. B. (1992). The role of country of origin information on buyers' product evaluation: an in-depth interview approach. *Enhancing Knowledge Development*, 3, 274–280.

Li, W. K., and Wyer, R. S. (1994). The role of country of origin in product evaluations: informational and standard-of-comparison effects. *Journal of Consumer Psychology, 3*(2), 187–212.

Mishra, S., Umesh, U. N., and Stem Jr, D. E. (1993). Antecedents of the attraction effect: an information-processing approach. *Journal of Marketing Research, 30*, 331–349.

Nagashima, A. (1970). A comparison of Japanese and US attitudes toward foreign products. *Journal of Marketing, 34*(1), 68–74.

Parvin, N., and Chowdhury, M. H. K. (2006). Consumer evaluations of beautification products: effects of extrinsic cues. *Asian Academy of Management Journal, 11*(2), 89–104.

Paswan, A. K., and Sharma, D. (2004). Brand-country of origin (COO) knowledge and COO image: investigation in an emerging franchise market. *Journal of Product and Brand Management, 13*(3), 144–155.

Peterson, R. A., and Jolibert, A. J. (1995). A meta-analysis of country-of-origin effects. *Journal of International Business Studies, 26*(4), 883–900.

Schaefer, A. (1997). Consumer knowledge and country of origin effects. *European Journal of Marketing, 31*(1), 56–72.

Shimp, T. A., and Sharma, S. (1987). Consumer ethnocentrism: construction and validation of the CETSCALE. *Journal of Marketing Research, 24*(3), 280–289.

Wall, M., Liefeld, J., and Heslop, L. A. (1991). Impact of country-of-origin cues on consumer judgments in multi-cue situations: a covariance analysis. *Journal of the Academy of Marketing Science, 19*(2), 105–113.

Watson, J. J., and Wright, K. (2000). Consumer ethnocentrism and attitudes toward domestic and foreign products. *European Journal of Marketing, 34*(9/10), 1149–1166.

Verlegh, P. W., and Steenkamp, J. B. E. (1999). A review and meta-analysis of country-of-origin research. *Journal of Economic Psychology, 20*(5), 521–546.

Zeithaml Valarie, A. (1988). Consumer perception of price, quality, and value: a means-end model and synthesis of evidence. *Journal of Marketing, 52*(3), 2–22.

M. Hanefi Topal, Mehmet Bölükbaş, and M. Kemal Bostan

The Public Debt and Unemployment Growth Nexus in the PIIGS (Portugal, Ireland, Italy, Greece and Spain) Countries and Turkey: Empirical Evidence

1 Introduction

As in the case of several other country groups, the European Union (EU) countries have faced increasing public debt and unemployment problems following the global financial crisis of 2008. The ratio between public debt and gross domestic product (GDP) rose to 78% in 2009 compared with 65% in 2007, whereas the unemployment was 9.5% in 2009 as opposed to the pre-crisis levels of 7.4% in 2007. Apart from the increases in public debt and unemployment, an alarming upside move in youth unemployment in the EU countries has also been observed. The average youth unemployment rate in the EU, which was about 15%, increased above 21% in 2009 (World Bank, 2016). The distortion in unemployment and youth unemployment are assumed to be related to public debt. Leão (2013) argues that the current low-interest-rate policy of the central banks forces governments with only the fiscal policy option. Therefore, governments tend to increase public expenditure and public debt in order to reduce unemployment.

The economic theory involves many conflicting assertions regarding the influence of fiscal policy instruments (including public debt) on employment. According to Keynes, the increase in unemployment arising out of lack of demand or recession may be prevented by means of the fiscal policies of the state aimed at employment boost. Yilmaz (2012) also emphasizes that public debt may be considered as an efficient policy action to reach full employment level in Keynesian economics. The adverse effects of debt on budget balance and the overall economy are more tolerated as opposed to the resulting production increase and the employment growth. In contrast, Monetarist and New Classical economists have differing policy visions. If elaborated, Monetarist economists—for instance— put forward the argument that the function of the state is to enhance free market economy dynamics rather than to ensure full employment. Monetarists acknowledge that the borrowing by the state to finance public expenditure or to tackle unemployment will create crowding-out effect and punish the private investments and employment. As Gordon (1987) stated, a stable monetary policy should be executed without state intervention and radical economic policies should be avoided. Taking a different approach towards the economic effects of public debt, New Classical economists claim that neither fiscal nor monetary policies are efficient. The approach, predicating that systematic errors will not be repeated, thanks to the rational decisions of rational individuals, emphasizes that active state interventions will disrupt the stability of the existing economic stability. In parallel with the statement by Slavin (2008), New Classical economists rule out all types of fiscal policies whether based on expenditure or public debt, and they claim that policies against inflation or recession will not produce real effects, on the contrary these policies will further destabilize the economy. As opposed to the policy inefficiency thesis of New Classical economics, the New Keynesian economics argues that fiscal and monetary policy practices may be efficient under economic instabilities such as unemployment and inflation. In the words of Heijdra and Ploeg (2002), the New Keynesians contemplate that this assumption may not signify an absolute policy inefficiency, although even the expectations of economic agents are rational. Nevertheless, Snowdon and Vane (2005) highlight that there is no uniform standpoint within New Keynesian economics as to the efficiency of the fiscal policies while reminding that there is some form of compromise on the applicability of activist policies.

When empirical literature on the relationship between public debt and unemployment is considered, the findings seem to endorse Monetarist and New Classical projections as against few studies supporting Keynesian arguments. For instance, in the study of Kurecic and Kokotovic (2016), a linear regression analysis conducted for five of EU15 countries regarding the effect of public debt on unemployment has exposed a statistically significant correlation between the variables. Concurrently, it has been emphasized within the study that there is strong causality between public debt and unemployment; hence, unemployment would rise about 2.7% in the event of a public debt increase similar to the increases in 2012 and 2013 in Portugal, Greece, Ireland and Italy. Another research that would be taken into account is the one conducted by Fedeli and Forte (2012) covering 19 Organisation for Economic Co-operation and Development (OECD) and 13 EU–OECD country groups for the period of 1981–2009. The research, addressing the relationship between public debt and unemployment, has defined fiscal deficit as a negative determinant of unemployment. The study by Korol and Cerkas (2015) focusing on Greece should also be mentioned with its conclusion arguing that a 1% increase in public debt increases unemployment rates by 0.46%. Oganna et al. (2016), on the other hand, have analysed the Nigerian economy between 1980 and 2015 and have asserted that 1% increase in public debt would lead to

1.6% increase in unemployment due to the long-term relationship between the two variables. Last but not least, Jimenez and Mishra (2010) have confirmed the distortionary effect of public debt increases on unemployment via their scholar work on the influence of increasing public debt on labour demand in the United States for the period of 1980–2008. The list of the studies on the relationship between public debt and unemployment may be extended; however, it should be noted that there are numerous valuable works studying the relationship between external debt and unemployment or the effects of fiscal policy instruments other than public debt on unemployment (see Holden and Sparrman, 2011; Ayyoub et al., 2012; Maqbool et al., 2013; Amaral and Lopes, 2015; Bianchi et al., 2015; Richard and Chinedu, 2015; Battaglini and Coate, 2016; Isaev and Masih, 2017).

The literature also contains several researches aiming to predict public debt's effect on unemployment and youth unemployment by adding the latter variable into the econometric model. The study by Kokotovic (2016) may be considered as a pioneer in this respect. The study sample consists of Greece, Croatia and Spain with the highest levels of youth unemployment followed by Germany, Denmark and Czech Republic with the lowest youth unemployment within the EU. The autoregressive distributed lag (ARDL) estimation results indicate that the youth unemployment is affected more by public debt compared with total unemployment in Croatia and Spain. The author has emphasized that new economic measures should be implemented to fight youth unemployment in the EU countries still bearing the destructive effects of the global financial crisis of 2008. Moreover, Sam and Pokhariyel (2016) have analysed the 1979–2012 period in Kenya and have utilized the ARDL estimation method to identify the economic determinants of youth unemployment. The findings have revealed a long-term and significant relationship between youth unemployment and the variables of population increase, foreign direct investments, GDP and public debt. It has also been stated that the positive impact of public debt on youth unemployment is too weak.

The overview of the earlier-mentioned studies reflects that the range of the related research is extensive in terms of their sample and time periods; however, the findings seem to converge in essence. This study analysing the PIIGS (Portugal, Ireland, Italy, Greece and Spain) countries and Turkey for the period of 1990–2015 on the causal relationship between public debt and unemployment (and youth unemployment) has several features that make it unique. The first feature to name is its sample covering different country groups from previous studies. The PIIGS countries have been selected as their recent economic indicators of public debt, unemployment and youth unemployment are generally high. Turkey, with converging high unemployment and youth unemployment rates albeit its relatively low public debt, is also included within the sample. The variables within the econometric model have been selected based on the works of Fedeli and Forte (2012), Oganna et al. (2016), Kurecic and Kokotovic (2016) and Kokotovic (2016). As the econometric method, in contrast, the bootstrap panel causality test proposed by Kónya (2006) allowing for panel heterogeneity and taking cross-sectional dependence into account has been utilized. This method allows the researcher to get individual results for each country and hence facilitates making comparisons between countries. The study also provides separate estimations in terms of public debt's effect on unemployment and youth unemployment. The extent of the change in public debt as a tool of fiscal policy through differing unemployment levels has been monitored as a modest contribution to the literature within this respect. Section 2 elaborates the data and the empirical methodology of the study, whereas Section 3 summarizes the findings. The concluding remarks assess the insights from the empirical analysis.

2 Data and methodology

The analysis of causality between public debt and unemployment – youth unemployment was conducted on PIIGS countries and Turkey through a 26-year period between 1990 and 2015. The reason to specify this time period is the significant rises in the unemployment rates of these countries recently. Within the study, the unemployment rate is defined as *(UN) = the number of the unemployed/active labour*, whereas the youth unemployment rate is *(YUN) = the number of the unemployed between the age of 15 and 24/active labour*; the data on unemployment have been taken from the World Bank's World Development Indicators. The public debt levels of the countries have been computed as *(PDEBT) = total debt stock of public sector/GDP*, whereas the data on public debt have been taken from the World Economic Outlook database of the International Monetary Fund (IMF).

In recent years, the PIIGS countries stand out with higher levels of public debt and unemployment rate (both total and youth). These negative attributes put them apart from the EU member countries. Turkey, on the other side, has strived to deal with high levels of unemployment (even higher levels of youth unemployment), although the public debt levels do not constitute a significant problem with notable downside momentum in recent era. The course of the specified countries' unemployment and public debt indicators is provided in the appendix. Unemployment and youth unemployment are common problems for the six countries. It should also be noted that the local economic crisis of 2001 had distortionary effects on Turkey's unemployment and public debt, while it is evident that the global financial crisis of 2008 had a significant impact on the PIIGS countries. Following the considerable recovery in unemployment levels of the PIIGS countries at the beginning of the 2000s, the unemployment has soared after the global financial crisis of 2008. In the post-crisis era, the deepest recession occurred in Spain and Greece. One in four people is still unemployed in Spain and Greece. What's more, one in two of the young people is unable to get a job. Although the total unemployment rates in the other three countries (Portugal, Ireland and Italy) are not as severe as in the former countries, the youth unemployment is still too high. These insights may also fit the issue of public debt. Only Italy and Greece had high levels of public debt; however, all five countries faced rapid rising in public debt following the crisis. In order to tackle the subsequent recession, these countries increased their public spending to stimulate the total demand; they tended to finance this public expenditure with additional public debt rather than levying more taxes. It has also been observed that these countries—except Ireland—still carry out this high public debt policy. Although we can talk about a mild recovery in these countries for the last couple of years, the impact of the global economic crisis is not over yet. Turkey's situation differs slightly from that of the PIIGS countries. In the relevant period, the most destructive factor on unemployment rates and public debt was the local economic crisis of 2001. The public debt and unemployment levels significantly increased after the crisis; however, the conduct of fiscal discipline and sound management of public finances made lowering the public debt possible. The same achievements couldn't be reached in terms of unemployment. The effect of the global financial crisis of 2008 on public debt and unemployment was negative but temporary. The public debt and unemployment that increased right after the crisis stabilized at their prior levels. In recent years, a renewed upside wave in unemployment levels has been observed despite the decreasing tendency in public debts. The asylum of about 4 million Syrian refugees and the uncertainties caused by internal/external political tensions have weighed significantly on the Turkish economy.

The empirical analysis of the study covers two different panel data models. The panel data model 1 is created to estimate the causality between public debt and unemployment, whereas the panel data model 2 is utilized to do the same for the causality between public debt and youth unemployment. The models are based on the bootstrap panel Granger causality test proposed by Kónya (2006). This test avails several advantages: First, it does not require pretests such as the stationarity and cointegration, and also it relies on a more realistic assumption as it allows for cross-sectional dependence. As the test allows panel heterogeneity, country-based comparisons are possible. The application of the test is two phased. In the first stage, whether cross-sectional dependence and panel heterogeneity are valid for the whole panel is tested. The second stage involves estimation of Granger causality for each country based on the method of seemingly unrelated regression (SUR).

The two basic assumptions of the bootstrap panel Granger causality test by Kónya (2006) are cross-sectional dependence and panel heterogeneity. Thus, they should be tested as the first step of the causality test. Cross-sectional dependence signifies whether the cross sections are correlated or not. If the countries are affected by the common factors, this is expected. As the dependence among the countries is high in today's world, it is of high probability that a shock regarding public debt or unemployment within a country will affect other countries as well. The estimation not taking cross-sectional dependence into account will be biased and inconsistent (Pesaran, 2004). In order to set cross-sectional dependence, Breusch and Pagan (1980) proposed Lagrange multiplier (LM) test statistic that provides the asymptotic Chi-square distribution with $N(N-1)/2$ degrees of freedom as shown in Equation (1):

$$LM_1 = T\sum_{i=1}^{N-1}\sum_{j=i+1}^{N} \hat{\rho}_{ij}^2 \ (1)$$

Within the LM test, the null hypothesis states that there is no cross-sectional dependence $(H_0 = cov(u_{it}, u_{jt}) = 0$ for all t and $i \neq t)$, whereas the alternative hypothesis is constructed as there is cross-sectional dependence for at least one pair $(H_1 = cov(u_{it}, u_{jt}) \neq 0$ for at least *one pair of* $i \neq t)$. $\hat{\rho}_{ij}$ is the pair-wise correlation coefficient of the residuals of ordinary least square (OLS) estimations for each i. The LM statistic is used to test cross-sectional dependence when $T \to \infty$ and N is constant, i.e. $T > N$. However, when N is high, the power of the LM statistic is limited. In order to tackle this issue, Pesaran (2004) suggested two different tests that display asymptotic standard normal distribution: LM_2 for $T \to \infty$ and $N \to \infty$ $(T > N)$, and CD (Cross-sectional Dependence) for cases in which N is high and T is relatively low, i.e. $N > T$. These test statistics are stated as indicated in Equations (2) and (3).

$$LM_2 = \left(\frac{1}{N(N-1)}\right)^{1/2} \sum_{i=1}^{N-1}\sum_{j=i+1}^{N} T\hat{\rho}_{ij}^2 - 1 \ (2)$$

$$CD = \left(\frac{2T}{N(N-1)}\right)^{1/2} \sum_{i=1}^{N-1}\sum_{j=i+1}^{N} \hat{\rho}_{ij} \ (3)$$

In cases where the group mean is zero as against the individual means being less/more than zero, LM_2 and CD tests fail in rejecting the null hypothesis that there is no cross-sectional dependence. To overcome this issue, Pesaran et al. (2008)—by utilizing the mean and the variance of the LM statistic—suggested bias-adjusted LM statistic with asymptotic standard normal distribution for cases in which $T \to \infty$ and $N \to \infty$. The bias-adjusted LM statistic is expressed in Equation (4). μ_{Tij} and are v_{Tij}^2, respectively, the mean and the variance of $(T-k)\hat{\rho}_{ij}^2$ as suggested by Pesaran et al. (2008):

$$LM_{adj} = \sqrt{\left(\frac{2T}{N(N-1)}\right)} \sum_{i=1}^{N-1} \sum_{j=i+1}^{N} \hat{\rho}_{ij} \frac{(T-k)\hat{\rho}_{ij}^2 - \mu_{Tij}}{\sqrt{v_{Tij}^2}} \quad (4)$$

Another assumption in the bootstrap panel Granger causality test proposed by Kónya (2006) is the heterogeneity of slope coefficients. In order to test this assumption, Swamy (1970) proposed Swamy slope homogeneity statistic. It should be highlighted, however, that this test is only efficient when $T > N$. Recently, Pesaran and Yamagata (2008) have put forth a different standardized version of Swamy's test that facilitates applicability to larger panels. Denoted as $\tilde{\Delta}$, the first step is to calculate the modified Swamy $(\tilde{S})$ statistic as illustrated in Equation (5):

$$\tilde{S} = \sum_{i=1}^{N} \left(\hat{\beta}_i - \hat{\beta}_{WFE}\right)' \frac{x_i' M_\tau x_i}{\tilde{\sigma}_i^2} \left(\hat{\beta}_i - \hat{\beta}_{WFE}\right) \quad (5)$$

Within the equation, $\hat{\beta}_i$ is the pooled OLS estimator, $\hat{\beta}_{WFE}$ weighted and fixed effect pooled estimator, M_τ the identity matrix and $\tilde{\sigma}_i^2$ the estimator of σ_i^2. As the next step, the standardized version of Swamy's statistic with asymptotic normal distribution is generated as in Equation (6):

$$\tilde{\Delta} = \sqrt{N} \left(\frac{N^{-1}\tilde{S} - k}{\sqrt{2k}}\right) \quad (6)$$

On the condition of $\sqrt{N}/T \to \infty$, the null hypothesis that slope coefficients are homogeneous when $(N,T) \to \infty$ $(H_0 : \beta_i = \beta; \text{ for all } i)$ is tested against the alternative hypothesis that slope coefficients are heterogeneous $(H_1 : \beta_i = \beta_j; \text{ for } i \neq j)$. Besides, Pesaran et al. (2008) suggested bias-adjusted $\tilde{\Delta}_{adj}$ test that is applicable for small samples and whose error terms are distributed normally as shown in Equation (7):

$$\tilde{\Delta}_{adj} = \sqrt{N} \left(\frac{N^{-1}\tilde{S} - E(\tilde{z}_{it})}{\sqrt{var(\tilde{z}_{it})}}\right) \quad (7)$$

In the second stage of the bootstrap panel Granger causality test proposed by Kónya (2006), Wald test statistics and bootstrap critical values are computed by means of SUR system estimation developed by Zellner (1962). As the critical values of cross sections are obtained by bootstrap, the series are handled with their initial values and the stationarity test on cross sections is not required. It is assumed through the analysis of the system that each equation has predetermined different variables and error terms that are correlated with each other. Wald test is also applied to examine the causality. The forecasted two sets of equations based on SUR system may be expressed as in Equations (8) and (9):

$$Y_{1,t} = \alpha_{1,1} + \sum_{j=1}^{ly_1} \beta_{1,1,j} Y_{1,t-j} + \sum_{j=1}^{lx_1} \gamma_{1,1,j} X_{1,t-j} + \varepsilon_{1,1,t}$$

$$Y_{2,t} = \alpha_{1,2} + \sum_{j=1}^{ly_2} \beta_{1,2,j} Y_{2,t-j} + \sum_{j=1}^{lx_2} \gamma_{1,2,j} X_{2,t-j} + \varepsilon_{1,2,t} \quad (8)$$

$$\vdots$$

$$Y_{N,t} = \alpha_{1,N} + \sum_{j=1}^{ly_N} \beta_{1,N,j} Y_{N,t-j} + \sum_{j=1}^{lx_N} \gamma_{1,N,j} X_{N,t-j} + \varepsilon_{1,N,t}$$

and

$$X_{1,t} = \alpha_{2,1} + \sum_{j=1}^{lx_1} \beta_{21,j} Y_{1,t-j} + \sum_{j=1}^{ly_1} \gamma_{2,1,j} X_{1,t-j} + \varepsilon_{2,1,t}$$

$$X_{2,t} = \alpha_{2,2} + \sum_{j=1}^{lx_2} \beta_{2,2,j} Y_{2,t-j} + \sum_{j=1}^{ly_2} \gamma_{2,2,j} X_{2,t-j} + \varepsilon_{2,2,t} \quad (9)$$

$$\vdots$$

$$X_{N,t} = \alpha_{2,N} + \sum_{j=1}^{lx_N} \beta_{2,N,j} Y_{N,t-j} + \sum_{j=1}^{ly_N} \gamma_{2,N,j} X_{N,t-j} + \varepsilon_{2,N,t}$$

Within the equations, Y is unemployment (and youth unemployment) rates, X public debt, N the number of countries t the time period, whereas α, β and γ are common factors and ε is the disturbance. The maximum lag length is denoted as l. The variation in lag length is allowed in equation systems; nevertheless, it is assumed that it does not vary by cross sections. The maximum lag length is set as 4, and the appropriate lag lengths for the systems have been determined according to Akaike information criterion (AIC) and Schwarz information criterion (SIC).

The estimation results may bring forth four different types of Granger causality (Kónya, 2006: 981):

1. Unidirectional Granger causality exists from X to Y when and $\gamma_{1,i} \neq 0$ and $\beta_{2,i} = 0$ for each i.
2. Unidirectional Granger causality exists from Y to X when and $\gamma_{1,i} = 0$ and $\beta_{2,i} \neq 0$ for each i.
3. Bidirectional Granger causality exists between X and Y if $\gamma_{1,i} \neq 0$ and $\beta_{2,i} \neq 0$ for each i.
4. Granger causality does not exist between X and Y if $\gamma_{1,i} = 0$ and $\beta_{2,i} = 0$ for each i.

3 Findings

The cross-sectional dependence and slope homogeneity test estimation results are reported in Table 1. Keeping in mind that in this study $T (=26) > N (=6)$ and CD test is more efficient when $N > T$, the cross-sectional dependence tests indicate that the null hypothesis of no cross-sectional dependence for the models is rejected according to the common results of three test statistics (CD_{LM1}, CD_{LM2} and LM_{adj}). Similarly, the null hypothesis of no cross-sectional dependence for unemployment (UN) and youth unemployment (YUN) are rejected based on all test statistics. Except the CD test statistics, all other test statistics exhibit the rejection of null hypothesis regarding the public debt series. Accordingly, it can be argued that cross-sectional dependence exists within the $PDEBT$ series. These findings suggest the public debt and unemployment shocks in the PIIGS countries and Turkey also affect other countries. According to the slope homogeneity test results, the null hypothesis that assumes the homogeneity of slope coefficients is rejected at 1% and 5% significance levels for the models 1 and 2, respectively. This finding infers that the causality between public debt and unemployment – youth unemployment may differ as of countries. What's more, the assumptions of the bootstrap panel Granger causality test proposed by Kónya (2006) are valid as cross-sectional dependence and panel heterogeneity are detected within the panel.

Table 1: Cross-sectional Dependence and Slope Homogeneity Test Results

Method	Model 1		Model 2		UN		YUN		PDEBT	
	Stats	Prob	Stats	Prob	Stats	Prob	Stats	Prob	Stats	Prob
Cross-sectional dependence										
LM$_1$	26.03**	0.038	79.62***	0.000	33.96**	0.003	67.26***	0.000	47.94***	0.000
LM$_2$	2.01**	0.022	11.79***	0.000	3.46***	0.000	9.54***	0.000	6.01***	0.000
CD	−2.77**	0.003	−0.532	0.297	−3.29***	0.000	−3.11***	0.000	−0.521	0.301
LM$_{adj}$	24.93***	0.000	16.19***	0.000	9.54***	0.000	19.80***	0.000	20.45***	0.000
Slope homogeneity										
$\tilde{\Delta}$	3.189***	0.000	2.222**	0.013						
$\tilde{\Delta}_{adj}$	4.200***	0.000	2.368**	0.009						

Notes: ***, **, and * denote the significance at 0.10, 0.05 and 0.01 levels, respectively. EC: estimated coefficients; Prob: probability; Stats: statistics.

The results of the bootstrap panel Granger causality test proposed by Kónya (2006) are reported in Table 2. According to the test results, there is no causality between public debt and unemployment (and youth unemployment) in Portugal. It may be inferred that there is unidirectional causality from public debt to unemployment and youth unemployment in Italy and Greece, whereas the direction of the causality is reversed (from unemployment and youth unemployment to public debt) in Ireland and Spain. It is also inferred that bidirectional causality exists between public debt and unemployment – youth unemployment in Turkey. When the estimated coefficients for the period of 1990–2015 in countries with statistically significant causal relationships are considered, public debt increased the unemployment and youth unemployment in Italy and Greece; in contrast, unemployment and youth unemployment led to an increase in public debt in Ireland and Spain. As of Turkey, public debt and unemployment – youth unemployment had reciprocal upside impact. The comparison of the coefficients shows the fact that the youth-unemployment-increasing effect of public debt is relatively higher in Italy, Greece and Turkey, whereas debt-increasing effect of total unemployment is again relatively higher in Spain and Turkey.

Table 2: Bootstrap Panel Granger Causality Test Results

Country	H_0: PDEBT ↛ UN				H_0: UN ↛ PDEBT				Results
	Wald Statistics[EC]	Bootstrap Critical Values			Wald Statistics[EC]	Bootstrap Critical Values			
		10%	5%	1%		10%	5%	1%	
Portugal	0.145	7.53	10.89	19.94	0.173	8.09	11.60	19.95	PDebt ↮ UN
Ireland	3.526	7.51	10.61	18.39	12.242** [2.00]	6.67	9.64	16.95	PDebt ← UN
Italy	8.922** [0.047]	5.31	7.86	15.10	0.058	4.74	7.02	12.61	PDebt → UN
Greece	16.052** [0.071]	9.03	12.96	22.41	0.093	5.19	7.76	15.58	PDebt → UN
Spain	2.642	5.69	8.30	16.45	13.795*** [0.59]	4.15	5.97	10.82	PDebt ← UN
Turkey	7.060* [0.033]	6.53	9.58	17.70	18.738*** [3.36]	6.14	9.18	17.48	PDebt ↔ UN

Country	H_0: PDEBT ↛ YUN				H_0: YUN ↛ PDEBT				Results
	Wald Statistics[EC]	Bootstrap Critical Values			Wald Statistics[EC]	Bootstrap Critical Values			
		10%	5%	1%		10%	5%	1%	
Portugal	2.749	8.05	12.36	22.65	0.127	7.51	10.85	20.54	PDebt ↮ YUN
Ireland	4.197	7.09	10.38	18.32	23.172*** [2.03]	6.06	8.95	15.87	PDebt ← YUN
Italy	12.277** [0.183]	4.94	7.20	15.31	1.146	4.63	6.79	12.76	PDebt → YUN
Greece	10.742* [0.116]	8.68	12.72	23.42	0.152	4.65	7.15	14.70	PDebt → YUN
Spain	3.212	5.51	8.25	15.28	14.115*** [0.35]	4.14	5.95	11.06	PDebt ← YUN
Turkey	6.963* [0.056]	5.74	8.45	15.73	12.034** [2.08]	5.52	8.19	15.04	PDebt ↔ YUN

Notes: ***, **, and * denote the significance at 0.10, 0.05 and 0.01 levels, respectively. Critical values obtained from 10,000 replications. EC: Estimated coefficients.

4 Conclusion

This study has analysed the causal relationship between public debt and unemployment – youth unemployment in the PIIGS countries and Turkey for the period of 1990–2015. Availing country-based comparisons, the estimation results of the bootstrap panel Granger causality test proposed by Kónya (2006) indicate that in five of the sample countries except Portugal, there is causality between public debt and unemployment (and youth unemployment). Public debt increases unemployment (and youth unemployment) in Turkey, Italy and Greece. Similar to numerous studies (i.e. Jimenez and Mishra, 2010; Fedeli and Forte, 2012; Korol and Cerkas, 2015; Kokotovic, 2016; Kurecic and Kokotovic, 2016), these findings do not support the Keynesian thesis that public debt has a positive effect on unemployment. On the contrary, it may be said that the results endorse policy inefficiency and debt's distortionary effect claims of the Monetarist and New Classical economics. Another conclusion to be made out of the analysis is that unemployment (and youth unemployment) has an increasing effect on public debt in Turkey, Ireland and Spain. In these economies—with tight monetary policies—fiscal policies are regarded as the only policy option albeit it is evident that public debt is not a proper and efficient remedy for unemployment.

References

Amaral, J. F. and Lopes, J. C. (2015). The Trade-off Unemployment Rate/External Deficit: Assessing the Economic Adjustment Program of the Troika (European Commission, ECB and IMF) for Portugal using an Input-Output Approach. Working Papers No. 2015/04, Lisbon School of Economics & Managements, Lisbon.

Ayyoub, M., Chaudhry, I. S. and Yaqup, S. (2012). Debt Burden of Pakistan: Impact and Remedies for Future. Universal Journal of Management and Social Sciences, 2(7), 29–40.

Battaglini, M. and Coate, S. (2016). A Political Economy Theory of Fiscal Policy and Unemployment. Journal of the European Economic Association, 14(2), 303–337.

Bianchi, J., Ottonello, P. and Presno, I. (2015). Unemployment, Sovereign Debt, and Fiscal Policy in a Currency Union. 2016 Meeting Papers 459, Society for Economic Dynamics, Toulouse.

Breusch, T. S. and Pagan, A. R. (1980). The Lagrange Multiplier Test and Its Applications to Model Specification in Econometrics. The Review of Economic Studies, 47(1), 239–253.

Fedeli, S. and Forte, F. (2012). Public Debt and Unemployment Growth: The Need for Fiscal and Monetary Rules. Evidence from OECD Countries (1981–2009). Economia Politica, 29(3), 409–437.

Gordon, R. J. (1987). "Wage Gaps vs. Output Gaps: Is There a Common Story for All of Europe?" NBER Working Papers 2454, National Bureau of Economic Research, Cambridge.

Heijdra, B.J. and Ploeg, F. (2002). The Foundations of Modern Macroeconomics. Oxford University Press, Oxford.

Holden, S. and Sparrman, V. (2011). Do Government Purchases Affect Unemployment? CESifo Working Paper Series 3482, CESifo Group, Munich, Germany.

Isaev, M. and Masih, M. (2017). The Nexus of Private Sector Foreign Debt, Unemployment, Trade Openness: Evidence from Australia. Munich Personal RePEc Archive Paper 79423, University Library of Munich, Germany.

Jimenez, C. I. G. and Mishra, A. K. (2010). The Effects of Public Debt on Labor Demand in the United States. 2010 Annual Meeting, February 6–9, 2010, Orlando, Florida.

Kokotovic, F. (2016). An Empirical Study of Factors Influencing Total Unemployment Rate in Comparison to Youth Unemployment Rate in Selected EU Member-States. Theoretical and Applied Economics, 3(608), 79–92.

Kónya, L. (2006). Exports and Growth: Granger Causality Analysis on OECD Countries with a Panel Data Approach. Economic Modelling, 23(6), 978–992.

Korol, O. and Cerkas, N. (2015). The Economic Impact of Foreign Debt in Greece. Baltic Journal of Economic Studies, 1(1), 105–112.

Kurecic, P. and Kokotovic, F. (2016). Relevance of Public Debt-to-GDP Ratio Correlation with Significant Macroeconomic Indicators. Macedonian Journal of Political Science, E-Proceeding of Papers, 3(7), 38–56.

Leão, P. (2013). The Effect of Government Spending on the Debt-to-GDP Ratio: Some Keynesian Arithmetic. Metroeconomica, 64(3), 448–465.

Maqbool, M. S., Mahmood, T. Sattar, A. and Bhalli, M. N. (2013). Determinants of Unemployment Empirical Evidences from Pakistan. Pakistan Economic and Social Review, 51(2), 191–207.

Oganna, C. I., Idenyi, O. S., Ifeyinwa, A. C. and Gabriel, N. U. (2016). The Implications of Rising Public Debt on Unemployment in Nigeria: An Auto Regressive Distributed Lag Approach. Asian Research Journal of Arts & Social Sciences, 1(1), 1–15.

Pesaran, M. H. (2004). General Diagnostic Tests for Cross Section Dependence in Panels. Working Papers in Economics No. 0435, Faculty of Economics, University of Cambridge, Cambridge, England.

Pesaran, M. H. and Yamagata, T. (2008). Testing Slope Homogeneity in Large Panels. Journal of Econometrics, 142(1), 50–93.

Pesaran, M. H., Ullah, A. and Yamagata, T. (2008). A Bias-Adjusted LM Test of Error Cross-Section Independence. The Econometrics Journal, 11(1), 105–127.

Richard, E. O. and Chinedu, N. G. (2015). Effect of Deficit Financing on Unemployment Rate in Nigeria: An Error Correction Model. International Journal of Small Business and Entrepreneurship Research, 3(7), 28–46.

Sam, S. O. and Pokhariyel, G. P. (2016). Modelling Economic Determinants of Youth Unemployment in Kenya. Journal of Emerging Trends in Economics and Management Sciences, 7(1), 31–38.

Slavin, S.L. (2008). Economics. McGraw-Hill Education, New York.

Snowdon, B. and Vane H. (2005). Modern Macroeconomics. Edward Elgar Publishing Limited, Massachusetts.

Swamy, P. A. (1970). Efficient Inference in a Random Coefficient Regression Model. Econometrica, 38(2), 311–323.

World Bank (2016). Unemployment Data. https://data.worldbank.org/indicator

Yılmaz, B. E. (2012). Gt ve Kamu Borçlanması Üzerine. In: Keynes'in Genel Teorisi Üzerine, Akalın, U. S., İncekara, A., ve İncekara, G., Ed., Kalkedon, İstanbul, 1–20.

Zellner, A. (1962). An Efficient Method of Estimating Seemingly Unrelated Regressions and Tests for Aggregation Bias. Journal of the American Statistical Association, 57(298), 348–368.

Appendix: Public Debt, Unemployment and Youth Unemployment Rates in the PIIGS Countries and Turkey (1990–2015)

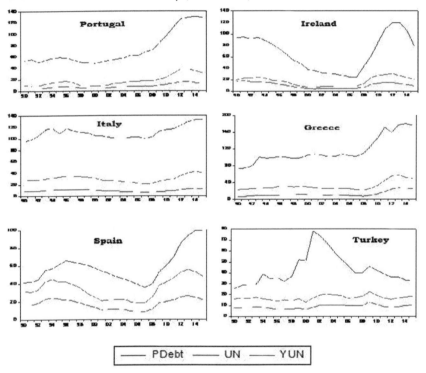

Ercan Yaşar and Mine Yaşar

Global Wealth and Aging Population

1 Introduction

Inequality has been an important issue in the history of humanity in terms of ensuring social justice and equality, and protecting social peace and moral values. Economically, the most important dimension of inequality is income inequality. Income inequality not only deepens socio-economic problems but also nourishes them; thus, it prevents the welfare enhancement effect of economic development from reaching large segments of society. Inequalities in income distribution are also important indicators of general economic inequalities. Inequalities in income and distribution have mechanisms that feed each other. There are many economic and social factors affecting income distribution. All macroeconomic policies must take unfair distribution of income into account because it causes some social problems that affect economic and political stability (Pehlivan, 2009: 19; Palaz and Öksüzler, 2013: 120).

Although the income gap and inequality between the social classes and the individuals are encountered in every period, problems of income inequality and poverty have gained particular importance along with industrialization and the capitalist market. The globalization process has an important influence on income distribution not only among countries but also within countries. Even among the citizens of the same country, very high differences can occur. Income distribution inequality is not a problem specific to only underdeveloped or developing countries. The more equitable distribution of income for developed countries has become an issue that must not be ignored, deferred, and urgent measures must be taken against (Musayeva, 2011: 395). For this reason, inequalities have become the most important issue of the discussions of the world economy. In recent times, income inequality has started to be vocalized not only by unions and leftist parties but also by international institutions and organizations such as the International Monetary Fund (IMF), the World Bank, and the Organisation for Economic Co-operation and Development (OECD). Because of the impact of the 2008 financial crisis, the global economy can't gain momentum, and the gathering of income and wealth in the hands of the "top layer" weakens the purchasing power of large sections of the local populace, so there is no strong demand for goods and services. This leads to the continuation of economic stagnation. According to the OECD's Inequality and Growth Report, the gap between the rich and the poor in OECD member countries has reached the highest level in the last 30 years. In the 1980s, the wealthiest segment of the population earned 7 times as much as the poorest segment of the population, but today this number has risen to 9.5 times (Kozanoğlu, 2014).

There is a very large literature on income inequality. However, most of the studies focus on income inequality, whereas studies on wealth distribution are relatively small and inadequate. Wealth inequality is related to income inequality. In fact, wealth injustice is one of the most fundamental causes of income inequality because wealth has an effect on income generation. For this reason, this study focuses on wealth distribution and its relation to demographic differences.

2 Wealth and Gini coefficient

Wealth is generally associated with savings, investments, our home, or with other forms of financial capital. However, the word wealth is a combination of "weal" (goodness) and "th" (condition) and means "condition of being good" (Anielski, 2003).

The wealth of a person or a household is measured by their possessions. A person's total wealth (or net wealth) also includes debts at the same time. Thus, the concept of wealth is different from the concept of income. Income is a flow variable whereas wealth is a stock variable. Wealth is the result of past spending and income, and at the same time, is influenced by decisions about investment, saving, and consumption, and by inheritance. Net wealth has a strong relationship with income. For example, people with high incomes tend to save more and as a result they accumulate more wealth. Although wealth tends to be more unevenly distributed than income, wealth inequality is associated with income inequality. Wealth consists of asset types such as land, real estate, agricultural assets, vehicles, cash savings, life insurance, pension funds, and personal properties (Staunton, 2015: 4).

In order to compare the distribution of wealth between countries, it is critical to make the same wealth definition. Wealth is defined as the current market value of all assets and net debt owned by households. According to international standards, assets include all financial and non-financial assets for which ownership rights can be applied and which have economic benefit. This definition includes all pension funds but excludes unspecified pension funds. It does not include prospective transfer payments of governments (due to the difficulty of observing market prices for such assets). The definition of wealth excludes human capital for the same reason (Zucman, 2016: 40).

The Gini coefficient defines the general distribution of wealth (or income) between 0 and 1. If the Gini coefficient is zero, it means that all the wealth is evenly distributed among all citizens and indicates "perfect equality". If the Gini coefficient is 1, it means that only one person has all the wealth and indicates "perfect inequality". The closer the coefficient is to 1, the greater the inequality; the closer the coefficient is to 0, the greater the equality (Staunton, 2015: 8).

Global wealth distribution

Because the inequality of wealth and income distribution has increased steadily over the last 40 years worldwide, these subjects are attracting much attention by researchers. The problem is not only that the more advanced economies do not lead to inequality at lower levels as suggested in Kuznets' theory, but at the same time they enter the vicious cycle of poverty because minority groups in wealthy countries cannot reach good education, health care, and social security. The disturbance of the mentioned minority groups can turn into a riot, in which everybody in the society, even the richest 1%, will suffer (Peshev, 2015: 29).

Many studies on income distribution in recent years have shown that global income inequality is high and does not decline over time (Bourguignon and Morrisson, 2002; Milanovic, 2002; Davies et al., 2009). In some regions, poverty and income inequality keep increasing. Davies et al. (2009) focused on predicting global wealth Gini coefficients in their study of estimating the global distribution of household wealth. They estimated that 10% of adults in the world had 71% of total household wealth and that the Gini coefficient for global wealth was 0.802 in 2000. In the same study, it was seen that wealth composition changed not only among developing countries but also among countries with the same income level. These variations can be explained by institutional and traditional differences, the importance of public pension funds, and other factors. The prominence of both financial assets and borrowing is rising sharply with per capita income and financial market development. On the other hand, the composition of household wealth in underdeveloped countries is still dominated by land and other material assets (Davies et al., 2009).

Wealth inequality is important because wealth is the determinant of many opportunities offered to individuals and households (such as investment opportunities for future education or the purchase of assets such as stocks or real estate that form the future income stream). The OECD argues that high wealth inequality can increase general inequality, which can reduce future economic growth. Wealth also provides financial assurance for times when income is declining. Those with more wealth have more possibilities to sustain their standard of living in times of low income. This can happen during lifetime in times of unemployment or illness. The distribution of wealth can be examined in two ways: The first is to rank households according to their wealth. This method shows wealth accumulation. The second method is to rank households according to their income. This method represents the wealth of different income groups (Australian Council of Social Service, 2015: 30).

The tendency of wealth inequality is changing, but it appears that it has increased since the 1930s. One of the key predictions of Thomas Piketty's book *Capital in the Twenty-First Century* is that if this trend continues, the inequality would reach the pre–World War I level, and the process of wealth demolition, expropriation, and taxation would be initiated. Two forces are working to reverse this long-term movement. In the first place, most of the capitalist economies face and are likely to face low production and revenue growth due to high growth factors such as employment-generating technological change, intense market competition, and high government spending. Low growth limits the ability of new groups and individuals to accumulate wealth. Second, the rate of return on capital is higher than the growth rate of developed economies and will continue to be higher. This is highly related to the opening of global markets for speculation of financial assets (Yates, 2016).

Thomas Piketty's book *The Capital in the Twenty-First Century* is based on a 15-year investigation dedicated to understanding the historical dynamics of wealth and income. His basic argument depends on the hypothesis that the rate of return of the capital (r) is higher than the rate of increase in revenue and production (g). He uses a comprehensive data set and provides political and historical evaluation to support his hypothesis. He originally focuses on distributional relations in his work and describes the fact that the accumulated wealth (r) grows faster than income (g) as "the fundamental contradiction of capitalism". He establishes a causality between the decline of inequality during certain periods and the shocks created by wars. He suggests an increasing tax rate on capital in order to help rid the rapidly rising global wealth inequality. However, the suggestion of an increasing tax rate on wealth requires global coordination and regional political integration (Piketty, 2014).

In addition, he has reached some conclusions about world wealth inequality, using data obtained from tax returns:

- In Europe, wealth inequality was at a fairly high level in the 19th century and lasted until 1914 (about 90% of total wealth in 1910 was shared by 10% of the population). Wealth inequality was then tilted until the 1960s and 1970s (10% of the population's share of wealth fell to 50–60% of total wealth due to taxes and other factors). It has increased moderately since 1980.

- In the United States, wealth inequality had shown a more moderate increase than in Europe until 1914, but it had risen much more strongly in recent years than in Europe.
- In both Europe and the United States, wealth inequality is now less extreme than in Europe compared to that in 1914 (Staunton, 2015: 5).

Global wealth reduced to $250 trillion in 2015 from the level of $262.4 trillion in 2014. In 2015, global assets totaled $250 trillion, down $12.4 trillion from the year 2014. One of the most important reasons for this decrease was the depreciation of the other currencies against the US dollar and thus the decrease in the US dollar–denominated assets of the measured assets in these currencies. According to Credit Suisse's 2016 Global Wealth Report, global wealth increased by 1.4% and reached to $256 trillion in 2016. However, creating wealth only adapted to population growth. As a result, the per capita wealth has remained unchanged for the first time since 2008 at about $52,800 in 2016. The United States and Japan have succeeded in generating additional wealth, and the United Kingdom has experienced a significant decline due to the depreciation of the currency. The Global Wealth Report asserts that global household wealth has been driven by an increase in financial assets since 2008. In 2016, this tendency was changing because of the increase in non-financial assets. In total, $4.9 trillion was added to immovable (real) assets whereas financial assets increased by $330 billion. The report also reveals the wealth disparities measured by the share of the richest 1% and the wealthiest 10%. The richest 10% has 89% of the wealth. According to the 2016 Global Wealth Report, when we look at the amount of wealth per capita among the world's major economies, Switzerland is the country with the highest per capita wealth. Switzerland is followed by the United States, the United Kingdom, France, Sweden, and Germany. According to the report, the world's most unequal country is Russia, where 1% of rich people control 74.5% of national wealth. In India and Thailand, 1% controls 60% of national wealth, and in Indonesia and Brazil, it is around 50% (Credit Suisse, 2016).

According to the report's global wealth pyramid, the widest part of the world's population constitutes the bottom layer of the pyramid. It is estimated that the wealth of 3.5 billion people (73% of the adult population of the world) was below $10,000 in 2016. An upper layer of pyramid (900 million people that make up 19% of the total world population) is estimated to have a wealth of between $10,000 and $100,000. The third layer of pyramid (7.5% of the world population) is estimated to have a wealth of between $100,000 and $1 million. It is estimated that the top layer of the pyramid and the wealthiest section of the world population (0.7% of the world population) has more than $1 million (Credit Suisse, 2016).

In Credit Suisse's report, the definition of wealth includes both financial and non-financial assets. Financial assets include debt securities, equity securities, and cash. Non-financial assets include mainly real estate, small businesses, and farms. Although the average wealth per adult is $51,600, net wealth (after deducting financial debt) per adult is $8,908. As the average income level of countries and the development of financial markets increase, the composition of total wealth also changes from non-financial assets to financial assets (Credit Suisse, 2016).

When the shares of selected countries in global wealth are examined, it is observed that the United States has the largest share with a wealth of $84,784 trillion and 33.2% of total wealth in 2016. Japan's share was 9.4% ($24,070 trillion), France's share was 4.7% ($11,891 trillion), Britain's share was 5.5% ($14,150 trillion), Italy's share was 3.9% ($9,973 trillion), and Canada's share was 3% ($3,756 trillion) in 2016. When the share of BRIC (Brazil, Russia, India, and China) countries in global wealth is examined, China's share was 9.1% ($23,393 trillion), India's share was 1.2% ($3,099 trillion), and Brazil's share was 1% ($2,537 trillion) in 2016. The share of Turkey in global wealth was around 0.4% ($1,063 trillion) in 2016 (Credit Suisse, 2016).

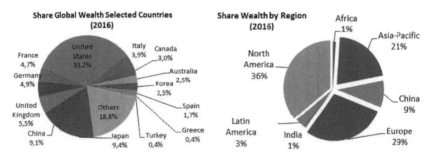

Source: Authors' calculations based on Credit Suisse's 2016 Global Wealth Databook.

"High-net-worth individuals" is a term used to identify individuals whose investable assets (such as stocks and bonds) exceed a certain amount. In the middle of 2016, it was estimated that there were 32.8 million high-net-worth individuals having wealth of between $1 million and $50 million per person. Majority of high-net-worth individuals (28.9 million) have wealth of between $1 million and $5 million per person. Majority of high-net-worth individuals settle in North America and Europe. About 8% of high-net-worth individuals inhabit in China, Latin America, India and Africa. Individuals whose net assets exceed $50 million are called ultrahigh-net-worth individuals. There were 140,900 ultrahigh-net-worth individuals in the world in 2016.

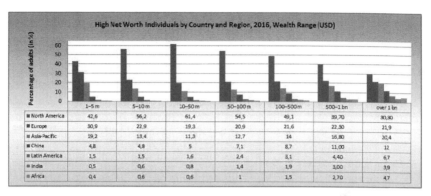

	1–5 m	5–10 m	10–50 m	50–100 m	100–500 m	500–1 bn	over 1 bn
▦ North America	42,6	56,2	61,4	54,5	49,1	39,70	30,30
▦ Europe	30,9	22,9	19,3	20,9	21,6	22,50	21,9
▦ Asia-Pacific	19,2	13,4	11,3	12,7	14	16,80	20,4
▦ China	4,8	4,8	5	7,1	8,7	11,00	12
▦ Latin America	1,5	1,5	1,6	2,4	3,1	4,40	6,7
▦ India	0,5	0,6	0,8	1,4	1,9	3,00	3,9
▦ Africa	0,4	0,6	0,6	1	1,5	2,70	4,7

Source: Authors' calculations based on Credit Suisse's 2016 Global Wealth Databook.

3 Per capita wealth and population age

The elderly population of developed countries keeps growing, and most of developed countries have an aging population. Graph 1 shows the relation between the share of 65+ population in the total population and the per capita wealth and indicates that the per capita wealth increases as the share of the elderly population increases. The country with the oldest population rate in the world is Japan with the rate of 25.7% and $192,720 wealth per adult. The country with the lowest proportion of elderly population is Burundi. The rate of Burundi's 65+ population is only 2.5% and the wealth per adult is $361. However, in the oil-rich countries such as Kuwait, Qatar, and the United Arab Emirates, the share of 65+ population in the total population is less than 2% and per capita wealth is $100,000. In Ukraine, 65+ population is around 15% and the per capita wealth level is around $1,254, the lowest level in Europe. The ratio of the total population of 65+ population in Turkey is 7.38%.

Graph 1: Relationship between wealth per capita and age 65+ in total population

Source: Authors' calculations based on Credit Suisse's 2016 Global Wealth Databook

When we look at the relationship between the share of 0–14 age population in the total population and the per capita wealth, we are confronted with the exact opposite of the relationship between the share of 65+ population in the total population and the per capita wealth. This relationship can be seen in Graph 2. The country with the lowest share of 0–14 age population in the total population in the world is Japan with 12.9%. Bosnia and Herzegovina with 13.5% and Italy with 13.9% follow Japan. The country with the highest share of the population between 0 and 14 years in the total population is Niger, where more than half of the population is in this age range. Niger is followed by Uganda with 48.1%. The per capita wealth of Niger and Uganda is $993 and $784, respectively.

Graph 2: Relationship between wealth per capita and age 0–14 in total population

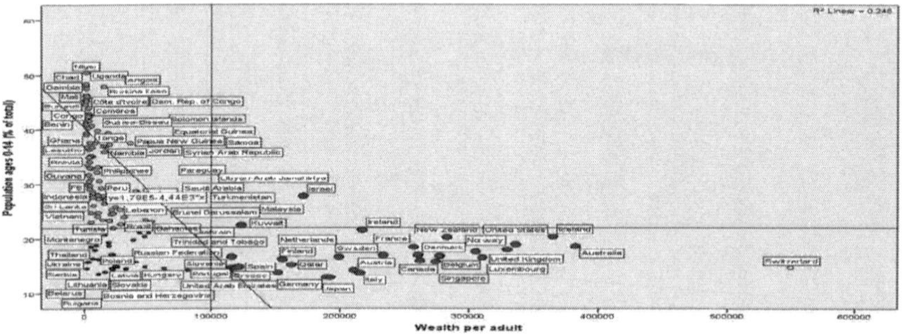

Source: Authors' calculations based on Credit Suisse's 2016 Global Wealth Databook.

4 Wealth per capita and life expectancy at birth

The high correlation between average life expectancy and income has been pointed out in many studies. It would not be surprising to expect a similar relationship between wealth per capita and life expectancy. This relationship has been shown in Graph 3. In countries with a high level of wealth per adult, the average life expectancy is higher than other countries. In Japan, where the average life expectancy is highest according to 2014 data, the per capita wealth is about $192,720. Similarly, in Switzerland, the average life expectancy is 82.8 years and the per capita wealth is $548,844.

In the world, the countries that have lower average life expectancy are also the countries that have lower wealth per capita. It is observed that the countries with the lowest wealth per capita in the world have the lowest average life expectancy. As can be seen in Graph 3, Swaziland is a country with a life expectancy of 48.9

and a per capita income of $3,900. The countries with the lowest life expectancy and the lowest per capita adult are located in Africa.

Graph 3: Relationship between wealth per capita and life expectancy at birth

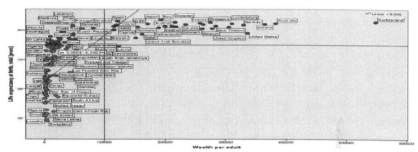

Source: Authors' calculations based on Credit Suisse's 2016 Global Wealth Databook.

When we look at the distribution of global wealth in 2016, it can be seen that the countries with a per capita wealth of more than $100,000 are the countries located in North America and Western Europe, Japan, Australia, and New Zealand. The countries with a per capita wealth of less than $5,000 are generally located in Central Africa. India, Pakistan, Iran and Kazakhstan are also the countries with a per capita wealth of less than $5,000. Ukraine and Belarus in Eastern Europe, and Guyana, Venezuela and Nicaragua in South America have per capita wealth of about $1,200 (see Graph 4).

Graph 4: Wealth per adult (2016)

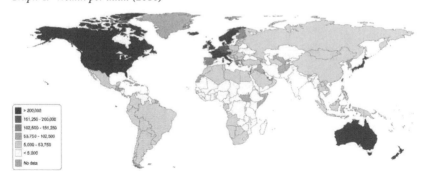

Source: Authors' calculations based on Credit Suisse's 2016 Global Wealth Databook.

Conclusion

With the increasing awareness of income inequality, the trend in wealth inequality has also become a matter of interest. Until recently, it was difficult to obtain empirical evidence on wealth inequality, but significant new evidence on wealth inequality is now available. In this study, the definition of wealth and global wealth distribution for selected countries are given. When we look at the shares of selected countries in world wealth, the United States, which owns 33.2% of the world's wealth, appears to be the richest country. The share of Turkey in global wealth is around 0.4% and $1,063 trillion. When we look at the amount of wealth per adult, the highest wealth per adult is in Switzerland with $562,000. In Turkey, the amount of wealth per capita is around $20,000. When we examine the amount of wealth of the world population, it can be seen that 73% of the world adult population has a wealth of less than $10,000 per adult, and the richest population of 0.7% of the world population has more than $1 million per adult. This situation reveals the unfairness of wealth distribution in the world. When we look at the relationship between the per capita wealth and the share of 65+ population in the total population, it can be observed that the per capita wealth increases as the share of the elderly population in total population increases except for petroleum-rich countries. In the oil-rich countries such as Kuwait, Qatar, and the United Arab Emirates, the share of 65+ population in the total population is less than 2% whereas per capita wealth is $100,000. It is also observed that the life expectancy decreases as the amount of wealth per adult decreases. The countries with the lowest expectancy of life and the lowest wealth per capita appear to be located in Africa.

References

Anielski, M. (2003), The Meaning of Wealth, ISSP Inside Newsletter, Ottawa, June 16.

Australian Council of Social Service (2015). "Inequality in Australia", the Australian Council of Social Service, Australia. http://www.acoss.org.au/wp-content/uploads/2015/06/Inequality_in_Australia_FINAL.pdf

Bourguignon, F. and Morrisson, C. (2002), "Inequality among World Citizens: 1820–1992", The American Economic Review, 92(4): 727–744.

Credit Suisse (2015), Global Wealth Databook. https://www.credit-suisse.com/

Credit Suisse (2016), Global Wealth Databook. https://www.credit-suisse.com/

Davies, J.B., Sandström, S., Shorrocks, A.B. and Wolff, E.N. (2009), "The Level and Distribution of Global Household Wealth", NBER Working Paper No. 15508, National Bureau of Economic Research, Cambridge.

Kozanoğlu, H. (2014), "Faiz Lobisi TUIK'i Atlattı", Birgün Gazetesi, August 30, 2014. http://www.birgun.net/haber-detay/faiz-lobisi-tuik-i-atlatti-79696.html

Milanovic, B. (2002), "True World Income Distribution, 1988 and 1993: First Calculations Based on Household Surveys Alone", Economic Journal 112(476): 51–92.

Musayeva, A. (2011), "Azerbaycan'da Gelir Dağılımi", Sosyal Siyaset Konferansları, 60(1): 393–432.

Palaz, S.Ş.Ö. and Öksüzler, O. (2013), "Eğitim Düzeyi Farklılıklarının Gelir Dağılımına Etkisi: Türkiye Örneği", Girişimcilik ve Kalkınma Dergisi, 8(2): 119–131.

Pehlivan, M. S. (2009), "Gelir Dağılımı Eşitsizliğine Devletin Müdahale Araçları: Sosyal Yardımlaşma ve Dayanışmayı Teşvik Fonu Örneği", Sosyal Yardım Uzmanlık Tezi, T.C. Başbakanlık Sosyal Yardımlaşma ve Dayanışma Genel Müdürlüğü, Ankara.

Peshev, P. (2015), "Analysis of the Wealth Inequality Dynamics in Bulgaria: Different Approach", Economic Alternatives, 4: 29–33.

Piketty, T. (2014), "Capital in the Twenty-First Century", Translated by Hande Koçak, İş Bankası Kültür Yayınları – İnceleme – Araştırma Dizisi, Belknap/Harvard University Press, İstanbul.

Staunton, C. (2015), "The Distribution of Wealth in Ireland", TASC, December, 3–28.

Yates, M.D. (2016), "Measuring Global Inequality", Monthly Review, 68(6). http://monthlyreview.org/2016/11/01/measuring-global-inequality/

Hikmet Gülçin Beken

Middle Income Trap: Conceptual and Theoretical Discussions

1 Introduction

Ensuring economic growth and development is one of the main targets of developed and developing countries. Development is a concept of process that involves both economic growth and structural transformations in the society. The importance of the sustainability of growth and development is indispensable. Developing countries should maintain a process from the low level of income to the middle and eventually to the high level of income. In this context, the middle income trap is both a threat and a challenge for many developing countries.

In this chapter first the middle income trap is defined. Then, the characteristics of countries that fall in the middle income trap are determined. Finally, the policy recommendations in order to escape from the middle income trap are analyzed.

2 How to define the middle income trap?

The poverty trap concept is used in the economic theory to describe the poor countries' structural problems that stuck them in a vicious circle, which they cannot succeed in to leave. Likewise, the middle income trap concept is derived from the poverty trap concept and used for the countries that cannot transform their economies from the middle income to the high income due to their structural problems (Itoh, 2012: 2).

Figure 1 provides development stages of an economy represented by the change in gross domestic product (GDP) per capita through time during the development process. Any point between A and B reflects a traditional community while any point between B and C indicates escaping from poverty trap and the beginning stages of development process. Point C shows the middle income level. If point C is regarded as the starting point, two different growth paths could be traced. If the economy follows the path from C to E, this means that the economy performed low growth rates and fall into the middle income trap. On the other hand, if the economy follows the path from C to D, this means that the economy caught a continuous and consistent growth trend and reached to the high level of income (Tho, 2013: 109).

Figure 1: Development stages of an economy

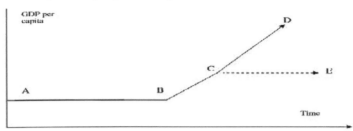

Source: Tho (2013: 109)

Middle income countries are trapped because they cannot compete with the production of low-price (wage) goods in the global system and they cannot develop their capacities to produce high-value-added goods to become competitive. Therefore, their problem is not only to be able to produce goods but also to be able to sustain growth and income increases by producing knowledge- and technology-intensive products (Paus, 2012: 116). A country, which experiences a transformation from low income level to middle income level, sustains competitiveness in international arena when moving from agricultural sector to the production of manufactured goods. When the country reaches the middle income level, the unqualified labor supply which is extracted from agriculture and being used in new production structure begins to contract with the increase in wage; also the revenues of imported technologies start to decrease. The increase in productivity, due to the technology-led catch-up effects and sectoral changes, will be disappeared. Then the country start losing its international competitiveness and this will also cause the country to get stuck in the middle income trap without reaching to the high income levels under the conditions of growth and output slowdowns (Agenor et al., 2012: 3).

Latin American and Middle East economies are examples that prove the accuracy of the middle income trap. Although many economies in these regions reached to middle income level in the 1960s and early 1970s, majority of them still remains in the middle income country category. Only 13 of 101 countries in the middle income level group in 1960 reached to the high level of income level in 2008 (World Bank, 2013: 12).

In the literature, there are some discussions about the concept of the middle income trap. Some find using the word of "trap" is not accurate and appropriate. Some argue that explanatory economic theories are not fully developed about the concept. Some argue that the theory lacks sound empirical findings (Cai, 2012: 50).

Some put forward that the definition of middle income trap depending on income levels and thresholds reveals different results due to using different base years and different definitions of per capita income. Some others argue that the high income level does not reflect real development of the economy including the technological and institutional capacity (Kanapathy et al. 2014: 11).

3 How to avoid the middle income trap

The middle income trap is a process that is caused by the decrease in marginal productivity of capital that is resulted from growth strategies of countries based on factor accumulation (Gill et al., 2007: 18). Especially, when East Asian newly industrialized countries are analyzed, the necessity of product diversification and the transformation through to the production of high-value-added goods could be seen as a way to escape from the middle income trap (Jankowska et al., 2012). If the policies adopted by East Asian countries are taken as an example for other countries in the middle income trap, their experience reveals that East Asian countries are successful in advanced infrastructure network development. Second, they are no longer those countries that imitate and import technologies but they become the ones that develop these technologies. Third, they are able to shift their labor force to the areas and regions that need labor force (Agenor et al., 2012: 5). Therefore, the productivity structure of countries and the characteristics of their exported goods will be decisive in their escape from the middle income trap (Felipe et al., 2012: 46).

In their study, Kharas and Kohli (2011: 286) mentioned three transformations needed for not falling into the middle income trap. First of all, the specialization in the production should be sustained. Second, important structural reforms, especially in education (knowledge and innovation based), must be adopted in order to sustain the increase in total productivity. Finally, in order to realize all these transformations and changes, the decentralization in decision-making process should be obtained. It is also important to remember that good governance and the private sector inclusion should also be maintained in terms of political administration and institutions. As argued by Armstrong and Westland (2016), the middle income trap is an economic phenomenon, but escaping it through deeper openness and financial reform is a political challenge since the vested interests obtained from the existing institutional structure in the country could show some resistance—for not losing its status-quo and power (Fabian, 2016).

High level of inequality in the economy could also be an important obstacle for escaping from the middle income trap. Egawa (2013) argues that high level of inequality causes the high level of saving rates, the decrease in capital effectiveness with the deterioration in capital distribution, and the slowdowns in growth. High level of inequality may affect the investment climate in a negative way since it makes more people feel themselves disadvantaged and creates discontents at the community level. This negative atmosphere in investments causes the growth to slow down and the country to fall into the middle income trap. Both of these mechanisms (economic and social) can affect each other and other explanatory factors that have impact on the middle income trap.

Ohno (2009: 28) defines industrialization and development consisting of five stages. Phase 0 indicates the pre-industrialization phase for a low income country that relies on foreign aids and subsistence agriculture. Phase 1 indicates having developing manufacturing industries that are built through foreign investments. Foreign direct investment accumulation and production increase takes place in phase 2. In phase 3, information and skills are internalized and the country starts producing high-quality products. Phase 4 is a period when the country starts to produce new products by its own and reaches to the global leading position in innovation and product design. The whole process cannot follow through a linear development pattern. Countries may be stuck in one of these five stages and may not be able to get into the next stage. Countries in stage 2 cannot reach stage 3 if they do not strengthen their human capital and they may fall into the middle income trap even though their income levels are high.

By using data between 1957 and 2007, Eichengreen et al. (2011) analyzed the experiences of countries presenting growth slowdown. Their study indicates that the slowdown of growth is experienced when GDP satisfies three conditions. First, average growth rate of these countries for seven years during fast-paced growth period is about 3.5%. Second, seven-year average growth rate decreases to 2% level during the slowdown period. Finally, slowdown starts when GDP per capita is more than US$10,000. According to their findings, economies face with growth slowdowns when their per capita income is about the level of $17,000. Their another study (2013: 12) suggests that the economies that have high level of elderly dependency ratio, very high level of investment rates, and undervalued currencies will most probably experience slowdowns in comparison to the countries that have high level of secondary and higher education and soaring share of high-technology products in total exports.

Study of Kanchoochat and Intarakumnerd (2014: 5) analyzes the factors mentioned in the literature that cause countries to fall and remain in the middle income trap. Inadequate quality of education and institutions, inadequate capabilities of producing and exporting higher technology products, inappropriate and insufficient role of the state in enhancing capabilities to produce and export higher technology products are the factors mentioned in the literature that cause countries to fall and remain in the middle income trap. In order to avoid the middle income trap, the state should create the right incentive systems, invest more in research and development and education, and support the industries having a comparative advantage focus on capabilities accumulation and industrial upgrading.

4 The middle income trap and Turkey

According to the study of Felipe et al. (2012), Turkey reached to the low middle income level in 1955 and to the high middle income group in 2005. Turkey spent nearly 50 years in the group of low middle income countries. During these fifty years, its average growth rate was around 2.5%. Altuğ et al. (2008) analyzed the factors determining the long-term growth performance of Turkey between 1880 and 2005. Their study reveals that the source of growth of Turkey is not total factor productivity but capital accumulation. Similar to the growth performance of Latin American countries, Turkey's growth trajectory is in a little association with human capital. Reforms and policy on the areas of human capital accumulation and endowment were implemented late. They were also not effective in stimulating growth and income as in East Asian and South European countries.

South Korea and Taiwan have successfully reached to the high income group by passing the middle income level without falling into the middle income trap. They implemented industrial, foreign trade, and innovation policies in an integrated and complementary way. They transferred technologies from more developed countries and implemented research and development activities (Tuncel, 2014: 53). As can be seen in Table 1, the ratio of research and development spending to gross domestic product is 4.15% in Korea and 3.47% in Japan while it is only 0.94% in Turkey in 2013. The ratio in Turkey is not able to reach even 1% throughout the years between 2006 and 2013. Turkey needs to create a convergence on this indicator in order to be among the high income level group countries.

Table 1: Research and Development Spending as Percentage of GDP

Geo/Time	2006	2007	2008	2009	2010	2011	2012	2013
Argentina	0.40	0.40	0.42	0.48	0.49	0.52	0.58	N.A
Brazil	0.99	1.08	1.13	1.12	1.16	1.14	1.15	N.A
China	1.38	1.38	1.46	1.68	1.73	1.79	1.93	2.01
Israel	4.19	4.48	4.39	4.15	3.96	4.10	4.25	4.21
Japan	3.41	3.46	3.47	3.36	3.25	3.38	3.34	3.47
Korea, Rep.	2.83	3.00	3.12	3.29	3.47	3.74	4.03	4.15

Geo/Time	2006	2007	2008	2009	2010	2011	2012	2013
Malaysia	0.61	N.A	0.79	1.01	1.07	1.06	1.13	N.A
Singapore	2.13	2.34	2.62	2.16	2.01	2.15	2.00	N.A
Portugal	0.95	1.12	1.45	1.58	1.53	1.46	1.38	1.37
Spain	1.17	1.23	1.32	1.35	1.35	1.32	1.27	1.24
Thailand	0.25	0.21	N.A	0.25	N.A	0.39	N.A	N.A
Turkey	0.58	0.72	0.73	0.85	0.84	0.86	0.92	0.94
USA	2.55	2.63	2.77	2.82	2.74	2.77	2.81	N.A

Source: World Development Indicators

According to World Trade Organization data (2015), China is the largest export economy in the world in 2014 with the share of 12.3% of total exports in the world. The volume of its exports amounts 2,343 billion dollar. China is followed by the USA ($1,621 billion, 8.5%) and Germany ($1,508 billion, 7.8%). Turkey's share of total exports is 0.8% with the amount of $158 billion export. The share of Turkey in total exports is not enough once we consider the fact that Turkey has implemented export-led growth strategy since 1980. Turkey needs to increase its export volume by finding new markets and developing new processes instead of selling more products to its current markets. Turkey should focus on demand structure based on prices, quality, and customer preferences. Therefore, innovation and product differentiation are the only ways to satisfy market demands both at local and international levels for countries in the middle income group (Kharas and Kohli, 2011: 285).

The composition of export products of a country is as important as its export volume. When we look at the share of high-technology exports as a percentage of manufactured goods, the figure was 47.18% for Singapore, 43.87% for Malaysia, and 25.37% for China while it is only 1.93% for Turkey (see Table 2).

Table 2: High-Technology Export as of Manufactured Exports

Geo/Time	2006	2007	2008	2009	2010	2011	2012	2013	2014
Argentina	7.05	6.59	9.02	8.69	7.50	7.48	7.70	9.84	6.68
Brazil	12.08	11.87	11.65	13.20	11.21	9.72	10.49	9.63	10.61
China	30.51	26.66	25.57	27.53	27.51	25.81	26.27	26.97	25.37
Israel	14.51	7.48	11.12	17.62	14.66	13.98	15.85	15.61	16.01
Japan	22.06	18.41	17.31	18.76	17.97	17.46	17.41	16.78	16.69
Korea, Rep.	32.15	30.54	27.60	28.73	29.47	25.72	26.17	27.10	26.88
Malaysia	53.84	52.28	39.92	46.57	44.52	43.39	43.72	43.57	43.87

Geo/Time	2006	2007	2008	2009	2010	2011	2012	2013	2014
Portugal	8.90	8.17	7.78	4.10	3.51	3.69	4.14	4.31	4.38
Singapore	58.07	45.21	49.38	48.14	49.91	45.16	45.29	46.99	47.18
Spain	6.38	5.11	5.31	6.23	6.36	6.47	6.99	7.67	7.00
Thailand	27.39	25.96	24.55	25.34	24.02	20.74	20.54	20.09	20.43
Turkey	1.85	1.89	1.62	1.74	1.93	1.84	1.83	1.88	1.93
USA	30.06	27.22	25.92	21.49	19.97	18.11	17.78	17.82	18.23

Source: World Development Indicators

The main problems related to Turkish foreign trade are high import dependency on intermediate and capital goods and the difference between export and import structure (Küçükkiremitçi, 2011: 32). Foreign trade technology structure of Turkey is presented in Table 3. In the analysis of technological structure of the products, it can be seen that Turkey mainly exports low–medium technology products (37.8%) and low technology products (30.4%). High technology products have the lowest share in the total exports (3.4%). Turkey mainly imports medium–high level technology products (41.9%) and high level technology products (12.8%). Thus, Turkey's competitiveness in high-value-added/high-technology products is very low.

Table 3: Technology Structure of Turkish Trade (as % of Total Exports and Imports)

Export Share (%)	2008	2009	2010	2011	2012	Import Share (%)	2008	2009	2010	2011	2012
Low Technology	28.3	31.7	32.6	32.3	30.4	Low Technology	12.9	14.2	14.1	13.5	13.2
Medium–Low Technology	37.7	34.4	31.8	32.5	37.8	Medium–Low Technology	33	28.3	28.6	30.4	32.1
Medium–High Technology	30.9	30.4	32.2	32	28.4	Medium–High Technology	41.5	42.8	42.8	43.2	41.9
High Technology	3.1	3.5	3.4	3.1	3.4	High Technology	12.5	14.7	14.5	12.9	12.8

Source: Eşiyok (2013: 8).

5 Conclusion

The main factors to cause to the middle income trap should be carefully analyzed considering the economic, social, and political structure of the countries. Inability to improve productivity due to lack of innovation, poor quality, and amount of higher education and the income distribution are the main barriers of countries that want to escape from the middle income trap.

In the analysis of the country cases trapped in the middle income level, Yılmaz (2014) emphasizes two factors as the main reasons of falling into the middle income trap: low level of human capital and negative structural transformations. Low level of human capital endowment would cause the low level of productivity and negative structural transformations would lead to low per capita income. Negative structural transformations also limit human capital accumulation. As a result of these two factors, which strengthen each other, an economy could not reach to the high income level and will not be able to escape from the middle income trap and vicious circle. In this context, main suggestions for avoiding the middle income trap are to make investment especially in human capital, to reform the institutions, and to adopt an appropriate governance structure (Drysdale, 2012).

References

Agenor Pierre-Richard, Otaviano Canuto and Michael Jelenic (2012). Avoiding Middle Income Growth Traps. Economic Premise, November, Number 98, World Bank.

Altuğ Sumru, Alpay Filiztekin and Şevket Pamuk (2008). Sources of Long-Term Economic Growth for Turkey, 1880–2005. European Review of Economic History, 12: 393–430.

Armstrong Shiro and Tom Westland (2016). Escaping the Middle Income Trap. East Asia Forum: Economics, Politics and Public Policy in East Asia and the Pacific (28 March 2016), http://www.eastasiaforum.org/2016/03/28/escaping-the-middle-income-trap/ (date accessed 21.04.2016).

Cai Fang (2012). Is There a Middle Income Trap? Theories, Experiences and Relevance to China. China & World Economy, 20(1): 49–60.

Drysdale, Peter (2012). Asia's human capital and the middle-income trap, East Asia Forum: Economics, Politics and Public Policy in East Asia and the Pacific, http://www.eastasiaforum.org/2012/07/23/asias-human-capital-and-the-middle-income-trap/ (date accessed 3.6.2016).

Egawa Akio (2013). Will Income Inequality Cause a Middle Income Trap in Asia? Bruegel Working Paper 2013/06, Bruguel Publications, Brussels, Belgium.

Eichengreen Barry Donghyun. Park and Kwanho Shin (2011). When Fast Growing Economies Slow Down: International Evidence and Implication for the Peoples Republic of China. NBER Working Paper No. 16919, National Bureau of Economic Research, Cambridge.

Eşiyok Bayram Ali (2013). Türkiye İmalat Sanayinin Teknolojik Yapısı: Sürdürülebilir mi?, http://www.inovasyon.org/pdf/B.AliEsiyok.Imalat.San.TeknoYapı.pdf (date accessed 3.6.2016).

Eurostat, http://ec.europa.eu/eurostat/statistics-explained/index.php/Glossary: Research_and_development_(R_%26_D) (date accessed 3.6.2016).

Fabian Mark (2016). Generalising the middle income trap. East Asia Forum: Economics, Politics and Public Policy in East Asia and the Pacific (28 April 2016), http://www.eastasiaforum.org/2016/04/28/generalising-the-middle-income-trap/ (date accessed 12.05.2016).

Felipe Jesus, Arnelyn Abdon and Utsav Kumar (2012). Tracking the Middle Income Trap: What is it, Who is in it, and Why?, Levy Economic Institute Working Paper No. 715. New York, NY: Levy Economics Insitute of Bard College.

Gill Indermit, Homi Kharas and Deepak Bhattasali (2007). An East Asian Renaissance: Ideas for Economic Growth. Washington, DC: World Bank.

Itoh Motoshige (2012). What is the Key to Long-lasting Growth in Asia? in National Institute for Research Advancement. The Middle Income Trap in Asia, NIRA Policy Review Series No. 58, Tokyo, Japan: The National Institute for Research Advancement.

Jankowska Anna, Arne J. Nagengast and Jose Ramon Perea (2012). The Middle Income Trap: Comparing Asian and Latin American Experiences, Policy Insights No. 96, OECD Development Centre. Paris, France: OECD Publishing.

Kanapathy Vijayakumari, Herizal Hazri, Pasuk Phongpaichit and Pornthep Benyaapikul (2014). Middle Income Trap: Economic Myth, Political Reality, Case Studies From Malaysia and Thailand. The Asia Foundation, https://asiafoundation.org/resources/pdfs/MiddleIncomeTrap.pdf (date accessed 17.4.2016).

Kanchoochat Veerayooth and Patarapong Intarakumnerd (2014). Tigers Trapped: Tracing the Middle-income Trap through the East and Southeast Asian Experience. Berlin Working Papers on Money, Finance, Trade and Development No. 4. Berlin, Germanay: University of Applied Sciences.

Kharas Homi and Harinder Kohli (2011). What Is the Middle Income Trap, Why Do Countries Fall Into It, and How Can It Be Avoided?. Global Journal of Emerging Market Economics, 3(3): 281–289.

Küçükkiremitçi Oktay (2011). Türkiye Sanayi Strateji Belgesi Temelinde İmalat Sanayinin Yapisal Analizi, http://inovasyon.info/pdf/O.Kucukkiremitci.2011.pdf (date accessed 12.05.2016).

Ohno Kenichi (2009). Avoiding the Middle Income Trap: Renovating Industrial Policy Formulation in Vietnam, ASEAN Economic Bulletin Vol. 26, No. 1, pp. 25–43.

Paus Eva (2012). Confronting the Middle Income Trap: Insights from Small Latecomers. Studies in Comparative International Development, 47(2): 115–138.

Tho Trân Vân (2013). The Middle-Income Trap: Issues for Members of the Association of Southeast Asian Nations, VNU Journal of Economics and Business, 29(2): 107–128.

Tuncel Cem Okan (2014). Orta Gelir Tuzağı ve İnovasyon Politikaları: Doğu Asya Deneyimi ve Türkiye İçin Dersler. Maliye Dergisi, Sayı 167: 40–70.

World Bank (2013). China 2030: Building a Modern, Harmonious, and Creative Society, The World Bank Development Research Center of the State Council, the People's Republic of China. Washington DC: World Bank.

World Bank, http://data.worldbank.org/news/new-country-classifications-2015, Washington DC: World Bank.

World Development Indicators, http://databank.worldbank.org/data/reports.asp x?source=2&type=metadata&series=GB.XPD.RSDV.GD.ZS#

World Development Indicators, http://databank.worldbank.org/data/reports.asp x?source=2&type=metadata&series=TX.VAL.TECH.MF.ZS#

World Trade Organization (2015). International Trade Statistics 2015. https:// www.wto.org/english/res_e/statis_e/its2015_e/its2015_e.pdf (date accessed 12.06.2016).

Yılmaz Gökhan (2014). Turkish Middle Income Trap and Less Skilled Human Capital. Central Bank of the Republic of Turkey. Working Paper No. 14/30. Ankara, Turkey: Central Bank of the Republic of Turkey.

M. Veysel Kaya and Yunus Kutval

The Reserve Options Mechanism in Turkey and a General Overview of the Reserve Option Coefficient

1 Introduction

The reforms undertaken in the context of the Strong Economic Transition Program in 2001 have caused radical changes in operations of the Central Bank and monetary policy in Turkey, whereby independency of the Central Bank has been emphasized and monetary policies have been implemented by an autonomous monetary policy board.

As a lender of last resort, the Central Bank plays a regulatory role on other banks in the economy. One of the regulations of the Central Bank is the required reserve ratio application. Within the scope of the required reserve ratio application, banks must keep some portion of their deposits as cash. This is a traditional policy tool of central banks both in Turkey and the world. However, unconventional policy measures have been implemented by central banks especially in emerging market economies recently. One of such measures is the reserve option mechanism. The Reserve Options Mechanism (ROM) was introduced by the Central Bank of the Republic of Turkey (CBRT) in September 2011 to fight against large swings in short-term capital flows and to keep stability in money markets. This mechanism allows banks to hold a certain fraction of their domestic currency required reserves in foreign currency or gold. The fraction is determined by the reserve option coefficient (ROC), which is determined by the Central Bank.

In the first part of the study, definition and process of ROM and its effect on financial stability are analyzed. In the second part of the study, the function and derivation of the ROC and its effect on the monetary liquidity of the banks are inspected.

2 The Reserve Options Mechanism

The CBRT gained experience after the 2001 financial crises in Turkey and 2008 Mortgage Crisis in the USA. At the end of the year 2010, the CBRT started to search for alternative policy instruments to support financial stability and to increase resistance of the economy against external financial crises and shocks (Küçüksaraç and Özel, 2012: 2; HSBC, 2013; Seval and Özdemir, 2013: 13). Hence, the CRBT has recently adopted the ROM to increase the resilience of the economy against external financial shocks and to reduce the possible adverse effects of volatile capital flows on macroeconomic and financial stability (Başçı, 2014; Alper, Kara and Yörükoğlu, 2012: 1). ROM is a monetary tool application that allows banks to keep a certain ratio of their Turkish Lira (TL) reserve requirements in foreign exchange (FX) or gold (Tokatlıoğlu and Saraçoğlu, 2013: 1; TCMB, 2012c: 2).

The CBRT has applied a number of legal regulations in order to eliminate the possible negative effects of reserve requirement ratios on bank profitability and credit. One of these regulations is allowing banks to keep a certain ratio of their TL reserve requirements in FX or gold (XTB, 2014; Glocker and Towbin, 2012: 8). ROM is a monetary tool application that allows banks to keep a certain ratio of their TL reserve requirements in FX or gold. By this application, the CBRT aims to increase the level of profitability of banks, to provide TL liquidity permanently to the market, and to reduce informal economy (Oduncu, Ermişoğlu and Çelik, 2013: 2). With this application, banks burden the lower gold cost instead of the higher repo cost. Moreover, since the said change will be positive for profitability, banks will enter into an intense competition with other banks during the period of collecting gold from the market in order to increase the gold they can keep in their reserves (Böcüoğlu, 2015: 21). As a result of these activities, the CBRT will register the gold in the informal status. With this decision, the need for banks' short-term TL will also be minimal (Miniane, 2013: 15).

2.1 General framework of ROM

ROM is basically a mechanism that allows banks to keep a certain ratio of their TL reserve requirements in FX and/or gold. The fraction of TL-required reserves that can be held in FX or gold is set by the reserve option ratio (ROR). The amount of FX or gold that can be held per unit of TL is called the ROC. For example, if the ROC is 3, banks have to hold 3 TL worth of FX or gold per 1 TL reserve requirement if they wish to utilize the ROM facility. Let us give an example to grasp the mechanism. Suppose that banks have to hold 100 TL reserve requirements in total for their TL liabilities. Let us assume that ROR for FX is 90 percent (i.e., banks can hold up to 90 percent of their TL reserve requirements in FX) and ROC is 1 (banks can hold 1 TL equivalent of FX per unit of TL reserve requirement). Let us further assume that the exchange rate for USD/TL is 1.8000. In this case, if the bank prefers to use the facility fully in USD, it has to hold 90 TL equivalent of USD, which is 90/1.8000 = 50 USD. If this is the case, banks will hold 50 USD (90 TL) plus 10 TL to fulfill their 100 TL of total reserve requirements (Alper, Kara and Yörükoğlu, 2012: 2).

If the ROC is set as 2 instead of 1, the banks will have to hold 2 TL equivalent of FX per 1 TL. In this case, if the banks wish to utilize the facility fully, they will hold 90*2 = 180 TL equivalent of FX for their 90 TL reserve requirements, which amounts to 180/1.8000 = 100 USD. ROC does not have to be constant across all tranches (Alper, Kara and Yörükoğlu, 2012: 2).

The figures below present some examples on how ROC can be set alternatively. The first graph in Figure 1 depicts the case of a constant ROC, which corresponds to the example discussed earlier. In the second graph, ROC increases linearly across RORs. In this case, the banks have to hold higher amounts of FX per unit of TL as ROR increases. The last graph demonstrates the current practice by the CBRT. Currently, the ROC increases with respect to reserve option; however, for practical implementation, the whole facility is divided into sections (5 percent tranches) and ROC is set as constant within each tranche (Alper, Kara and Yörükoğlu, 2012; TCMB, 2013: 5).

Figure 1: Some examples for the setting of ROC

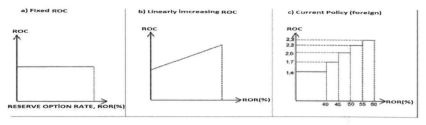

Source: Alper, Kara and Yörükoğlu (2012: 2)

2.2 Construction of ROM

The build-up phase of the ROM is engineered at a gradual pace in order to smooth the transition process of the banks. As a first step, banks are allowed to hold a fraction of their TL reserve requirements in FX or gold with a uniform ROC at 1. The system was enhanced and further developed in time to construct a mechanism that will work as an automatic stabilizer eventually (Özatay, 2012; Başçı ve Kara, 2011). Hence, the CBRT has changed the ROC levels by setting higher coefficients for higher RORs.

Figure 2 summarizes the build-up phase of the ROM in 8 steps. The construction of the ROM (for FX) has started in September 2011 by setting the ROR at 10 percent; i.e., allowing the banks to hold 10 percent of their TL reserve requirements in FX (I). ROR was raised to 20 percent in October (II) and further to 40 percent in November (III). Up to this point, the ROC was uniform (and equal to 1) across all tranches. Differentiation of ROC from 1 started in June 2012 when the ROM was increased to 45 percent from 40 percent, with a ROC of 1.4 for the incremental 5 percent (IV). Afterwards, the ROR was increased to 50 and 55 percent in two consecutive steps and ROC was set at 1.7 and 1.9, respectively, for each additional 5 percent tranches (V and VI). In the next step, the ROR was raised to 60 percent with a ROC of 2 for the incremental 5 percent. Moreover, with this move, ROC for the 0–40 percent tranche was increased to 1.1 from 1 (VII). Finally, in September and October 2012, ROC was increased by 0.2 and 0.1 percentage points, respectively, for all tranches (VIII).

Figure 2: Construction of ROM

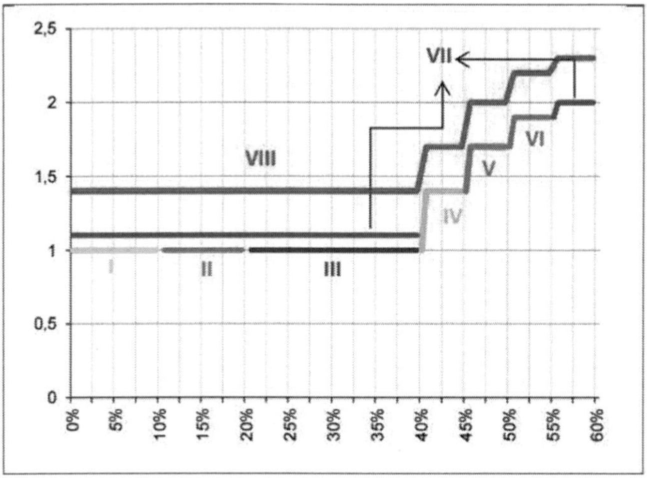

Source: Alper, Kara and Yörükoğlu (2012: 6)

2.3 ROM and financial stability

ROM limits the appreciation pressures of TL during acceleration in capital inflows by inducing banks to hold a higher ratio of their TL reserve requirement liabilities in FX while it limits depreciation pressures during a deceleration in capital inflows by inducing banks to hold a lower ratio of their TL reserve requirement liabilities in FX. Thus, the ROM may limit both the market volatility through the automatic stabilizer mechanism. With the application of the ROM, the CBRT aims to strength FX reserves and FX reserves accumulated by banks will serve as a buffer during capital outflows (Kara, 2012: 25). As shown in Figure 3, ROM has contributed an average of US$50 billion to the CBRT's total reserves by the end of 2013, while the reserve contribution of FX-required reserves has averaged US$30 billion (TCMB, 2013).

Figure 3: Foreign exchange-required reserves and contribution of ROM to gross reserves

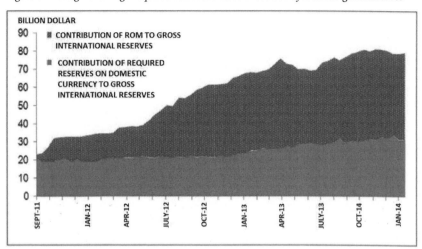

Source: TCMB (2013).

3 The reserve option coefficient

The amount of FX or gold that can be held per unit of TL is called the ROC (Alper, Kara and Çelik, 2012: 5; Başçı and Kara, 2011). ROC is an important element of the ROM system that the Central Bank put in place to ensure the flexibility lost in the FX market. In 2010, the Central Bank initiated a new era in the Monetary Policy Committee (Para Politikası Kurulu, PPK) meeting and has put 100 percent domestic instrument into practice. Instead of interest rate corridor, ROM was started to be used during that period. The Central Bank, which pulls down the upper corridor of the interest corridor, provides the quantitative easing through the loans, while the flexibility lost in the FX market is sustained by a new required reserve application that includes the ROC (Eğilmez, 2012; Ayyıldız, 2012). For example, suppose that the reserve option tranches (ROT) are similar to the date 7 June 2013, the exchange rate for USD/TL is 2, and a bank wants to keep 60 percent of its TL-required reserve as FX, then the bank should provide the Central Bank with 54.75 dollar per 100 TL-required reserves:

30*(1.4/2)+5*(1.5/2)+5*(1.8/2)+5*(2.2/2)+5*(2.5/2)+5*(2.7/2)+5*(2.8/2)
= 54.75

Thus, 54.75 dollar is withdrawn from the market (see Figure 4).

Figure 4: The reserve option coefficients and the ROT

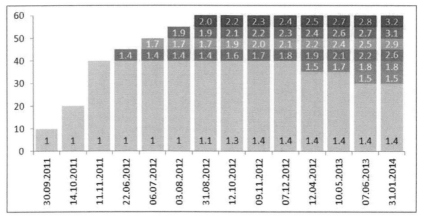

Source: TCMB (2013).

The interest rate corridor tool was used as a main monetary policy tool before using the ROM. The interest rate corridor mechanism ensures that short-term market interest rates are independent of the interest rate of the Central Bank (Değerli ve Fendoğlu, 2013). Excessive depreciation of TL is prevented by FX sales interventions and increasing upper level of interest rate corridor. On the other hand, the Central Bank allowed overnight interest rates to decrease by keeping interest rate corridor wide when global risk expectancy is high (Bürümcekçi and Sezgin, 2013; Başçı and Kara, 2011). Thus, while maintaining a tight stance for credits, it has also prevented the further appreciation of the TL. There are two basic benefits from the interest rate corridor (Oduncu, Ermişoğlu and Çelik, 2013: 48):

1. The use of credit and exchange rate channels in different directions in line with the objectives of inflation and financial stability.
2. The flexibility of the Central Bank's stance against daily frequency in the market.

However, interest rate corridor undermines risk perceptions toward Turkey and creates undesirable pressure of interest volatility toward economic activities. Moreover, it leads to considerable decrease in the FX reserves of the Central Bank.

The following reasons also contributed to use of the ROM instead of interest rate corridor (TCMB, 2012c and 2012a):

1. Slow performance of the economic activity and the need to support the economy through loans,
2. Improvement of global risk appetite and stabilization of TL with the possibility of additional monetary loosening in developed countries,
3. The Central Bank's settling of FX reserves on a strong ground.

If we summarize the results and benefits of ROC application: Permission of banks to keep fraction of their required reserves as FX or gold at the Central Bank will increase the TL liquidity of banks. Hence, the cost of TL funding is lowered for banks whose daily transactions are mostly made in TL. The ROC application also encourages banks to borrow cheaper FX from abroad. The main advantages of ROC application for the CBRT are twofold (Demirhan, 2013: 584; Başçı and Kara, 2011):

1. The CBRT increases its FX reserves.
2. The effect of the currency substitution has also been reduced due to increased FX reserves of the CBRT.

4 Conclusion

Recently, traditional monetary policies have been replaced by modern stabilizers. One of these stabilizers is the ROM. The ROM is developed to fight against the negative effects of inflation targeting, exchange rate policies, and short-term capital flows. With the introduction of ROM, an optional operating system has emerged in which both commercial and investment banks in market maintain their domestic currency liquidity.

The ROM system, which has been implemented since 2012, is operated by the ROC, which is determined according to the conjuncture. This system, which enables banks to obtain FX at a lower cost from foreign markets, increases not only the foreign currency liquidity capability of the Central Bank but also the FX reserves of the Central Bank. It also ensures that the neoliberal movements in capital and money markets affect positively the economy by filtering markets from speculative flows.

According to the principle of accountability and transparency, the Central Bank should share the policy coefficients to be used under the ROM applications with the public. This can also contribute the scientific studies to be made on the required reserves and in turn to the development of optimal policies.

References

Alper, K., Kara, A. H. and Yörükoğlu, M. (2012). "Rezerv Opsiyon Mekanizması", TCMB Ekonomi Notları, Sayı: 2012–28. http://www.tcmb.gov.tr/wps/wcm/connect/79085fc2-6da0-44cf-a7f1-d0a64a15a9e4/EN1228.pdf?MOD=AJPERES&CACHEID=79085fc2-6da0-44cf-a7f1-d0a64a15a9e4.

Ayyıldız, Z. (2012). "Rezerv Opsiyon Katsayısı Nedir?" http://kanalfinans.com/egitim/rezerv-opsiyon-katsayisi-nedir.

Başçı, E. (2014). "Rezerv Opsiyon Mekanizması" http://www.hurriyet.com.tr/erdem-basci-doviz-depo-piyasasindaki-faizi-indirebiliriz-27215590.

Başçı, E. and Kara, H. (2011). "Finansal İstikrar ve Para Politikası". TCMB Çalışma Tebliği, No:11/08. 2011.Ankara, Turkey: Türkiye Cumhuriyet Merkez Bankası.

Böcüoğlu, M. A. (2015). "Rezerv Opsiyon Mekanizmasının Banka Davranışlarına Etkisi". Uzmanlık Yeterlilik Tezi. TCMB Piyasalar Genel Müdürlüğü. Ankara, Turkey: Türkiye Cumhuriyeti Merkez Bankası.

Bürümcekçi, H. and Sezgin, N. (2013). "Merkez Bankası'nın en yeni silahı ROK Nedir?" http://neo-ekonomi.com/rok-nedir-merkez-bankasi/.

Değerli, A. and Fendoğlu, S. (2013). "Otomatik Dengeleyici Bir Politika Aracı Olarak Rezerv Opsiyon Mekanizması: Döviz Kuru Beklentilerinden Bulgular". Türkiye Cumhuriyeti Merkez Bankası Çalışma Tebliği, 13/28. http://www.tcmb.gov.tr/wps/wcm/connect/TCMB+TR/TCMB+TR/Main+Menu/Yayinlar/Arastirma+Yayinlari/Calisma+Tebligleri/2013/Sunum+51 Access Date: 05.12.2015.

Demirhan, B. (2013). "Türkiye'de Yeni Yaklaşım Çerçevesinde Para Politikalarının Finansal İstikrarı Sağlama Yönünde Uygulanması". Afyon Kocatepe Üniversitesi İktisadi İdari Bilimler Fakültesi Dergisi, 15(2): 567–589. http://www.iibfdergi.aku.edu.tr/pdf/15_2/25.pdf.

Eğilmez, M. (2012). "Karşılıklar Politikası ve Rezerv Opsiyon Katsayısı". http://www.mahfiegilmez.com/2012/11/karslklar-politikas-ve-rezerv-opsiyon.html.

Glocker, C. and Towbin, P. (2012). "Reserve Requirements for Price and Financial Stability: When Are They Effective?". International Journal of Central Banking, 8(1): 65–113.

HSBC (2013). "Expanding the Reserve Requirement Framework". http://www.hsbc.com.tr/HSBCYatirim/Arastirma/research/pdf/Economy/CBRT-Mar13.pdf.

Kara, A.H. (2012). "Küresel Kriz Sonrası Para Politikası". TCMB Çalışma Tebliği No: 12/17. https://www.researchgate.net/profile/Hakan_Kara/publication/254423678_Kuresel_kriz_sonrasi_para_politikasi/links/5406baf90cf23d9765a7ff2b/Kueresel-kriz-sonrasi-para-politikasi.pdf

Küçüksaraç, D. and Özel, Ö. (2012). "Rezerv Opsiyonu Mekanizması ve Optimal Rezerv Opsiyonu Katsayılarının Hesaplanması". TCMB Çalışma Tebliği No: 12/32. http://www.tcmb.gov.tr/wps/wcm/connect/ccdc3f45-c3bc-4d76-a43f-feb4b73edcc2/WP1232.pdf?MOD=AJPERES&CACHEID=ROOTWORKSP ACEccdc3f45-c3bc-4d76-a43f-feb4b73edcc2.

Miniane, J. (2013). "Turkey". https://www.imf.org/external/pubs/ft/scr/2013/cr13364.pdf.

Oduncu, A., Ermişoğlu, E. and Çelik, Y. (2013). "Merkez Bankası'nın Yeni Enstrümanı Rezerv Opsiyonu Mekanizması ve Kur Oynaklığı". Türkiye Bankalar Birliği Bankacılar Dergisi, (86): 43–52.

Özatay, F. (2012). "Bir Finansman Mühendisliği Örneği Olarak ROM". http://www.radikal.com.tr/yazarlar/fatih_ozatay/bir_finansman_muhendisligi_ornegi_olarak_rom-1105531.

Seval, B. and Özdemir, K. A. (2013). "2000'li Yıllardan Günümüze Değişen Türkiye Ekonomisi". SERPAM (Sermaye Piyasaları Araştırma ve Uygulama Merkezi). http://serpam.org/wp-content/uploads/TE_1.pdf.

TCMB (2012a). Online Bülten. (28). http://www.tcmb.gov.tr/wps/wcm/connect/14cdae5a-4898-42c7-a7dc-4087642253e4/Bulten28.pdf?MOD=AJPERES.

TCMB (2012b). "2013 Yılında Para ve Kur Politikası". TCMB, Ankara.

TCMB (2012c). "Zorunlu Karşılıklarda Rezerv Opsiyon Mekanizması". http://www.tcmb.gov.tr/wps/wcm/connect/8dfb08f7-ed9c-4a9d-9764-f6cee27c7d4d/bolumIV5.pdf?MOD=AJPERES&CACHEID=ROOTWORKSPACE8dfb08f7-ed9c-4a9d-9764-f6cee27c7d4d.Access Date: 06.12.2015.

TCMB (2013). "2014 Yılında Para ve Kur Politikası". TCMB, Ankara.

Tokatlıoğlu, Y. and Saraçoğlu, B. (2013). "Yeni Bir Para Politikası Aracı: Rezerv Opsiyon Mekanizması". EY Uluslararası Ekonomi Kongresi I (EYC2013), Ekim 24–25, 2013, Ankara, Türkiye (No. 291). www.ekonomikyaklasim.org/eyc2013/?download=Paper%20291.pdf.

XTB (2014). "Detaylı Enstrüman Analizi-USDTRY Rezerv Opsiyon Mekanizması" http://www.xtb.com.tr/forex-analizler/26122013-dea-1346,20131226,124700.

Haydar Akyazı and İbrahim Al

Globalization and Monetary Policy

1 Introduction

Globalization can be defined as the integration of cross-border markets and increasing mutual dependency of states on political and economic policies. There are different scenarios regarding when globalization began. "According to different authors, globalization has been going on either since the first movement of people out of Africa into other parts of world, or since third millennium BC (when according to Andre Gunder Frank the World System emerged), or only since the great geographical discoveries, or in the nineteenth century, or after year 1945, or only since the late 1980s" (Grinin and Korotayev, 2014: 33). In the literature, there is no consensus concerning either when globalization began or what it means and its effects. The main reason of this situation is that globalization has the highly complicated, comprehensive, dynamic, and permanent characteristics.

The 1980s is the period that differentiates globalization from the past. This period is called as the new wave of globalization and has its own unique characteristics. These characteristics can be summarized as the adaptation of the majority of developing countries to the global markets, marginalization of the rest of the developing countries in the world economy, decreasing income and increasing poverty levels in marginalized developing countries, and the increasing significance of international migration and capital flows (The World Bank, 2000: 31). With a new wave of globalization, the world economy has transformed deeply and comprehensively since the mid-1980s. Integration of real and financial markets is the main indicator of this transformation. This process also directly affects the execution of monetary policies (Moutot and Vitale, 2009: 5).

The aim of this study is to investigate the impacts of globalization on monetary policy and central banking. The rest of the chapter is organized as follows. Section 2 discusses the term of globalization and its effects on monetary policy and central banking. Section 3 focuses on the effects of globalization on the monetary transmission mechanism. Section 4 analyzes the relationship between globalization and future of central banking and discusses the reflections of globalization on monetary policy strategies. Section 5 concludes.

2 Overall reflections of globalization on monetary policy and central banking

There are many definitions of globalization. Globalization may be described as "increasing and intensified flows between countries of goods, services, capital, ideas, information and people, which produce crossborder integration of a number of economic, social and cultural activities" (Wynne, 2005: 2). From a more technical and different perspective, globalization "is a transplanetary process or set of processes involving increasing liquidity and the growing multi-directional flows of people, objects, places and information as well as the structures they encounter and create that are barriers to, or expe-dite, those flows ..." (Ritzer, 2011: 2).

Globalization has deep impacts on many areas including economics. Globalization also leads to changes in monetary policy and central banking. The impacts of globalization on monetary policy and central banking can be summarized as follows:

- Globalization in financial markets may cause significant inefficiency and uncertainty in a country's monetary transmission mechanism. The global integration in financial markets may result in inability of central bank to control domestic interest rates and accordingly the failure of monetary policies' sufficiency in affecting price stability. In other words, the interest rate channel may not work effectively. In addition, fluctuations in exchange rates and asset prices might cause uncertainty in the monetary transmission mechanism.
- Globalization may affect inflation dynamics. Globalization may contribute to both decrease and increase in the global inflation. On the one hand, globalization contributes to the formation of a common culture about the benefits of price stability and breaks the inflation expectations. In this context, globalization has played an important role in providing a consensus on the central bank's primary objective to be price stability. On the other hand, central banks started having difficulty in maintaining price stability due to the price volatilities experienced in international food, energy, and other commodities due to globalization.
- Advances in information and communication technologies along with globalization create difficulties in central banks' control of money supply. The proliferation of new payment instruments such as electronic money reduces the demand for central bank money and causes negative effect on the interaction between monetary policy instruments and objectives. These developments may lead to the emergence of new monetary policy tools and some changes in

the monetary policy objectives and strategies. For example, in many countries monetary targeting and then exchange rate targeting have been abandoned; inflation-targeting strategy has been widely implemented instead. Moreover, central banks started to focus on not only price stability but also financial stability.

- Advances in information and communication technologies along with globalization have made access to information easier, rapid, and largely cost-free than ever before. As a result of this radical change in access to information, the expectations of economic actors and the management of those expectations in accordance with the policy objectives have become even more important. Indeed, the effective management of economic actors' expectations becomes very important for the management of monetary policies for central banks. The central banking started to be defined as "the art of managing and guiding expectations".

- With globalization, concepts such as the transparency, accountability, and independence of the central banks have become more spoken.

- Globalization causes the Phillips curve to become flatter. Globalization weakened the relationship between domestic growth and domestic inflation and led to dependence of domestic inflation on overseas growth (production).

- Globalization has led to an increase in the frequency of economic crises and the contagion of the crises. Increasing global uncertainty and volatility create serious problems for central banks in implementation of monetary policy.

With the increase in the number of global crises, the questions have been raised regarding the role and structure of the central banks to achieve international coordination on the one hand, and whether it is possible to benefit from international coordination through monetary policy rule on the other hand. Globalization also weakened effectiveness of some of targeting policies. There are three targeting policies: monetary targeting, exchange rate targeting, and inflation targeting. Globalization weakened effectiveness of monetary targeting and exchange rate targeting policies. With globalization, the monetary aggregates fail to signal about the state of monetary policy and ultimately fail to be a good nominal anchor for inflation expectations (Mishkin, 2004: 501; Mishkin, 2006: 11). For these reasons, in New Zealand, Canada, and UK, central banks have begun to abandon the monetary targeting strategy since the mid-1980s. This situation is best described by the President of Central Bank of Canada: "We did not abandon monetary aggregates, they abandoned us" (Hammond, 2012: 5).

After adopted by some countries such as Argentina, Mexico and Turkey, and achieved partial success in reducing inflation, exchange rate targeting strategy is also abandoned because of the problems such as increasing capital movements caused by globalization. Since the 1990s, monetary targeting and exchange rate targeting have been abandoned and inflation targeting has started to be used by central banks instead. Nowadays, inflation targeting is considered to be the most appropriate monetary policy strategy for central banks.

3 Effects of globalization on monetary transmission channels

Monetary transmission mechanism is a process that the monetary policy decisions cause changes in real gross domestic product and inflation (Taylor, 2006: 11). Bernanke (2007) points out that when the impact of globalization of financial system on monetary policy is investigated, starting point should be the monetary transmission channels. There are three basic monetary transmission channels, namely interest rate channel, asset price channel (foreign exchange channel and stock price channel), and credit channel (bank lending channel and the balance sheet channel) (Mishkin, 1996).

Interest rate channel is based on a traditional Keynesian investment/saving-liquidity preference/money supply equilibrium (IS-LM) analysis. According to this channel, when money supply (MS) changes, real interest rate (r), investment spending (I), aggregate demand (AD), and output (y) change, respectively. For example, if the MS increases, r decreases and I increases, and hence AD and y increase. According to the exchange rate channel, when money supply changes, real interest rate (r), exchange rate (E), net exports (NX), aggregate demand (AD), and output (y) change. For instance, if the MS increases, r decreases, E and NX increase, and accordingly AD and y increase. According to the credit channel when the supply of money changes, bank deposits (D), bank loans (L), investment (I), aggregate demand (AD) and output (y) change. For example, if the MS increases, D, L, and I increase, hence AD and y increase[1].

3.1 Interest rate channel

The interest rate channel of monetary policy will be more effective if domestic financial markets are not developed enough. Liberalization of capital movements in line with globalization could strengthen interest rate channel. However, financial

---

1   In this study, only the explanations of interest rate channel, exchange rate channel, and credit channel is given since they are directly related to the topic. For details see; Mishkin F.S. (1996), "The Channels of Monetary Transmission: Lessons for Monetary Policy", *NBER Working Paper Series*, 5464.

globalization would have a negative effect on the effectiveness of the interest rate channel especially in small and open economies. In the globalization process although the effectiveness of the interest rate channel does not completely disappear, it dramatically decreases. According to Tahir (2012: 29), growing financial globalization has a negative effect on the relationship between domestic savings and domestic investment, and thereby the relative importance of traditional interest rate channel decreases.

Meier (2013: 26) investigates the effects of financial globalization on monetary transmission channels by using the new Keynesian dynamic stochastic general equilibrium models. He suggests that the financial integration as a result of globalization has a negative impact on interest rate channel since it leads to lower transaction costs and higher holding of foreign assets. Lower transaction costs may negatively impact the control of monetary policy on domestic spending because it enables domestic economic actors to finance their consumption by borrowing from abroad. As a result, this situation weakens the interest rate channel. However, Mishkin (2008) argues that globalization does not have any effect on interest rate channel's impact on economy. Even if domestic interest rates are influenced by foreign interest rates due to globalization, the central bank will continue to affect long-term interest rates and domestic credit costs by influencing short-term interest rates. Thus, the central bank's impact on output and inflation will continue since central banks still have a chance to affect demand and output by influencing short-term interest rates.

3.2 Exchange rate channel

Exchange rate is the key concept in international monetary theories and it has three significant roles. First of all, expected change in exchange rates affects the return on assets hold in several currencies. These return differentials lead to emergence of international capital flows in order to obtain optimal returns. Second, currency exchange rates influence export and import by affecting relative prices of good/services and labor in different countries. Finally, past and expected exchange rate changes affect inflation rate via exchange rate channel (Taylor, 2006: 3). Globalization has made short-term interest rates much more dependent on external financial developments compared to the previous period and consequently the sensitivity of interest rates to the differences of exchange rates among countries has increased (Kamin, 2010: 33). This situation increases the efficiency of the exchange rate channel. Tahir (2012: 29) asserts that the increase in international trade and financial globalization strengthens the exchange rate channel. However, growing international competition may reduce the effectiveness of exchange rate channel (Tahir, 2012: 2).

The changes in exchange rates have the power to change net export, ultimately aggregate demand and production. For example, if the central bank implements tight monetary policy, interest rates will rise and this will lead to domestic currency appreciation. The domestic currency appreciation will decrease exports while increasing imports. Thus, net exports will decrease and hence aggregated demand will decrease. With the increasing share of internationally traded goods and services in economy, globalization may increase the role of the exchange rate channel while decreasing the role of interest rate channel. In this framework, globalization has increased the sensitivity of economy on exchange rates. With financial globalization, demand for domestic and foreign assets has become more sensitive to international return differentials. Meier (2013: 26) focuses on this subject from the asset price perspective. Financial integration allows economic actors hold more foreign assets in their portfolios. In this case, a monetary policy that leads to currency appreciation increases return of foreign assets and thus the wealth of economic actors.

3.3 Credit channel

Banks have critical role on monetary transmission channels in the countries whose financial system is dominated by banking sector. Cetorelli and Goldberg (2008) argue that globalization has a deep and pervasive impact on the transmission of monetary policy. Domestic-owned banks display significant sensitivity to monetary policy and enhance the effect of credit channel. However, foreign-owned banks can curb the efficiency of credit channel. For example, a central bank can follow a contractionary monetary policy to reduce domestic aggregate demand. However, foreign-owned and global banks can still continue to extend credit by receiving funds from their home countries and foreign sources. On the contrary, a shock to home country of foreign banks can also be transmitted to host country. Thus, the efficiency of credit channel and ability of central bank to affect markets via this channel will be reduced by the counteractions of foreign-owned banks. Hence, the impact of monetary policy through the credit channel on domestic markets diminishes over time as globalization progresses. Ananchotikul and Seneviratne (2015) examined the effect of foreign banks on monetary transmission channels under financial globalization. They found that foreign-owned banks are less responsive to monetary policy of host country.

4 Globalization and future of central banking

With the use of information and communication technology widely in the monetary sector, some electronic payment instruments such as "the e-cash," "the network money," and "e-money" have become popular. This process known as "cashless world" or "cashless society" may have an important influence on monetary policy and central banking. The possible effects of electronic money usage are as follows:

- Limit the central bank's ability to control money supply,
- Increase the velocity of money,
- Decrease international monetary control,
- Increase the money multiplier,
- Decrease the currency-to-deposit ratio,
- Decrease the reserve-to-deposit ratio.

Thus, monetary base, money multiplier and money supply become unstable, and it will be difficult for the central bank to enact monetary policy and to follow monetary targeting. Foresights about the effect of spreads of electronic money can be divided into two groups:

First group of researchers argue that there will not be a radical change in the field of central banking and monetary policy due to the spread of electronic payment instruments owing to information and communication technology developments (Goodhart, 2000; Freedman, 2000; Woodford, 2000). Their argument can be summarized as follows:

- There is no significant change in basic principles, main goals, and objectives of the central bank's monetary policy.
- There has been no electronic payment instrument that can replace the central bank's money since the beginning of the central banks. Moreover, this kind of payment instruments will be riskier instruments than the central bank money.
- Central banks can apply legal provisions on electronic money to compensate for the decrease in their seigniorage revenue.
- As a public institution, central banks never go bankrupt. They can increase demand for their money by increasing interest rates.

Second group of researchers argue that there will be a radical change in the field of central banking and monetary policy due to the spread of electronic payment instruments owing to information and communication technology developments (King, 1999; Dowd, 1998; Friedman, 1999; White, 2001). Their argument can be summarized as follows:

- Because of technological innovations, some functions of central bank such as the final settlements can be fulfilled by the private sector without a central bank.

- The interaction and communication between monetary policy and the market may weaken because of technological innovations. This means a significant reduction in the effectiveness of monetary policy.
- It is irrelevant to discuss whether the technological innovation will reduce the central bank's effectiveness. Because central banks have historically never worked efficiently and effectively.
- Technological innovations will reduce the demand for the central bank's money. This will eliminate completely the effectiveness of monetary policy. This will lead to a significant loss of seigniorage revenue of the central bank.

In retrospect, some of the arguments outlined in these two groups became reality, some of them partially came true, and some have not come true. Despite everything, central banks have continued to maintain their existence. However, implemented monetary policies have started to confront with major challenges. In fact, the 2008 Global Crisis has displayed the ineffectiveness of conventional monetary policy in times of crisis. Nevertheless, there are still rooms for central banks to use new methods of monetary policy.

5 Conclusion

Globalization of financial markets has critical impacts on monetary policy and central banking. The effects of globalization on monetary policy and central banking can be summarized as follows:

- Interest rate and domestic credit channels of the monetary transmission channels have been weakened by globalization in financial market.
- As a result of the globalization of product, service and factor markets, and also integration of the developing countries into the global economy, goods and services have become cheaper in the world trade. Hence the prices of imported goods become cheaper and consequently, inflationary pressures are reduced in the domestic market.
- Introduction of new payment instruments such as electronic money has accelerated the debate on the future of the central banking.
- With the liberalization of the capital movements and financial liberalization, globalization leads to ineffectiveness of exchange rate and monetary targeting regimes. Instead, inflation targeting has become popular under the conditions of globalization.

References

Ananchotikul, N. and Seneviratne D. (2015). Monetary Policy Transmission in Emerging Asisa: The Role of Banks and the Effects of Financial Globalization. *IMF Working Paper,* WP/15/207, 1–34, International Monetary Fund, Washington, DC.

Bernanke, B. S. (2007). Globalization and Monetary Policy. http://www.federalreserve.gov/newsevents/speech/bernanke20070302a.htm [accessed on 15.08.15].

Cetorelli, N. and Goldberg L. S. (2008). Banking Globalization, Monetary Transmission and the Lending Channel. *Deutsche Bundesbank Discussion Paper Series 1: Economic Studies*, 21/2008, 1–37.

Dowd, K. (1998). Monetary Policy in the 21st Century: An Impossible Task?. *Cato Journal*, 17, 327–331.

Freedman, C. (2000). Monetary Policy Implementation: Past, Present and Future—Will Electronic Money Lead to the Demise of Central Banking?. *International Finance*, 3, 221–227.

Friedman, B. M. (1999). The Future of Monetary Policy: The Central Bank as an Army with Only a Signal Crops?. *International Finance*, 2, 321–338.

Goodhart, C. A. E. (2000). Can Central Banking Survive the IT Revolution?. *International Finance*, 3, 189–209.

Grinin, L. E. and Korotayev, A. V. (2014). Origins of Globalization in the Framework of the Afroeurasian World-System History. *Journal of Globalization Studies*, 5(1), 32–64.

Hammond, G. (2012). State of the Art of Inflation Targeting, Bank of England. CCBS Handbook No. 29, London.

Kamin, S. B. (2010). Financial Globalization and Monetary Policy. *Board of Governors of the Federal System International Finance Discussion Papers*, 1002, 1–51.

King, M. (1999). Challenges for Monetary Policy: New and Old. *Paper Prepared for the Symposium on "New Challenges for Monetary Policy"* Sponsored by the Federal Reserve Bank of Kansas City at Jackson Hole, Wyoming, http://www.bankofengland.co.uk/archive/Documents/historicpubs/speeches/1999/speech51.pdf.

Meier, S. (2013). Financial Globalization and Monetary Transmission. *Federal Reserve Bank of Dallas Globalization and Monetary Policy Institute Working Paper,* 145, 1–42. Federal Reserve Bank of Dallas, Dallas.

Mishkin, F. S. (1996). The Channel of Monetary Transmission: Lessons for Monetary Policy. *NBER Working Paper Series, 5464*, 1–27, The National Bureau of Economic Research, Cambridge, MA.

Mishkin, F. S. (2004). The Economics of Money, Banking, and Financial Markets. Seventh Edition, Addison-Wesley, Boston, MA.

Mishkin, F. S. (2006). Monetary Policy Strategy: How Did We Get Here?. *NBER Working Paper Series, 12515*, 1–44, The National Bureau of Economic Research, Cambridge, MA.

Mishkin, F. S. (2008). Globalization, Macroeconomic Performance and Monetary Policy. *NBER Working Paper Series, 13948*, 1–15, The National Bureau of Economic Research, Cambridge, MA.

Moutot, P. and Vitale, G. (2009). Monetary Policy Strategy in a Global Environment. *European Central Bank Occasional Paper Series, 106*, 1–42, European Central Bank Frankfurt, Germany.

O'Rourke, K. and Williamson, J. G. (2000). When Did Globalization Begin?. *NBER Working Paper Series, 7632*, 1–42, The National Bureau of Economic Research, Cambridge, MA.

Ritzer, G. (2011). Globalization: The Essential. Wiley–Blackwell, Chichester.

Tahir, M. N. (2012). Relative Importance of Monetary Transmission Channels: A Structural Investigation: Case of Brazil, Chile and Korea. Universite de Lyon. 1–41. http://ecomod.net/system/files/Relative%20Importance%20of%20Mon etary%20Transmission%20Channels%20AStructural%20Investigation%20 Case%20of%20Brazil%2C%20Chile%20and%20Korea.pdf.

Taylor, J. B. (2006). "Implications of Globalization for Monetary Policy", Academic Consultants Meeting Federal Reserve Board, 28 September 2006, 1–14, Board of Governers of the Federal Reserve System, Washington, DC.

The World Bank (2000). Globalization, Growth, and Poverty. A Copublication of the World Bank and Oxford Press, Washington, DC.

White, L. H. (2001). In What Respects Will the Information Age Make Central Banks Obsolete?. *Cato Journal*, 21, 219–224.

Woodford, M. (2000). Monetary Policy in a World Without Money. *NBER Working Paper Series, 7853*, 1–47, The National Bureau of Economic Research, Cambridge, MA.

Woodford, M. (2001). Monetary Policy in the Information Economy. *NBER Working Paper Series, 8674*, 1–70, The National Bureau of Economic Research, Cambridge, MA.

Woodford, M. (2007). Globalization and Monetary Control. *NBER Working Paper Series, 1339*, 1–74, The National Bureau of Economic Research, Cambridge, MA.

Wynne, M. A. (2005). Globalization and Monetary Policy. *Federal Reserve Bank of Dallas Southwest Economy*, 4, 1–8.

Afşin Ahmet Kaya, Elif Çelenk Kaya, and Ceren Kaya

Situation Analysis of Public Hospitals in the Eastern Black Sea Region in Terms of Disaster Management

1 Introduction

Disasters are unexpected and undesired situations in which a society is under threat, local interventions are insufficient, national resources are required to be mobilized, and great losses of life and property are sustained (Drabek, 1996: 2–3). Disasters are natural, technological, and man-induced events that require many institutions and organizations to work in coordination. They cause physical, economic, and social losses for individuals and affect societies or human populations by stopping or intercepting normal life and human activities. They are sudden devastating events that are difficult to be stopped by humans and cause losses of life and property. An event or series of events need to cause loss of life or property in order to be considered as a "disaster" (Şahin and Sipahioğlu, 2002: 15). The magnitude of the disaster or catastrophe is usually measured with losses of life, injuries, structural damages, and economic losses caused by them (Bozkırlı, 2004).

The single most effective action that can be taken against disasters is to conduct research, develop plans, and put them into action in order to escape damages caused by them and minimize their effects on the society. In order to provide timely and effective health services during disasters, it is vital that health workers are prepared for a disaster. The main purpose of the disaster management in health institutions is to minimize the damage to the health-care providers and consumers of health services in disaster situations. "Disaster management" includes all activities that inform people about natural events in their vicinity, teach about reasons and consequences of disasters in detail, and demonstrate how to remain unaffected or affected as little as possible from these events in case of recurrence. The concept of modern disaster management involves pre-disaster protection activities such as preparation, forecasting, early warning, and mitigating losses and damages. On the other hand, "crisis management" involves post-disaster activities such as risk management, impact analysis, intervention, recovery, and reconstruction (Kadıoğlu, 2008). In this context, an effective disaster management includes all activities that are necessary before, during, and after the disaster (Demirci and

Karakuyu, 2004). Disaster management is a continuous and repeating process rather than a process that ends prominently (Lettieri et al., 2009).

This study aims to evaluate the current situation of public hospitals in the central districts of the Eastern Black Sea Region of Turkey in terms of disaster management and to propose recommendations in accordance with results of the comparison among hospitals in the region.

2 Disaster management in hospitals

Undoubtedly, health-care institutions and hospitals are among the most needed units in case of emergencies such as disaster and war. Preparedness of hospitals in case of such threats prevents a possible state of panic and allows for immediate medical response to the highest number of injured people. In order to prepare hospitals to the disasters, plans must be made with a certain discipline level and according to certain standards, and these plans must be reviewed prior to disaster and be taught to the entire personnel.

Hospital Disaster Plan aims to prevent and mitigate risks related to disasters and emergencies and ensures preparedness against disasters and emergencies. It is a disaster recovery system that suggests a systematic approach that can be applied by all sorts of health institutions (HAMER, 2009). It is a disaster recovery system whereby assistance is extended in the time of chaos following a disaster, disaster responders have very clear definitions of their tasks, regular records are continued to be kept, and a common language is used in every place of the disaster area.

Hospitals' location, service capacity, and facilities have decisive importance in achievement of aims and objectives of Hospital Disaster Plan. In this regard, first of all, hospitals' structural and nonstructural elements, personnel, and operation features must be perfectly defined (Sağlık Bakanlığı, 2015). Then, hospital personnel must enhance their professional skills in order to provide adequate health-care service before, during, and after the disaster (Hsu, 2004).

Hospital Disaster Plan

- plays a role in formation of long-term damage mitigation strategies;
- helps with correct management of resources;
- is both a necessity and an opportunity;
- is important in damage mitigation and prevention;
- is the new concept of disaster response throughout the world;
- is an accreditation process required by the Ministry of Health of Turkey in all hospitals;

- is taken into account by all international auditing organizations in the accreditation process of hospitals;
- ensures active preparedness and risk mitigation in case of disasters;
- is formed by attention and responsibility of hospital management and personnel;
- requires risk analysis in all cases;
- must involve risk analysis and budgeting.

If the hospital sustains damages due to internal or external disasters and no measures are taken, the community will be affected psychologically and a strong public pressure will be formed against authorities. That is why, health personnel and disaster coordinators must be constantly informed and trained with in-service trainings regarding disaster plans, recovery, first aid, emergency aid, communication, working under stress, triage, basic life support, carrying techniques, and legal responsibilities.

Considering that emergency units of hospital will have more work to do than ever during a disaster, it must be ensured that services should be standard and they should be provided within the shortest time possible. In order to provide the best service within the shortest time possible during a disaster, disaster plans should be prepared, tested, constantly renewed, and improved on a provincial or even a national level prior to the disaster.

3 Method

This cross-sectional and descriptive study aims to evaluate the current situation of public hospitals in central districts of the Eastern Black Sea Region in Turkey in terms of disaster management and to propose recommendations in accordance with results of the comparison among these hospitals. The study examines what kind of plans, which are prepared for internal and external extraordinary situations, hospitals have in place and what measures are taken by these hospitals in accordance with these plans and recommendations. The universe of the research consists of public hospitals located in central districts of the Eastern Black Sea Region in Turkey. No sample selection was performed, and seven hospitals that agreed to participate in the study were included in the study. The study was conducted between April 15, 2016 and June 3, 2016 by using the face-to-face interview method. The hospitals interviewed within the scope of the study are as follows: Gümüşhane Public Hospital, Ordu Public Hospital, Giresun University Prof. Dr. A. İlhan Özdemir Public Hospital, Trabzon Kanuni Education and Research Hospital, Bayburt State Hospital, Artvin Public Hospital, and Rize State Hospital.

Questionnaire of the study is based on a survey on "Hospital Organization in Disasters and the Status of Hospitals in Izmir" conducted in 1996. The questionnaire consists of 34 questions under 12 headings (hospital disaster planning, ambulance, security, evacuation plan, pharmacy, emergency unit plan, food services, chemical and radioactive accidents, communication, generator, and morgue). The questions in the questionnaire examine the availability of items required in disaster management. The questionnaire was used to collect data through face-to-face interviews and was applied to unit chiefs or managers of hospitals.

4 Findings

Research results indicate the following:

- All hospitals in the region have a disaster plan in which institutions to be collaborated in case of disaster is determined and all units in hospitals had easy access to this plan.
- All hospitals under the study have an annual schedule for hospital disaster drills.
- All hospitals under study have a crisis room and a written copy of the disaster plan in the crisis room except for Gümüşhane, Trabzon, and Bayburt Public Hospitals.
- All hospitals having a crisis room have multiple communication devices except for Rize Public Hospital. Availability of multiple communication devices in the crisis room allows for better conditions for communication, which is one of the most important needs during a crisis.
- Except for Artvin Public Hospital, all hospitals having a crisis room have a spare lighting device in the crisis room.
- All hospitals under study have an evacuation plan in case of an emergency situation in the hospital, and these plans include directions for outpatient and inpatient exit gates and hospitals to transfer patients.
- The triage plan, which determines the patient priority in emergency units of hospitals, is in place in all hospitals under study.
- All hospitals under study have a sufficient number of ambulances, which have critical importance in emergency cases. However, the provinces of Artvin and Rize, in spite of having a sufficient number of ambulances, don't have a provincial plan for ambulance provision.
- Ambulances of hospitals in all provinces have a detailed map of the city and the region, except for Trabzon, Bayburt, and Rize.
- Buildings of all hospitals were disaster resistant, except for Giresun, Trabzon, and Bayburt.
- All hospitals under study have special security units and early warning system in case of fire. However, it was noted that hospital security in Trabzon and

Artvin Public Hospitals was not adequate for emergency cases. Because hospitals are primary institutions in emergency and disaster cases, the adequacy of building security and special security units is among principal factors that should be considered.

- All hospitals under study have a disaster communication plan. All hospitals except for Bayburt Public Hospital have a public relations specialist to communicate with the press in case of a disaster.
- All hospitals included in the study have critically important drugs in stock.
- All hospitals except for Artvin Public Hospital have a disaster plan for food services.
- All public hospitals included in the study have a spare generator, and the maintenances of these generators are performed on a regular basis.
- Except for Trabzon Public Hospital, all hospitals under the study have a health plan for the chemical and radioactive accidents and don't have equipment to be used in such cases.
- The areas to be used as temporary morgues are designated in Gümüşhane, Ordu, and Giresun Public Hospitals in case of disasters.

5 Conclusion and recommendations

Our study on public hospitals in the Eastern Black Sea Region in Turkey reveals that although all public hospitals in the region have a disaster plan in which institutions to be collaborated in case of disaster are determined and all units in these hospitals have an easy access to this plan, there are some shortcomings in some criteria such as building durability, provision of additional ambulances in case of a disaster, temporary morgue sites, crisis room planning, and uninterrupted communication during a disaster.

A success in disaster management in hospitals requires the following:

- Training of the personnel
- Collaboration and continuous information sharing with hospital stakeholders
- Good risk analysis
- Damage mitigation activities
- Elimination of structural defects
- Disaster plan in line with realities of the hospital
- Hospital disaster drills performed on a regular basis

Also, disaster plans must be updated on a regular basis taking changing environmental conditions and evolving technologies into account. Existing disaster plans may be improved with a good SWOT (strengths, weaknesses, opportunities, threats) analysis, periodic checks, and controls. These improvements ensure that health-care service providers and consumers are affected from disasters on a minimal level.

References

Bozkırlı, K. (2004). "Afet ve Felaketlerde Hastane Hizmetlerinin Yonetimi: Bir Alan Calısması." Gazi Universitesi, Sosyal Bilimler Enstitusu, Yayınlanmamıs Bilim Uzmanlığı Tezi, Ankara.

Demirci, A. and Karakuyu, M. (2004). "Afet Yönetiminde Coğrafi Bilgi Teknolojilerinin Rolü." Doğu Coğrafya Dergisi, 9(12), 67–101.

Drabek, T. E. (1996). "The Social Dimensions of Disaster." FEMA, Fort Collins, CO.

Hacettepe Üniversitesi Afet Uygulama ve Araştırma Merkezi (HAMER) (2009). "Acil ve Afet Durumlarında Sağlık Yönetimi Kursu." Hacettepe Halk Sağlığı Anabilimdalı, Ankara.

Hsu, E. B. (2004). "Effectiveness of Hospital Staff Mass-Casualty Incident Training Methods: A Systematic Literature Review." Prehospital and Disaster Medicine, 19(3): 191–199.

Kadıoğlu, M. (2008). "Küresel Iklim Değişikliğine Uyum Stratejileri." Kar Hidrolojisi Sempozyumu Bildiri Kitabı, 27–28 Mart 2008, DSİ VII, Bölge Müdürlüğü Erzurum, 69–94.

Lettieri, E., Masella, C. and Radaelli, G. (2009). "Disaster Management: Findings from a Systematic Review." Disaster Prevention and Management, 18(2): 117–136.

Sağlık Bakanlığı (2015). "Hastane Afet Ve Acil Durum Planı (HAP) Hazırlama Klavuzu." Sağlık Bakanlığı, Ankara.

Şahin, C. and Şipahioğlu, Ş. (2002). "Doğal Afetler ve Türkiye." Gündüz Eğ. ve Yay, Ankara.

Rana Özyurt Kaptanoğlu

Marketing of Health Tourism in Turkey and the World

1 Introduction

The privatization efforts in the health sector have brought competition into the sector particularly after 2011. The increase in the number of alternative health services enabled consumers to choose among alternatives. Thus, marketing of the health services has become important, especially for private health providers.

In this study, the history of the health tourism, factors affecting demand for the health tourism, policies promoting the health tourism, health tourism in Turkey and the world, and analysis of health tourism in Turkey have been examined. The main focus of the study is the marketing of health tourism. How standard marketing methods are adapted to health tourism are examined with examples.

2 Health tourism

It is not easy to express tourism with a single definition because it is a multifaceted and complex phenomenon. When the origins of the tourism word are examined, the word "tournus," which means "turning, moving, turning around" in Latin, and "tourner" and "tour" words in French are confronted (Dinçer, 1993: 5). The concept of "tourists" began to be used first by the English. The word "tourism" began to be used after the usage of the word "tourists" in the 1800s. The concept of health tourism emerged as a result of traveling and accommodating for the purpose of treatment apart from the purpose of just traveling. Health tourism is the organized trips to the outside of the periphery for the protection, development, and improvement of the mental and physical well-being of people (Carrera and Bridges, 2006: 447). The aim of health tourism is to improve and protect the health as well as meeting the nutritional and entertainment requirements within a certain period of time (Aydın, 2012: 92).

Researchers indicate that people's travel for health purposes dates back to the second half of the first millennium BC (Güleç, 2011: 17). Patients were treated with thermal water in the Mediterranean countries in the ancient Greek Empire, whereas Europeans went to the Nile for the thermal treatment in the 18th century (Aydın, 2012: 92). Afterward, health-oriented travels diversified, developed rapidly, and started to be called "alternative tourism" (Çelik, 2009: 4). Health tourism is quite different from other tourism forms whereby health tourism is vital, not-postponed, and all-year-round tourism. Within the last century, treatment destinations have been concentrated in the countries that have relatively lower costs and fewer waiting periods. Nowadays, countries such as Cuba, Costa Rica, the Philippines, Singapore, and Colombia are among the leading destinations for travel (Aydın, 2012: 92).

3 Classification of health tourism

Medical tourism, thermal tourism, elderly tourism, and disabled tourism are considered as the types of health tourism.

> Medical tourism: Medical tourism mostly involves eye and teeth treatment, aesthetic surgery, cardiovascular surgery, prosthetic treatment, and infertility treatment (Aydın, 2012: 93). Advanced treatments (radiotherapy, Cyber Knife, etc.) and transplantation are other areas of medical tourism. The needs of medical tourists are met by hospitals and qualified personnel (Kılıçaslan, 2016: 36).

> Thermal tourism: It is the oldest type of health tourism. Thermal and spa-wellness tourism is perhaps the most ancient type of health tourism. Water treatment (hydrotherapy), seawater treatment (thalassotherapy), mud treatment, and climate treatment are types of treatments offered during thermal tourism.

> Elderly and disabled tourism: The elderly population has increased in recent years in the world, especially in Western European countries. In some countries, the elderly population is more than 25% of the total population. As age progresses, the need for treatment and care also increases. Rehabilitation services, sightseeing tours, various therapies, nursing care services, and special trips for disabled and elderly people are some types of services of this tourism.

4 Health-care marketing

The marketing of health care is a concept that emerges toward the end of the 1970s. Although health services have been developing rapidly over the past 50 years, neither doctors nor agencies need institutional marketing of health services until the last 10 years. The marketing of the service is a new concept for the health sector, and importance of it keeps increasing in the sector (Corbin et al., 2001: 7).

Despite the fact that every individual has right to reach health services, health services have become a part of business administration due to high costs, increasing supply, lack of consumer's knowledge about health, diversity of consumer needs, increase in demand, and changes in doctor–patient relations. Marketing of health services can be defined as the process of determining the needs of the consumers, shaping the services for the needs, generating new services, and encouraging the use of the offered services (Odabaşı, 1994: 30).

Kennett et al. (2005: 417) identified eight main marketing tasks for health-care services. These tasks include screening of the business environment (e.g., demographic, legal, technological, and social aspects), understanding of competing markets, understanding of the customer's decision-making process and purchasing behavior, deciding on what products and services will be presented, segmenting the market according to service types, determining the prices of the products, communicating with consumers and customers, and developing relationships with different organizations to distribute products.

The marketing of health services is more difficult than the marketing of both commodities and other services. The main reasons for this are that health services aren't desired product and cause negative feelings. That is why the focus point in the marketing of health services must be gathered on the benefits of service. In this case, institutions and organizations should be informed about the long-term changes of the consumers they serve, which requires follow-up for a while. This process will benefit consumers, shed light on future services, and play an important role in the development of consumer and customer relationships. Each health-care service will have a lifetime value in the consumer (Wolf, 2001: 13).

The marketing of health services is different from other sectors a number of ways. Table 1 summarizes these differences.

Table 1: Differences of Health-Care Marketing

The exchange doesn't always happen with the consent of both sides. For example, a consumer with a mental imbalance often does not receive services on demand.
The principle of change in the service offered is generally governed by the law and the government. A new regulation can reduce the profit of the organization (Odabaşı, 1994: 31).
There are two different target markets for nonprofit organizations. One of these is customers such as the other institutions and the other is the donor. The financing of services depends on the availability of resources (Harcar, 1991: 39).
Potential consumers think doctors as a health-care provider in the case of medical intervention, and nurses and caregivers as a health-care provider in the case of services in hospitals and nursing homes. This adds human factor as a fifth factor to the marketing besides product, price, distribution, and promotion (Odabaşı, 1994: 31).
Health insurance institutions can also intervene in pricing (Harcar, 1991: 39).
The price sensitivity to the service is less than other services, and the pricing is mostly in the hands of the physicians. In addition, the consumer has no chance to negotiate the price because the service is based on a doctor–patient relationship (Harcar, 1991: 39).

Only distribution of medicines and materials fit the classical marketing understanding. Distribution in health care is related to how the service will be served to the consumer (Harcar, 1991: 39).
It is not possible to measure the quality of the service provided (Odabaşı, 1994: 3). As the quality perception varies from one consumer to the next, even if the service is the same, the changing expectations can be perceived by the consumer at different values. In addition, there is no guarantee that every intervention will be successful as it is the person who gives the service.

5 Status of health tourism in the world

Since the mid-1990s, health tourism has become an alternative tourism type due to globalization and competition in the sector. Countries such as India, Cuba, Costa Rica, Thailand, Singapore, Colombia, and Malaysia are the most preferred countries for health tourism. Latecomers in the sector have to compete with Singapore, Malaysia, and Thailand. They have to offer prices lower than these countries and advertise in airports (Connell, 2006: 1093).

Thailand became prominent in medical tourism as a result of successes in gender exchange operations in the 1970s. In the following years, it increased its effectiveness in the medical tourism market with cosmetic surgery (Connell, 2006: 1095). The "Bumrungrad International Hospital," the largest investment in Thailand's medical tourism in 2000, is one of the top 10 medical tourism hospitals in the world. Since 2004, Thailand has started to implement a new medical tourism investment policy and aimed to position itself as the medical tourism center of Asia. In the World Bank's easy investment index, Thailand became the sixth country in the world and the second country in Asia. For those seeking to invest in medical tourism, Thailand has included policies such as national taxation exemptions, facilities for medical supplies, and the reduction of procedures into the national policies (Dinçer et al., 2016: 38).

After the 1997–1998 Asian economic crisis, Malaysia started to search for ways to escape from the crisis, and in this context, it decided to use the potential of medical tourism. Most of the tourists who prefer medical tourism services in Malaysia constitute travelers from countries in the Far East region. One of Malaysia's greatest advantages in this area is that it offers surgical operations with short waiting periods. Apart from this, it has become a preferred position in the medical tourism market by presenting medical activities with alternative health activities and tourism products (Dinçer et al., 2016: 38).

Although the quality of health-care services in European countries is high, expensive health care and long waiting periods force patients to seek health care from other countries. Especially in the areas of hip, heart, and lung operations and infertility treatment, health services are obtained from other countries (Gülen and Demirci, 2012: 109).

Panama, Brazil, Costa Rica, Hungary, Malaysia, India, Jordan, Thailand, Singapore, and South Korea are the leading countries in health tourism around the world. The following are the reasons why these countries attract health tourists (Barca et al., 2013:70):

1. Less developed countries: Less developed countries such as Sudan, Somalia, Afghanistan, and Libya send their patients abroad because of the lack of health service provision and the number of health-care staff within the country.
2. Asian countries: Asian countries such as Pakistan, Iraq, and Syria send their patients abroad because of the lack of health service provision and the number of personnel.
3. The United States and European countries: The United States and European countries send their patients abroad because of the high cost of health care and the long waiting periods.
4. Countries with a lot of elderly population: Inadequate number of health-care staff, large number of elderly population, and high cost of maintenance make patients in such countries to go abroad for health-care services.

6 Status of health tourism in Turkey

Medical tourism is a new concept and a new field for Turkey. It presents new opportunities to Turkey and attracts attention of all parties of the sector. Turkey has medical tourism potential in the areas of eye and teeth treatment, and aesthetic, oncology, orthopedic, cardiovascular, and brain surgeries. Table 2 presents the chronology of health tourism in Turkey.

Table 2: Chronology of Health Tourism in Turkey

Talking about health tourism started	1990–2000
Health tourism was on the agenda	2000–2005
Nonprofit organizations, and public and private sectors had health tourism awareness	2005–2010
Health tourism took part in the strategic action plan	2010–2014
The Ministry of Health established Health Tourism Unit	2010
Legislations and regulations about health tourism were issued	2011
The vision of 2023 included targets about the Ministry of Health	2011
The World Health Organization pointed out Turkey's health tourism potential, and health tourism potential became a government policy in Turkey	2011

7 Health-care services for foreigners in Turkey

Health-care services for foreigners can be classified as emergency health-care services provided for foreign residents in Turkey for a short time, health-care services
provided to those coming from abroad for treatment purposes, and health-care
services provided to foreign residents in Turkey for a long time.

> Emergency health-care services provided for foreign residents in Turkey for a short time:
> Emergency health-care services are provided to tourists coming to Turkey for the purpose
> of trade, tourism, meeting and congress, etc.

> Health-care services to those coming from abroad for treatment purposes: Health-care
> services are provided to tourists coming from neighboring countries, Central Asia,
> and developed countries (the United States and European countries). Besides, within
> this scope there are health-care services provided to Turkish immigrants coming from
> European countries.

> Health-care services provided to foreign residents in Turkey for a long time: Health-care
> services are provided to consular staff and foreigners living in touristic cities for a long time.

8 Distribution of health tourists in Turkey by country of origin

The following are the reasons and distribution of health tourists in Turkey by
country of origin:

1. Countries with a large population of Turks due to various reasons (Germany, Holland,
   France, etc.)
2. Developing countries suffering from service difficulties due to lack of infrastructure
   and physicians (Balkan countries, Turkic Republics in Central Asia)
3. Countries where health services are expensive (the United States, England, and Germany)
4. Countries with long waiting periods due to supply and demand unbalance (England,
   Holland, and Canada)
5. Countries sending a definite number of patients to Turkey under bilateral agreements
   (Afghanistan, Yemen, Sudan, etc.)

When we look at the number of international patients in Turkey, there is a decrease in the number of international patients in 2016 compared to 2015 due to
data collection problems, local terror events, and regional events. Decrease in
the total number of international patients is more severe in private health institutions than in public health institutions: the number of international patients
in public sector health institutions decreased by about 8%, whereas the number
of international patients in private health institutions decreased by about 26%
(Yıldırım et al., 2017: 7).

Among the first 10 countries from where international patients came to Turkey for receiving health services in 2015, Libya ranked first with 45,118 patients, whereas it ranked fourth in 2016 with a decrease in rate by approximately 57%. Germany ranked third with 30,366 patients in 2015, whereas it ranked first in 2016 with 21,759 patients. When we look at the top 10 countries from where international patients come to Turkey, it is seen that international patients come from countries that are 3.5- to 4-hour flight distances, the neighboring countries, the countries where the Muslim population is dominant, the countries where the immigrant citizens are predominant, and the countries that many tourists come from (see Table 3) (Yıldırım et al., 2017: 8).

Table 3: Top 10 Countries That International Patients Come from, 2015 to 2016

2015				2016			
Country	Medical Tourism	Tourist Health	Total	Country	Medical Tourism	Tourist Health	Total
Libya	37,470	7,648	45,118	Germany	4,863	16,896	21,759
Iraq	18,993	13,632	32,625	Azerbaijan	12,318	8,496	20,814
Germany	7,261	23,105	30,366	Iraq	11,026	7,973	18,999
Azerbaijan	17,668	10,944	28,612	Libya	12,855	6,140	18,995
Russia	4,350	11,502	15,852	Syria	1,919	12,589	14,508
Syria	2,419	12,587	15,006	Turkmenistan	2,684	5,944	8,628
Turkmenistan	4,616	7,941	12,107	England	1,266	6,864	8,130
England	1,543	8,128	9,671	Holland	1,385	5,711	7,096
Afghanistan	3,169	6,094	9,263	Russia	2,371	4,387	6,758
Holland	1,663	6,268	7,931	Saudi Arabia	2,179	3,568	5,747
Total	**99,152**	**107,849**	**206,551**	**Total**	**52,866**	**78,568**	**131,434**

Source: Yıldırım et al. (2017).

As it can be seen in Table 3, 52% of the international patients from the top 10 countries came within the scope of tourism health, whereas 48% of them came within the scope of medical tourism in 2015. In 2016, 60% of the international patients from the top 10 countries came within the scope of tourism health, whereas 40% of them came within the scope of medical tourism (Yıldırım et al., 2017: 9).

The health tourism regulates the seasonal and geographical distribution of tourism activities and contributes to the health economics of countries. The health tourism is important in terms of both treating patients in better and economically favorable environmental conditions and reducing the intensity in large and crowded cities. In this context, the advantages of health tourism can be listed as shown in Table 4.

Table 4: Advantages of Health Tourism

It provides international acceptance of countries as a global health-care provider.
It contributes to the development of international relations.
It provides global marketing and medical trade.
It provides patient satisfaction.
Income from foreign tourists contributes to the economic prosperity of the countries.
Medical tourism provides cost advantages to developing countries compared to developed countries.
Opportunities provided with foreign patients also provide better service to local patients in their own countries.
It increases the employment by allowing year-round tourism.

Source: Altın et al. (2012).

9 Conclusion

When the causes of medical tourism patients' preference for hospitals abroad are examined, it can be seen that the hospital's reputation and price factors are the most influential factors. These factors are followed by recommendation of previous patients and the effectiveness of promotion activities. The quality of the health services, lower costs compared to other countries, the suitability of climatic conditions, the number of holiday opportunities, short waiting periods, existence of specialist hospitals, and adequate technological equipment are the reasons of medical tourism patients' preference for hospitals in Turkey (Table 5).

Table 5: Reasons of Medical Tourism Patients' Preference for Hospitals in Turkey

Health-care services in Turkey are cheaper than other countries.
Hospital capacities in Turkey are adequate and physician quality is good.
Turkey serves both the Western and the Eastern countries due to its geographical location.
Foreign language knowledge of health personnel in Turkey is of high level.

When we look at the distribution of income from medical tourism and the number of patients in Turkey, Western European countries with 185 million people market size seem to have a significant market potential for Turkey. Considering idle capacity of private sector hospitals in Turkey, the health tourism is expected to increase productivity of these hospitals. The public sector, which aims to exist with a small share in the sector, should support the sector with adequate physicians, hospitals, and infrastructures. Policies about marketing of health tourism potential of Turkey should be implemented (Kılıçarslan, 2016: 95).

References

Altın, U., Bektaş, G., Antep, Z. and İrban, A. (2012). "Sağlık Turizmi ve Uluslararası Hastalar İçin Türkiye Pazarı." Acıbadem Üniversitesi Sağlık Bilimleri Dergisi, 3(3): 157–163.

Aydın, O. (2012). "Türkiye'de Alternatif Bir Turizm; Sağlık Turizmi." KMÜ Sosyal ve Ekonomik Araştırmalar Dergisi, 14(23): 91–96.

Barca, M., Akdeve, E. and Gedik, B. (2013). "Türkiye Sağlık Turizm Sektörünün Analizi ve Strateji Önerileri." İşletme Araştırmaları Dergisi, 5(3): 64–92.

Carrera, P.M. and Bridges, J.F.P. (2006). "Globalization and Healthcare: Understanding Health and Medical Tourism." Expert Review of Pharmacoeconomics & Outcomes Research, 6(4): 447–454.

Çelik, A. (2009). "Sağlık Turizmi Kapsamında Termal İşletmelerde Sağlık Hizmetleri Pazarlaması ve Algılanan Hizmet Kalitesi: Balçova Termal İşletmesinde Bir Uygulama." Yüksek Lisans Tezi, Dokuz Eylül Üniversitesi, İzmir, Türkiye.

Connell, J. (2006). "Medical Tourism; Sea, Sun, Sand and Surgery." Tourism Management, 27(4):1093–1100.

Corbin, C.L., Kelley, S.W. and Schwartz, R.W. (2001). "Concepts in Service Marketing for Healthcare Professionals." The American Journal of Surgery, 181(1): 1–7.

Dinçer, M.Z. (1993). Turizm Ekonomisi ve Türkiye Ekonomisinde Turizm. Filiz Kitabevi, İstanbul, Türkiye.

Dinçer, M.Z., Aydoğan Çiftçi, M. and Karayılan, E. (2016). "Gelişmekte Olan Ülkelerde Medikal Turizm: Türkiye'nin Tayland, Malezya ve Hindistan'a Göre Potansiyelinin Değerlendirilmesi." İstanbul Üniversitesi Sosyal Bilimler Dergisi, 1: 34–60.

Güleç, D. (2011). "Sağlık Turizmi Kapsamında (Sağlıklı Yaşlanma) Uygulamaları ve Yaşlı Bakımı: Türkiye Değerlendirmesi." Yüksek Lisans Tezi, Gazi Üniversitesi, Ankara, Türkiye.

Gülen K. and Demirci, S. (2012). Türkiye'de Sağlık Turizmi Sektörü. İstanbul Ticaret Odası Yayınları, İstanbul, Türkiye.

Harcar, T. (1991). "Sağlık Hizmetleri Pazarlaması." Pazarlama Dünyası Dergisi, 5(25): 38-40.

Kennett, P.A., Henson, S.W., Crow, S.M. and Hartman, S.J. (2005). "Key Tasks in Healthcare Marketing: Assessing Importance and Current Level of Knowledge." Journal of Health and Human Services Administration, 27(3-4): 414-424.

Kılıçarslan, M. (2016). "Sağlık Hizmetlerinde Bütünleşik Model Önerisi Yalın Sağlık (İsraf)." Doktora Tezi, Beykent Üniversitesi, İstanbul, Türkiye.

Kördeve, M. (2016). "Sağlık Turizmine Genel Bir Bakış ve Türkiye'nin Sağlık Turizmindeki Yeri." Uluslararası Sağlık Yönetimi ve Stratejileri Araştırma Dergisi, 2(1): 51-61.

Odabaşı, M. (1994). Sağlık Hizmetleri Pazarlaması. Eskişehir Anadolu Üniversitesi Yayın No. 799, Açıköğretim Fakültesi Yayın No. 409. Anadolu Üniversitesi Açıköğretim Fakültesi Yayınları, Eskişehir, Türkiye.

Wolf, E.J. (2001). "A New Approach to Healthcare Marketing", Healthcare Executive, 16(1): 12-16.

Yıldırım, H.H., Konca, M., Aydın, M.A., Diktaş, H., Otuzoğlu, M. and Okumuş, N. (2017). Türkiye Uluslararası Hasta Raporu 2015-2016. Sağlık Bakanlığı Sağlık Hizmetleri Genel Müdürlüğü Sağlık Turizmi Daire Başkanlığı, Ankara, Türkiye.

Vildan Oral and Afşin Ahmet Kaya

The Concept of Disaster Waste and Disaster Management: A Conceptual Analysis

1 Introduction

Due to its geographical location, geological and topographical structure, and climate characteristics, Turkey is among the countries that frequently encounter natural disasters that cause great loss of life and property (Altinbilek et al., 1997: 3). The number of houses damaged by various hazards in Turkey in the last 70 years is around 600,000. Sixty-six percent of this is caused by earthquakes, 15% by floods, 10% by ground slides, 7% by rock falls, and 2% by meteorological events and avalanches. As can be seen, the most destructive part of these natural disasters is earthquakes; realities and scientific forecasts indicate that many earthquakes will take place in the Anatolian geography (Özkul and Karaman, 2007: 251; Şengün, 2005: 1384). In addition to the loss of lives and property damages in disasters, disaster wastes emerging in disaster consequences or in the intervention stage constitute a great risk for both people and the environment. One of the biggest difficulties that arise after a major disaster (building or bridge collapse, flood, earthquake, hurricane, etc.) is the management of the wreckage brought by the disaster (Luther, 2010: 1). Proper handling of large quantities of ambulatory wastes constitutes a tremendous task for the government in the earthquake zone (Xiao et al., 2012: 109).

Disaster debris can disrupt the improvement of social and economic conditions in the affected area, threaten public health and the environment, and prevent health care and search and rescue services delivered to victims and disaster victims (Brown and Milke, 2009: 1). In order to provide all these assistance and intervention services, an effective transportation network needs to be established. For this reason, clearing disaster wrecks from transport networks is the first step for both intervention and recovery phases (Özdamar et al., 2014: 249). It is possible to reach survivors quickly and ensure effective evacuation, but only if the debris problem is resolved efficiently. In the first step, up to 72 hours immediately after the disaster, debris in the discharge routes and major roads should be cleaned to provide traffic flow to the affected area. In the second step, debris in all the roads must be collected, arranged, transported, temporarily stored, disposed of, or recycled (Özdamar et al., 2014: 249). According to Reinhart and McCreanor (1999: 3), the amount of waste generated after a catastrophe can be 5–15 times the annual waste generation rate of a community. If solid wastes caused by disasters can't be removed safely and properly, they may lead to secondary disasters because they can infiltrate into groundwater and surface waters and cause pestilence, bad smell, and image pollution (Aydın and Kara, 2003: 574). That is why, the responsible units should determine the amount of waste generated when disasters occur, ensure that they are collected in temporary storage areas, and determine the appropriate collection methods and recycling options (Asari et al., 2013: 290). In Turkey, the task of debris removal is given to the Ministry of Environment as the main solution partner, and the Ministry of Interior and Urbanization (local governments) and private sector are determined as support solution partners within the scope of the Turkey Disaster Response Plan (TDRP). The Ministry of Environment and Urbanization has been designated as the institution responsible for the coordination of debris removal activities in the disaster area. The following points are counted within the duties and responsibilities of the debris removal service group (AFAD, 2013: 20):

- ➤ To determine the debris casting areas.
- ➤ To ensure that debris of buildings, factories, and surroundings are removed after the search and rescue work is finished.
- ➤ To destroy and dismantle damaged buildings that have to be demolished.

However, because TDRP was not active in the 1992 Erzincan and in the 2011 Van earthquakes, there are no official data about their positive and negative aspects. After the 2011 Van earthquake, a disaster that may cause great destruction hasn't occurred in Turkey. Thus, TDRP hasn't been applied to a disaster whose size is equivalent to the Van and Erzincan earthquakes.

2 The concept of disaster wastes and disaster management

The concept of disaster wastage is not used much in the literature. According to Berg et al. (2013: 4), disaster wastage is defined as waste generated both in the disaster period as a direct result of the disaster and in the post-disaster period as a result of poor waste management.

According to the US Environmental Protection Agency, disaster wastes consist of human and animal remains, a mixture of soil and sediment, rubble, plant cover, personal effects, hazardous materials, and domestic and clinical waste (Karunasena et al., 2012: 386). According to Reinhart and McCreanor (1999: 3), wastes are of considerable diversity, but they include concrete, asphalt, metal, green waste, plastic, sand, soil and rock, wall coverings (gypsum board), wood, glass, white goods, household waste, furniture, and personal items.

Researchers indicate that about 70–90% of the demolition waste is recoverable and consists of recycled concrete, brick, and fine dust (Xiao et al., 2012: 109). For example, the Wenchuan earthquake produced approximately 100 million tons of bricks, 80 million tons of concrete, 8 million tons of plastic, 10 million tons of metal, and 2 million tons of interior decoration material debris (Hu and Sheu, 2013: 118). Land road fillings, road pavements, pavement structures, fillings, coatings, and concrete bricks or blocks are suitable to be used as spare material for construction aggregates (Xiao et al., 2012: 109). The recycling or disposal of disaster wastes will benefit environment and society from many points such as sociocultural, psychological, and economic.

The 1995 Hyogoken-Nanbu earthquake (Mw: 7.2) was the first major earthquake affecting Japan's developed urban areas since the 1923 Great Kanto earthquake. Approximately 200,000 public and private buildings and houses were demolished and also many roads and bridges collapsed. Therefore, approximately 20 million tons of debris emerged after this sudden earthquake (Hayashi and Katsumi, 1996: 349). The Andrew Hurricane in 1992 produced 43 million yd^3 (11,610,000 tons) waste in Miami-Dade district, the Northridge earthquake in 1994 produced 7 million yd^3 (1,890,000 tons) waste in southern California, the Iniki Hurricane in Hawaii produced 5 million yd^3 (1,350,000 tons) waste, and the Hugo Hurricane in Carolina produced 2 million yd^3 (540,000 tons) of green waste (Reinhart and McCreanor, 1999: 3). In the Wenchuan earthquake, the total amount of building waste produced in the main disaster zone was about 380 million tons (Xiao et al., 2012: 116) (See Table 1).

Table 1: Disaster Waste Amounts Reported in Other Studies

Year	Type of Disaster	Waste Amount
2010	Haiti Earthquake	About 23–60 million ton
2009	L'Aquila Earthquake, Italy	About 1.5–3 million ton
2008	Wenchuan Earthquake, China	20 million ton
2005	Katrina Hurricane, USA	76 million m^3
2004	Frances and Jeanne Hurricanes, USA	3 million m^3
2004	Tsunami, India	10 million m^3 (only Indonesia)
2004	Charley Hurricane, USA	2 million m^3
1999	Marmara Earthquake, Turkey	13 million ton
1995	Great Hanshin-Awaji Earthquake, Japan	15 million ton

Source: Brown et al. (2011: 1090).

When all these figures are taken into account, it is possible to perceive the great-ness of the result. Coping with a waste of this magnitude creates an extra burden for both victims and governments, and delays in the transportation of medical care, crews, and disaster victims and in providing shelter, food, and fresh water resources (Solis, 1995: 1). Bad wastage management in debris lifting efforts in-creases these problems and may result in a slow and costly remediation work that may create public health and environmental risk in both short and long periods (Brown and Milke, 2009: 1).

3 Disaster wastes and disaster management in Turkey

Material and moral losses are inevitable when considering the natural, techno-logical, and human disasters that occur in Turkey and in the world today. In ad-dition to all these losses, a new problem has emerged at the rehabilitation stage of the integrated disaster management. Wastes of various sizes occur as a result of natural disasters and management of these wastes appears as a new problem. The main aim of this study is to determine the systems, techniques, and methods to cope with such a problem in Turkey.

Literature review reveals that there are a wide variety of wastes as a result of various natural disasters. Disaster wastes include concrete, asphalt, metal, green waste, plastic, sand, soil and rock, wall coverings, wood, glass, electronic and white goods, household waste, furniture, and personal items. In many countries in the world, most of these wastes are separated, recycled, and reused through appropriate factories. However, disaster wastes that emerged during the 1999 Marmara, 1992 Erzincan, and 2011 Van earthquakes have not been recycled. The resulting wastes were either used for sea filling or temporarily stored in areas designated by municipalities. After the Van earthquake, iron debris was separated from structural wastes and the rest was taken to the storage area.

3.1 Erzincan earthquake (March 13, 1992)

The Erzincan Plain is located in the first-degree earthquake zone on the North Anatolian Fault Zone, which is located in the east-west direction of Turkey. For this reason, the deformations on the zone occasionally affected the Erzincan Plain and Erzincan. According to historical records, Erzincan was destroyed 11 times by earthquakes (Kurtuluş, 1993: 311). One of these earthquakes occurred on March 13, 1992, at a depth of 16 km with 6.9 (Richter) magnitude. The 1992 Erzincan earthquake is an example of how earthquakes affect urban areas (Şengezer, 1993: 404). During the 1992 Erzincan earthquake, 522 people according to official records and 2,500 people according to informal sources lost their lives. Most of the damage occurred in Erzincan and Üzümlü and nearby towns (Kurtuluş, 1993: 310) (See Figure 1).

Figure 1: Erzincan earthquake violence map

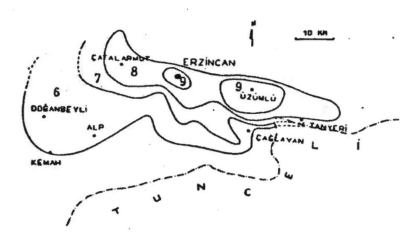

Source: Kurtuluş (1993: 313).

According to the study of Kurtuluş in 1993, 948 houses and 825 workplaces were heavily, 2,311 houses and 309 workplaces were moderately, and 5,822 houses and 230 workplaces were slightly damaged from 26,495 dwellings in the center of Erzincan. In Üzümlü town and its villages, 444 houses were heavily, 488 houses were moderately, and 944 houses were slightly damaged (Kurtuluş, 1993: 318). In Erzincan, the average damage of residential units was 25% and the average damage of workplaces was 43% (Sengezer, 1993: 406) (See Table 2).

Table 2: 1992 Erzincan Earthquake Damage Report

Rid/Heavy Damage	Moderate Damage	Slight Damage	Undamaged	Total
5,807	8,934	13,401	16,529	44,671

Source: Gökçe and Tetik (2012: 115).

The wreck resulting from the earthquake could be removed in about 2 months with 500 heavy-duty machines belonging to various government agencies. Wrecks of 1,530 houses, 139 workplaces, 1 bank, 1 gallery, 1 hotel, 2 schools, and 2 hospitals were removed by these machines and workers (Gökçe ve Tetik,

2012: 118). Five percent of brick building, 9% of prefabricated houses, 34% of half-timbered houses, and 35% of concrete houses were damaged in the city (Şengezer, 1993: 407). Except from household waste, white goods, and electronic devices, the majority of the wastes are concrete and iron. Stone, brick, and mud-brick constituted wastes from half-timbered houses. The earthquake did not affect only the region but also the Erzincan-Refahiye state road from 13 km to 45 km. The road was covered with small stones that could be cleared by 950 lorries. These stones covering the road caused the transportation to be cut off (Çetinkaya, 1993: 382). This disruption in transportation has potential to disrupt many activities such as health, nutrition, shelter, search, and rescue. After the 1992 Erzincan earthquake, Turkey spent about 650 million dollars for the rehabilitation and reconstruction works with the help of the World Bank (Gökçe ve Tetik, 2012: 118). Thus, the 1992 Erzincan earthquake reveals once more that disaster wastages are the invisible face of disasters and need to be tackled by a plan.

3.2 Van earthquake (October 23, 2011)

On October 23, 2011, at 1:40 am an earthquake with 7.0 (Mw) magnitude occurred in the city of Van in Turkey. The hypocenter of the earthquake was the village of Tabanli. Two weeks after this earthquake, a new earthquake with 5.7 (Mw) magnitude occurred in the town of Edremit, 16 km away from Van city center, on November 9, 2011, at 9:20 pm. Due to the earthquake, 644 people lost their lives and 1,966 people were injured. Most of the loss occurred in Erciş district (AFAD, 2014: 10). Approximately 187,000 structures were examined within the scope of damage assessment plan. About 49,000 heavily damaged structures were identified (AFAD, 2014: 11). As of January 24, 2012, the list of the buildings to be dismantled and wrecked is given in Table 3. The list is based on Van Special Provincial Administration Report.

Table 3: Van Earthquake Damage Report

Place	Building			Debris			
	Decided To Be Demolished	Demolition Finished	To Be Demolished	Demolished with Earthquake	Demolished with Workforce	Total Debris	Removed
Erciş	119	51	68	80	51	131	131
City Center	108	71	37	24	71	95	83
Total	227	122	105	104	122	226	214

According to Disaster and Emergency Management Presidency's Van earthquake report, 76% of the houses, 79% of the workplaces, and 82% of the barns were damaged. The undamage rate was 23%. Due to the earthquake, 36,203 dwellings, 2,884 workplaces, and 9,602 ranches were destroyed or seriously damaged (See Table 4). The size of the structural damage in the villages close to the city center was higher than that in the other regions. Approximately 89 of every 100 houses inspected in the villages close to the city center were damaged (AFAD, 2014: 11).

Table 4: Damage Condition of Buildings after the Van Earthquake

Damage Condition	Housing	Workplace	Barn	Total
Ripped/Heavily Damaged	36,203	2,884	9,602	48,689
Moderately Damaged	18,181	3,907	395	22,483
Slightly Damaged	58,374	7,992	6,692	73,058
Undamaged	34,864	3,952	3,590	42,406
Total	147,622	18,735	20,279	186,636

Source: AFAD (2014: 23).

According to Van Provincial Directorate of Environment and Urbanism, 81 buildings were destroyed in Van-Erciş immediately after the earthquakes that took place in 2011, and a total of 1,000 tons of debris wastes were collected with an average of 15 tons per building. About 300 tons of debris wastes emerged from Van city center. The resulting disaster debris was poured into the areas determined by the municipality. The debris is still in temporary storage areas.

When the records of the Ministry of Environment and Urbanization for the relevant years were examined, it was noticed that there is no information about the excavated soil and demolition wastes in the Environmental Impact Assessment Reports. All wastes belonging to the city center were stored in the irregular warehouse area on the Van-Özalp road. There is no information about quantities, transportation, storage, and disposal of wastes.

4 Discussion

The study of Xiao et al. (2012) suggests that recycling method should be used as the main method and using building wastes in reconstruction projects should be used as the supplementary method for the Wenchuan earthquake in China. The density of the disaster wastes in the earthquake is composed of concrete and brick materials. The recycling of these materials has been carried out through large crushing machines and complex processes. In contrast to recycling, reuse steps have been achieved with simple tools.

The study of Şengün (2005) focuses on the 1999 Marmara earthquake and analyzes the damage caused by this earthquake. The study states that it wouldn't be useful by itself to specify the location of wastage. The study informs that earthquake wastes before the Marmara earthquake were disposed randomly to roadsides whereas earthquake wastes of the Marmara earthquake were disposed to sea as filling material or river banks.

The study of Aydın and Kara (2003) presents that solid wastes are accumulated in settlements in an uncontrolled way in an emergency situation in Turkey. As a result of this, the individuals staying more than 6 months in the temporary shelters in these areas have to cope with epidemics. It has been revealed that waste management plays second fiddle because of disasters and food problems. It is emphasized that waste management is a problem that can be solved, and local authorities and the government should work together for the solution of this problem.

Researchers indicate that disposal and recycling of disaster wastes in Turkey is very limited. In the Van earthquake, only the iron parts were separated in various forms and the remaining debris was kept in the poured areas. Although glass fragments, stone, bricks, and so on can be used as asphalt material for roads, they are kept in temporary storage areas. Systems and technical means should be established to recycle these wastes whereby economic burden of these wastes will also decrease.

5 Conclusion and recommendations

Actions regarding storage, decomposition, recycling, and disposal of wastes after possible disasters should be in the plans prepared for post-disaster recovery in Turkey where disasters are inevitable. Debris removal should be included in the disaster scenarios, and the temporary storage areas for the disaster wastes in the post-disaster recovery stage should be determined by Geographic Information Systems programs. Building stock, building age, concrete class, soil properties, and so on should be determined for provinces and districts bearing disaster risks in order to determine the possible amount of disaster wastage. Projects should be carried out for waste disposal and recycling. Private sector and the state should work together to remove disaster debris quickly and cheaply. Agreements between private sector and the state should be made before such disasters happen. Hence, it is possible for the state to save time, money, and burden from the possible debris removal works. Geophysical and engineering studies on the wastes to be generated after disasters are carried out and mathematical and technical solution proposals are put forward in Japan and Sri Lanka. Similarly, projects and innovations for solving disaster waste problems should be put forward in Turkey.

References

AFAD. (2013). "Türkiye Afet Müdahale Planı (TAMP)". T.C. Başbakanlık Afet ve Acil Durum Yönetimi Başkanlığı, Ankara.

AFAD. (2014). "Müdahale İyileştirme ve Sosyoekonomik Açıdan 2011 Van Depremi". T.C. Başbakanlık Afet ve Acil Durum Yönetimi Başkanlığı, Ankara.

Altınbilek, D., Ans, T., Baş, R., Belen, E., Büyükdevres, M., Çancı, K., Ergünay, O., Evren, F. and Gülkan, P. (1997). "T.C. Başbakanlık Doğal Afetler Koordinasyon Baş Müşavirliği- Doğal Afetler Genel Raporu". Başbakanlık Afet ve Acil Durum Yönetimi Başkanlığı, Ankara.

Asari, M., Sakai, S., Yoshioka, T., Tojo, Y., Tasaki, T., Takigami, H. and Watanabe, K. (2013). "Strategy for Separation and Treatment of Disaster Waste: A Manual for Earthquake and Tsunami Disaster Waste Management in Japan". Journal of Material Cycles and Waste Management, 15: 290–299.

Aydın, M. E. and Kara, G. (2003). "Acil Durumlarda Katı Atık Yönetimi". TMMOB V. Çevre Mühendisliği Kongresi, Ekim 2003, Ankara.

Berg, P., Bjerregaard, M. and Jönsson, L. (2013). "Disaster Waste Management Guidelines". United Nations Office for the Coordination of Humanitarian Affairs Emergency Preparedness Section, Switzerland.

Brown, C. and Milke, M. (2009). "Planning For Disaster Debris Management". The WasteMINZ 21st Annual Conference, 14–16 October 2009. Christchurch, New Zealand.

Brown, C., Milke, M. and Seville, E. (2011). "Disaster Waste Management: A Review Article". Waste Management, 3: 1085–1098.

Çetinkaya, M. (1993). "13 Mart 1992 Erzincan Depreminde Yol Hasarları". TMMOB 2. Ulusal Deprem Mühendisliği Sempozyumu, 10 Mart 1993. Ankara, Turkey.

Gökçe, O. and Tetik, Ç. (2012). "Teoride ve Pratikte Afet Sonrası İyileştirme Çalışmaları". AFAD Yayınları, Ankara.

Hayashi, H. and Katsumi, T. (1996). "Generation and Management of Disaster Waste". Special Issue of Soils and Foundations Japanese Geotechnical Society, 36: 349–358.

Hu, Z. and Sheu, J. (2013). "Post-Disaster Debris Reverse Logistics Management under Psychological Cost Minimization". Transportation Research Part B, 55: 118–141.

Karunasena, G., Rameezdeen, R. and Amaratunga, D. (2012). "Post-Disaster C&D Waste Management: The Case of COWAM Project, City of Galle, Sri Lanka". 6th International Conference and Workshop on the Built Environment in Developing Countries 4–5 December 2012. Australia.

Kurtuluş, C. (1993). "13 Mart 1992 Erzincan Depremi ve Sonuçları". TMMOB 2. Ulusal Deprem Mühendisliği Sempozyumu 10 Mart 1993. Ankara, Turkey.

Luther, L. (2010). "Managing Disaster Debris: Overview of Regulatory Requirements, Agency Roles and Selected Challenges". CRS Report for Congress. Washington DC: Library of Congress, Congressional Research Service.

Özdamar, L., Tüzün, D. and Ergüneş, B. (2014). "Coordinating Debris Cleanup Operations in Post Disaster Road Networks". Socio-Economic Planning Sciences, 48: 249–262.

Özkul, B. and Karaman, E. (2007). "Doğal Afetler İçin Risk Yönetimi". TMMOB Afet Sempozyumu, 5–7 Aralık, Ankara.

Reinhart, D.R. and McCreanor, P.T. (1999). "Disaster Debris Management—Planning Tools". Final Report, US Environmental Protection Agency Region IV. United States Environmental Protection Agency, Washington, DC.

Solis, G.Y. (1995). "Disaster Debris Management", Final Report, the Disaster Preparedness Resources Centre, the University of British Columbia for Emergency Preparedness, Canada.

Şengezer, B. (1993). "13 Mart 1992 Erzincan Kentinde Meydana Gelen Hasarın Mahallelere Göre İrdelenmesi". TMMOB 2, Ulusal Deprem Mühendisliği Sempozyumu, 10 Mart, Ankara.

Şengün, H. (2005). "Deprem Ve Katı Atık Sorunu". Uluslararası Deprem Sempozyumu 23–25 Mart, Kocaeli.

Xiao, J., Xie, H. and Zhang, C. (2012). "Investigation on Building Waste and Reclaim in Wenchuan Earthquake Disaster Area". Resources, Conservation and Recycling, 61: 109–117.

Menekşe Varol Kılıçarslan

Innovation in the Health Sector

1 Introduction

Taking into consideration the changing and increasing population structure, the importance given to human health, and changing care needs, innovative activities in the health sector are needed to provide health services in a good quality, timely, and effective manner. In addition, health-care enterprises should continue to innovate by constantly following up developments in technology and diagnosis and treatment methods, training programs, government policies, and changes in management approaches. The realization of innovative activities and their sustainability can be achieved by providing the necessary support for the research and development, motivating the employees, providing adequate resources, and supportive policies of the governments.

In today's competitive strategies, it is not enough for the companies that want to maintain their lives to just provide the products and services requested by the customers. Firms have to orient and guide their customers' demand for goods and services. The first expansion of the concept of innovation was in the 1960s. The first definition was made by Schmookler in 1966. Schmookler defines innovation as a technical change that is made by firms as a result of a new product, service, method, and input development (Elçi, 2006: 78).

In Turkey, the concept of innovation began to be spoken about in the mid-1990s. Innovation performance of Turkey is relatively low compared to countries in the EU. Innovation affects life cycles of firms and the welfare of countries. It is a dynamic concept that is affected by technology, product life cycle, and globalization. Both organizations and countries need to involve in innovative activities in order to catch up with the rapidly increasing competition. They have to be an innovative culture in order to accomplish this purpose (Kaptanoğlu, 2016: 45).

2 Definition of innovation

The word *innovation* is derived from the Latin word "Innovatus" and means the use of new methods in social, cultural, and administrative environments (Elçi, 2006: 12). Some definitions of innovation in the literature are given in Table 1.

Table 1: Different Definitions of Innovation in the Literature

Author	Definition
Drucker (1985)	Innovation is an entrepreneurial tool and it enables entrepreneur to get the resources needed to bring wealth (Sarı and Işık, 2011: 538).
Porter (1990)	Innovation provides new business methods and competitive advantage as well as new Technologies (Sarı and Işık, 2011: 538).
Rogers (1995)	It is an object, practice or idea that is perceived as new from the point of individuals (Sarı and Işık, 2011: 538).
Damanpour (1991)	It is defined as new ideas as being created, developed and adapted for the success of the firm (Sarı and Işık, 2011: 538).
Trott (1998)	In this definition, innovation is considered as a management process. It is defined as the management of all activities of a new or improved product (Sarı and Işık, 2011: 538).
Pervaiz (1998)	It is defined as creating added value in order to be able to adapt to the changes happening in the surrounding environment (Pervaiz, 1998: 32).
Schumpeter (1978)	Presentation of available resources with new compositions (Schumpeter, 1978: 65).
TUSİAD (2003)	Innovation is a process that transforms technology and science into social and economic benefit (TUSİAD, 2003: 23).
Korkmaz (2004)	It is the activities of thought or technology development, new product – production management, and marketing activities (Korkmaz, 2004: 11).
Kırım (2006)	It is emphasized that a new thing and innovation are not the same. He pointed out that a new thing should be advantageous and remove the price sensitivity in the market in order to be regarded as an innovation (Kırım, 2006: 6).
Elçi (2006)	It is the transformation of knowledge into social and economic benefit (Elçi, 2006: 2).
Uzkurt (2008)	Innovation is not a single activity, but subprocesses have emerged as the result of interaction among them (Uzkurt, 2008: 19).
Güleş and Bülbül (2004)	It is the first time presentation or usage of a policy, program, system, product, service, or process by firms (Güleş and Bülbül, 2004: 125).
Savaşçı and Kazançoğlu (2004)	It is the transformation of new ideas into the economy (Savaşçı and Kazançoğlu, 2004: 518).

According to Pervaiz (1998), the innovation reflects organizational culture and it is an advantage for organizations to adapt themselves into the internal and external environments. At the same time, the cultural structure of organizations indicates the way of understanding of innovation within the organization.

The definition of innovation varies according to different perspectives in the literature (see Table 2).

Table 2: Innovation Definitions with Different Perspectives

Innovation from the Point of Marketing	Innovation means product development processes and marketing based on market changes, developments, new products/services for needs and expectations.
Innovation from the Point of Management	Innovation means the orientation of the firm to internal and external sources to ensure that new ideas are formed.
Innovation from the Point of Technology	Innovation means using technological sources, changes, and developments for the product improvement.

Source: Savaşçı and Kazançoğlu (2004: 518)

Innovation-related entrepreneurship needs academic and commercial collaborative works. Twenty percent of the drugs in the US and European markets are produced in India (Elçi, 2006: 129). In this study, the product, process, marketing, service, and organizational innovations in the Oslo guide are explained in relation to the health sector. Some of these innovation terms are:

Product Innovation: It can be defined as the development of a brand new product or the improvement of an existing product. Product innovation has a considerable importance in terms of competitive advantage of firms (Johne, 1999: 6).

Marketing Innovation: A new marketing method that covers all promotional activities (design, packaging, positioning, promotion, etc.) is called marketing innovation. The aim of marketing innovation is to be able to respond to needs in the market better and to be positioned in a new market. The most prominent feature of the marketing innovation is the use of an unprecedented marketing method by the company (Papinniemi, 1999: 97).

Service Innovation: It involves the development of a new, dissimilar and different service, and the development of existing service by a firm to attract more customers. The provision of remote health care through telemedicine application is an example for service innovation.

Organizational Innovation: It involves the use of a new organizational management. This innovation may involve within or outside the organization. Growth strategies such as merging with other companies and buying other companies are not accepted as innovations (Aktürk, 2016: 74). However, if the company renews its organizational methods as never before after the growth strategies, it is accepted as an organizational innovation (OECD, 2005: 56).

Process Innovation: It involves development of a new or significantly modified process. In these innovation techniques, there is a serious change in equipment and software.

Producing different products, reducing costs, and making product differences has made a serious improvement in the process (OECD, 2005: 53).

For successful innovation, organizational structure and processes it involves are very important. Since the innovation is a process that is not end and it is an uninterrupted process, the organizational structure must be in continuous research and development. Table 3 presents the characteristics of the organizational structure that prevents and supports innovation (Pervaiz, 1998: 384).

Table 3: The Characteristics of the Structure of the Organization that Hampers and Supports Innovation

Characteristics of Mechanical Structure that Prevents Innovation	Characteristics of Organic Structure that Supports Innovation
• Hierarchical, • Long decision-making chain and slow decision-making process, • Many rules and procedures, • Limited individual freedom, • Strict procedures and separation of departments, • Bureaucratic, • Top-down ordering, bottom-up reporting, • Formal written communication.	• Flow of information from top to bottom • Flexibility in rules, • Removal of hinders between teams and departments • A working environment in which ideas are expressed and considered, • Easy adapting to new situations • Hierarchical deprivation • Face to face communication without bureaucracy

Source: Pervaiz (1998: 384)

Reactions of employees to the innovation happening in the firm and changes in behavior and attitudes of employers in the process of innovation depend on the culture of the organization (Uzkurt, 2008: 136–138). Innovative companies should give importance to staff empowerment. Staff empowerment makes employees feel happier and confident individuals, increases their knowledge and experience, and enables them to control difficulties and events they will encounter. Staff empowerment requires employees to work where they feel they are most fit for the aim of the organization. There is a linear relationship between customer orientation and customer satisfaction. Customer orientation or customer focus is defined as the innovation process prepared in line with the needs of the target customers. Thus, the customer-focused performance and profitability measurement is made within the organization. Innovative firms are obliged to be closer to their customers (Durna, 2002: 226).

3 Innovation in the health sector

Nowadays demand for better health care has increased due to increase in the number of complicated illnesses, aging of societies, increase in income level, technological advances, and extension of health-care coverage all over the countries (Toprak, 2013: 21). Health-care providers need innovation to keep pace with increasing demands, changing care needs, and changes in management understanding. The health-care sector is a place of constant change and development. It is aimed to improve the quality of services through innovation for providing faster, more convenient, and more effective health-care services (Uzuntarla et al., 2016: 199).

Innovation in the health-care sector takes place in the areas of medicine, medical devices and technology, new diagnostic and treatment methods, training programs, government policies, and management approaches. The dimensions of innovation in health-care services are addressed by Ayhan (2011) as follows:

Call Center: They are centers where operators provide medical consultation services to callers.

Electronic Medical Record: It is the electronically held medical report. Electronic medical records provide a more efficient way of monitoring patients' health histories.

Biometric Identifier Smart Cards: They are cards with chips that verify the ID information of the patient with fingerprint or iris scan and enable medical records to be moved from one server to another.

Telemedicine (Web Camera): It is providing remote health-care services with patients in different places through information technologies such as web camera.

Remote Diagnosis: It is the diagnosis with remote medical equipment and remote devices.

Mobile Phone Technology: Mobile phones are used to facilitate health-care services. For example, it may include reminding patients to take medication, giving text messages, and informing about laboratory results. Mobile phones can also be used by the hosts to report medical information to the center (for example, a patient's AIDS-diagnosed report).

Tele-kiosks: Tele-kiosks are small units equipped with a telephone or computer where patients can receive health information.

Clinical Decision Support Software: It is the software that allows the user to make more accurate diagnosis and standardize the procedures of health-care services.

Toprak (2013) reports that only 61 firms out of the surveyed 526 private health companies displayed innovative activities. No statistically significant relationships between financial performance and innovation were found. However, statistically significant relationship was found between the financial performance of medical firms and innovation. Thus, it has been concluded that the private health sector does not pay enough attention to innovation activities and does not display any financial performance improvement depending on innovation except medical firms. Research results indicate that firms need to follow developing and changing technology, to be more inclined to innovate, and to allocate more resources to research and development departments.

The use of medical devices in Turkey reached a market size of $1.9 billion by the end of 2010. It is seen that approximately 85% of the medical devices in the market are imported. It is anticipated that the proportion and varieties of medical devices will increase at every stage of health-care services parallel to the flow of health care from hospitals to homes and increased computer-assisted operations and practices (Sengün, 2016: 196). It is necessary to support innovations in the field of medical devices by increasing resources for research and development activities. Resources allocated for health expenditures in Turkey increased from 12.3% in 2014 to 10.4% in 2015. Hence, resources for research and development to carry out innovations should be increased.

At the end of 2002, the Turkish health-care system needed to undergo drastic changes in many areas due to cost increases in the provision of health services, limited capacity of the public pension system, and the questioning of public health management by citizens. That is why the Health Transformation Program started to be implemented in 2003 (Sağlık Bakanlığı, 2012: 55–56).

The Health Transformation Program aims to establish a structure in which preventive and primary health-care services will have priority. Improving the health of citizens and the health-care workers' positions is the driving point of innovations in this area. In this context, the source devoted to preventive and primary health services increased by 2.7 times between 2002 and 2011 (Sağlık Bakanlığı, 2012: 105). Adaption of family medicine system in primary health care was the very first innovation carried out in the program. Family medicine system aims at achieving the simplest treatments in the shortest time possible for all citizens. Thus, palliative care was reduced to the level of primary health care. Meanwhile, the health-care-at-home system was also introduced with the thought that many simple treatments can easily be met at home. The health-care-at-home services are provided by both Ministry of Health and the Ministry of Family and Social Policy, whereby health-care-at-home services are provided by Ministry of Health while the other social care and support services are provided by the Ministry of Family and Social Policy (Memişoğlu and Kalkan, 2016: 662).

Another innovation brought by the Health Transformation Program to the health sector is the collection of public hospitals under one management (Sağlık Bakanlığı, 2012: 197). One of important innovations realized is the allowance of citizens to benefit from the private sector hospitals with their social security. This stimulated hospital investments of private sector. Meanwhile, restructuring of hospital services was carried out and the principle of local administration was applied into hospital management (Sağlık Bakanlığı, 2012: 199–200).

Innovations were also made in the field of patient rights. In this context, the Patient Rights Unit was set up in all hospitals, the right to choose the doctor was given to the patients, and call centers were activated for the request of patients (Sağlık Bakanlığı, 2012: 205–207).

E-health system was established with objectives of providing standardization of health data, establishing data analysis support and decision support systems, accelerating data flow among e-health users, establishing electronic personal health records, increasing resource savings and productivity, supporting scientific studies, and accelerating the national adoption of the e-health concept. Within the scope of e-health, national standards were developed in health information systems, information and communication platform was established under the name of Health-Net, and electronic systems such as institutional resource planning and decision support systems were established (Sağlık Bakanlığı, 2012: 233–239).

One of the main goals of the Health Transformation Program is to ensure continuous quality improvement in health services. In the first stage, an additional payment system based on performance was implemented while at the second stage, the Institutional Performance and Quality Improvement research was conducted to enhance the quality in health service delivery. Thus, a comprehensive hospital evaluation system was established. The hospital evaluation system includes evaluations about access to health service, service infrastructure, processes, patient satisfaction, and the degree of reaching the specified targets (Sağlık Bakanlığı, 2012: 310).

Since the health sector is an area where prices are constantly rising, disease patterns change, and technology usage in diagnosis and treatment services keeps increasing, difficulties arise in carrying out the health-care service delivery by only public sector (Memişoğlu and Kalkan, 2016: 661). At this point, the Ministry of Health in Turkey introduced the Integrated Health Campuses and City Hospitals under public–private partnership.

4 Conclusion

The health sector has a wide range of innovations in terms of providing services such as hotel services, education, and patient counseling as well as diagnosis, treatment, and rehabilitation services. It is necessary to motivate employees by providing information accessibility, training opportunities, and technology for the sustainability of innovative activities in health institutions (Ekiyor and Arslantaş, 2015: 132).

The reform process in the health sector in Turkey has developed in parallel with the EU countries. While expanding the scope of social policies in the health sector on the one hand, Turkey continues to take precautions for enhancing market economy and to make organizational changes that give the public hospitals more autonomy (Memişoğlu and Kalkan, 2016: 661). In this process of change, desired results were not obtained initially due to budget deficit of the social security system, failure to establish supply chain system, administrative uncertainty of city hospitals, failure of digital hospitals to adapt to system, failure of hospital information system to integrate between units, and failure of home care services to function in accordance with other units.

There is a need for the government's supportive policies in the health sector in order to support research and development efforts that provide innovations in the field of medical devices and technology, the pharmaceutical industry, new diagnostic, and therapeutic methods.

References

Aktürk, E. (2016). "Kurumsal Yönetim Çerçevesinde Uygulanan Etik Kurallara İlişkin Algı: Bankacılık Sektöründe Bir Araştırma", Beykent Üniversitesi Doktora Tezi, İstanbul.

Ayhan, E. (2011). "Sağlık Hizmetleri Pazarlamasında İnovasyonun Önemi Malatya'da Faaliyet Gösteren Hastanelerde Bir Uygulama", Gaziantep Üniversitesi Sosyal Bilimler Enstitüsü, Yüksek Lisans Tezi, Gaziantep.

Durna, U. (2002). "Yenilik Yönetimi", Ankara: Nobel Yayın Dağıtım.

Ekiyor, A. and Arslantaş, S. (2015). "Sağlık Sektöründe İşgören Motivasyonunun İnovasyon Performansına Etkileri", Çankırı Karatekin Üniversitesi Sosyal Bilimler Enstitüsü Dergisi, 6(2): 113–136.

Elçi, Ş. (2006). "İnovasyon—Kalkınmanın ve Rekabetin Anahtarı" (2. Baskı). Ankara: Nova Yayınları.

Güleş, H.K. and Bülbül, H. (2004a). "Yenilikçilik: İşletmeler İçin Stratejik Rekabet Aracı", Ankara: Nobel Yayın Dağıtım.

Güleş, H.K. and Bülbül, H. (2004b) "İşletmelerde Proaktif Bir Strateji Olarak Yenilikçilik: 500 Büyük Sanayi İşletmesi Üzerine Bir Uygulama", Dokuz Eylül Üniversitesi İşletme Fakültesi Dergisi, 4(1): 40–55.

Johne, A. (1999). "Successfull Market Innovation", European Journal of Innovation Management, 2(1): 3–16.

Kaptanoğlu, O.R. (2016), "Algılanan Değer, Müşteri Tatmini Ve Marka Bağlılığı İlişkisi, Marka Tutumları Ve Ürün İlgi Düzeylerinde Farklılığın Rolü Üzerine Bir Araştırma", Beykent Üniversitesi Doktora Tezi, İstanbul.

Kırım, A. (2006). "Kârlı Büyümenin Reçetesi İnovasyon", İstanbul: Sistem Yayıncılık.

Korkmaz, N. (2004). "Sorularla Yenilikçilik (İnovasyon)", İstanbul: İstanbul Ticaret Odası Yayınları.

Memişoğlu, D. and Kalkan, B. (2016). "Sağlık Hizmetlerinde Yönetişim, İnovasyon ve Türkiye", Süleyman Demirel Üniversitesi İktisadi ve İdari Bilimler Fakültesi Dergisi, 21(2), 645–665.

OECD, Frascati Kılavuzu (2005). "Araştırma ve Deneysel Geliştirme Taramaları İçin Önerilen Standart Uygulama", çev. TUBİTAK, 3.baskı.

Öklem, G. (2011). "Türkiye'nin Avrupa Birliği'ne Üyelik Sürecinde Sağlıkta İnovasyon", İstanbul: Tüsiad Yayınları.

Papinniemi, J. (1999). "Creating a Model of Process Innovation for Reengineering of Business and Manufacturing", International Journal of Production Economics, 60–61: 78–110.

Pervaiz, A. (1998). "Culture and Climate for Innovation", European Journal of Innovation Management, 1(1): 30–34.

Sarı, Z.E. and Işık, Ö. (2011). "İnovasyon ve Stratejik Yönetim Sinerjisi: Stratejik İnovasyon", Celal Bayar Üniversitesi Sosyal Bilimler Dergisi, 9(2): 520–556.

Savaşçı, İ. and Kazançoğlu, Y. (2004). "İşletmelerin Yenilik Yaratma Sürecinde Serbest Bölgelerin Rolü", Eskişehir: 3. Ulusal Bilgi, Ekonomi ve Yönetim Kongresi Bildiriler Kitabı, 25–26 Kasım 2004, Eskişehir.

Sağlık Bakanlığı (2012). "Sağlık İstatistikleri Yıllığı 2012", Ankara: T.C. Sağlık Bakanlığı.

Schumpeter, J. (1978). "The Theory of Economic Development", New York: Oxford Univ. Press.

Şengün, H. (2016). "Sağlık Hizmetleri Sunumunda İnovasyon". Haseki Eğitim ve Araştırma Hastanesi Haseki Tıp Bülteni, 54: 194–198.

Toprak, C. (2013). "Özel Sağlık Sektöründe İnovasyon: Özel Sağlık Sektöründe İnovasyon Ve Finansal Performans İlişkisi", Başkent Üniversitesi Sosyal Bilimler Enstitüsü, Yüksek Lisans Tezi, Ankara.

TÜSİAD (2003). "Ulusal İnovasyon Sistemi, Kavramsal Çerçeve, Türkiye İncelemesi ve Ülke Örnekleri", İstanbul: TÜSİAD Yayınları.

Uzkurt, C. (2008). "Yenilik Yönetimi ve Yenilikçi Örgüt Kültürü", İstanbul: Beta Yayınları.

Uzuntarla Y., Ceyhan, S. and Fırat, İ. (2016). "Sağlık Kurumlarında Yenilikçilik: Bingöl İli Örneği", Bingöl Üniversitesi Sosyal Bilimler Enstitüsü Dergisi, 6(11): 189–201.

Elif Çelenk Kaya and Necla İrem Ölmezoğlu

Evaluation of Miners' Knowledge Level Regarding Occupational Health and Safety

1 Introduction

Mineral and mining sector has an essential place in the lives of people and society. Throughout history, mineral and mining sector has been one of the factors playing an active role to reach technology and welfare that developed countries have. Along with agriculture, mining is one of the two basic production areas that meet raw material needs of societies. It is unlikely that human life can be sustained without mining activities. Today, almost everything that is indispensable for our lives, from the cars we use to the houses we live in, is produced by the products obtained from the mining activities. In the world, the USA, China, South Africa, Canada, Australia and Russia are counted among the countries where mining is powerful.

The richest countries in terms of world mineral reserve and important mineral ores in these countries are presented below:

- South African Republic: Gold, platinum group metals, manganese, chromium, aluminum
- China: Iron ore, lead, manganese, molybdenum, tin, zirconium, zinc and phosphate
- Canada: Uranium, zinc, gold, copper, nickel, cobalt, iron ore, petrol and natural gas
- Australia: Coal, iron ore, rutile, zinc, lead and uranium
- USA: Lead, molybdenum and phosphate ores

Turkey's complex geologic and tectonic structure is the cause of the existence of various mineral deposits. While 90 types of mineral are produced around the world, 60 types of mineral are produced in Turkey. Turkey ranks 28th in total mining production value and 10th in mineral diversity among 132 countries in the world according to General Directorate of Mineral Research and Exploration data (Ernst & Young, 2011).

Turkey is rich in raw materials, especially industrial raw materials, some metallic minerals, lignite and geothermal resources. Turkey has 2.5% of raw material reserves, 1% of coal reserves, 0.8% of geothermal potential and 0.4% of metallic mineral reserves in the world. Turkey has 72% of the world boron minerals and is the largest producer of them in the world (TBMM, 2010).

Approximately 30 million people work in mines around the world and approximately one third of them work in coal mines. Mining is a huge sector that interest almost 300 million people. This sector is at the top of the hardest and the most difficult sectors requiring special knowledge, experience, proficiency and continuous inspection due to the risks it has by nature. Possibility of encountering occupational accidents and illnesses in this labor-intensive sector is higher compared to other sectors.

Big accidents such as explosions, fires, and collapses in mines end up with disaster and cause death of many people. Although today's technology has developed considerably to avoid these accidents, mineral and mining is the leading sector where accident and death risk are maximum. Whereas 1% of the workers around world work in mines, 8% of serious accidents happen in mineral and mining sector. That is why the International Labor Organization (ILO) adapted ILO Hours of Work (Coal Mines) Convention in 1931 (No. 31). Safety and Health in Mines Convention (No. 176) and its accompanying Recommendation (No. 183) were adapted in 1995.

Mobile machines used in mines contain derv and hydraulic liquids, and these are explosive and combustive. Electrical devices and diesel motors are sources for firing and burning. It is very risky to combine materials with flammable and explosive properties and the equipment that will ignite them.

Cristal quartz (silica granules) is the most common dust that workers encounter in mines and quarries. When stones containing silica are broken, crashed or crumbled, inhalable silica dust comes out. Inhaling this dust is really dangerous. As a result, a type of pneumoconiosis disease named as silicosis is caused by long exposure to this dust. This dust also causes autoimmune diseases such as tuberculosis, lung cancer and arthritis.

Inhalable coal mine dusts are also extremely dangerous. There are silica, lime and clay within these dusts. Miners intensively contact with coal mine dusts when they work in narrow places underground. As a result, coal miner pneumoconiosis is caused by long exposure to coal dust. Inhaling coal dusts intensively can cause chronic bronchitis and emphysema.

Many machines are used in mineral and mining sector. These machines make really loud noise because of their working requirements. Moreover, indoor area prevents noise propagation underground and this can become a serious threat for the ears. Ionized radiation is also one of the important dangers in mineral and mining sector. Radon can emerge when explosives used for digging up hard rocks in mines melt the stones and it penetrates into the depths of the mines. Because radon is a carcinogenic gas, inhaling or being exposed to it for a long time can cause lung cancer.

In general, mineral and mining sector reserves many dangers such as fire, floods, explosions, and collapses that can cause massive deaths. In addition to these dangers, improper ventilation, damaged fortification systems, dust, non-ergonomic working conditions, noise, vibration, manual handling, electric shocks, insufficient lighting, psychologic problems and bad hygienic conditions are risk factors in this sector. Furthermore, factors such as overfatigue and human errors, long working hours in shifts, heat, and heavy working conditions are other risks in this sector (Rossetti et al. 2009).

Considering all these risks, it is necessary to evaluate knowledge level of people who work in this sector and then provide training by determining their shortcomings. Hence, this study aims to evaluate occupational health and safety awareness levels of people who work in mineral and mining sector.

2 Research method

People who work in a mine in Gümüşhane constitute the universe of the research. Survey used in the research consists of 23 main questions; 2 of which consist of 5 subquestions and 1 of which consists of 4 subquestions. Questions in the survey are dichotomous (double choice; yes/no) and multiple choice (5-point Likert scale) questions. In multiple choice questions, scoring was made by giving 5 points to "Always/Strongly Agree/Excellent" choice and 1 point to "Never/Strongly Disagree/Very Poor" choice. As a result of scale's validity and reliability analysis, Cronbach's alpha value was found out as 0.633.

3 Findings

Demographic characteristics of survey participants are given in Table 1. All of the research participants are male. Majority of the research participants are high school and primary school graduates. Among them, 11.8% of participants are in the 18–25 age group, 35.3% of them are in the 26–30 age group, 36.5% of them are in the 31–40 age group, and 16.5% of them are in the 41 years and above age group. Majority of survey participants have less than 5 years experience. Survey is conducted on both administrative personnel and workers in the mineral and mining sector; 18.8% of the survey participants are administrative personnel while 81.2% of them are workers.

Table 1: Demographic Characteristics of Research Participants

Level of Education	N	%	Gender	N	%
Primary School	31	36.5	Female	0	0
High School	35	41.2	Male	85	100
Associate Degree	4	4.7	**Experience**	**N**	**%**
Undergraduate	14	16.5	Less than one year	16	18.8
Graduate	1	1.2	1–5 Years	48	56.5
Age	**N**	**%**	6–10 Years	11	12.9
18–25	10	11.8	11 Years and Above	10	11.8
26–30	30	35.3	**Position**	**N**	**%**
31–40	31	36.5	Administrative Personnel	16	18.8
41 and Above	14	16.5	Worker	69	81.2
Total	85	100	Total	85	100

To understand participants' knowledge level regarding occupational health and safety, four questions were asked to the participants (see Table 2). In response to the question of "What is your knowledge level about occupational health and safety?," 47.1% of the participants said good, 12.9% of them said excellent, 31.8% of them said average, 5.9% of them said poor and 2.4% of them said very poor. When opinions of participants about occupational safety of workplace were asked, 44.7% of the participants answered good, 4.7% of them answered excellent, 34.1% of them answered average, 12.9% of them answered poor and 3.5% of them answered very poor. In response to the question of "On which level do you know the risks of your duty?," 21.2% of the participants said excellent, 43.5% of them said good, 28.2% of them said average, 4.7% of them said poor and 2.4% of them said very poor. When their opinions about occupational safety of workplace were asked, 44.7% of the participants said good, 4.7% of them said excellent, 34.1% of them said average, 12.9% of them said poor and 3.5% of them said very poor. Finally, it was asked to the participants on which level they knew their rights when they had an occupational accident and it was determined that 38.8% of them had knowledge at good level and 10.6% of them had knowledge at excellent level.

Table 2: Participants' Knowledge Level Regarding Occupational Health and Safety

	Very Poor		Poor		Average		Good		Excellent	
	N	%	N	%	N	%	N	%	N	%
What is your knowledge level related to occupational health and safety?	2	2.4	5	5.9	27	31.8	40	47.1	11	12.9
What is your opinion about occupational safety of your workplace?	3	3.5	11	12.9	29	34.1	38	44.7	4	4.7
On which level do you know the risks of your duty?	2	2.4	4	4.7	24	28.2	37	43.5	18	21.2
On which level do you know your rights when you have an occupational accident?	6	7.1	16	18.8	21	24.7	33	38.8	9	10.6

Survey questions include questions about reasons of occupational accidents (see Table 3). Among participants, 25.9% stated that occupational accidents always happened because of not using personal protective equipment while 35.3% pointed out that occupational accidents often happened due to not using personal protective equipment. Further, 29.4% of participants stated that occupational accidents rarely happened because of inexperience. Similarly, 24.7% of participants mentioned that occupational accidents rarely occurred because of inattention.

Table 3: Participants' Answers to the Questions Related to the Reasons of Occupational Accidents

	Never		Rarely		Sometimes		Often		Always	
	N	%	N	%	N	%	N	%	N	%
Inexperience	10	11.8	25	29.4	18	21.2	22	25.9	10	11.8
Inattention	9	10.6	21	24.7	19	22.4	18	21.2	18	21.2
Not using personal protective equipment	9	10.6	5	5.9	19	22.4	30	35.3	22	25.9
Long working hours	15	17.6	20	23.5	29	34.1	12	14.1	9	10.6
Intense work pressure	5	5.9	16	18.8	30	35.3	24	28.2	10	11.8

Participants' opinions about propositions related to the occupational health and safety are given in Table 4.

In this study, participants' opinions are asked regarding their participation levels related to the questions about occupational health and safety. Majority of participants agree (50.6%) and strongly agree (27.1%) with the proposition of "Majority of occupational accidents and illnesses can be prevented". Thus we may conclude that occupational accidents and illnesses can be prevented if necessary precautions are taken. This conclusion is also supported by the answers of other propositions. Majority of participants disagree (23.5%) and strongly disagree (54.1%) with the proposition of "Obeying occupational health and safety rules is waste of time". Apart from these, majority of the participants think that employer, employee and the state should work together to avoid occupational accidents.

Table 4: Participants' Answers about the Propositions related to Occupational Health and Safety

	Strongly Disagree		Disagree		Neutral		Agree		Strongly Agree	
	N	%	N	%	N	%	N	%	N	%
Majority of occupational accidents and illnesses can be prevented.	4	4.7	5	5.9	10	11.8	43	50.6	23	27.1
Obeying occupational health and safety rules is waste of time.	46	54.1	20	23.5	8	9.4	4	4.7	7	8.2
Preventing occupational accidents and illnesses is the responsibility of the employer.	5	5.9	19	22.4	11	12.9	32	37.6	18	21.2
Preventing occupational accidents and illnesses is the responsibility of the employees.	6	7.1	18	21.2	12	44.1	38	44.7	11	12.9
Preventing occupational accidents and illnesses is the responsibility of the state.	3	3.5	22	25.9	17	20	29	34.1	14	16.5

Question of "Do you have any knowledge about Occupational Health and Safety Act No. 6331?" may enable us to evaluate participants' knowledge level about Occupational Health and Safety Act No. 6331 introduced on June 30, 2012.

Among the participants, 88.8% stated that they had knowledge about the act while 11.2% stated that they did not have any knowledge about the act (see Table 5).

One of the rights given to the workers is right to avoidance of the work with Article 13 of Occupational Health and Safety Act No. 6331. Right to avoidance of the work is a right given to a worker/employee regarding occupational health and safety. According to the article, workers exposed to serious and imminent danger shall file an application to the committee or the employer in the absence of such a committee requesting an identification of the present hazard and measures for emergency intervention. The committee shall convene without delay and the employer shall make a decision immediately and write this decision down. The decision shall be communicated to the worker and workers' representative in writing. In the event that the committee or the employer takes a decision that is supportive of the request made by the worker, the worker may abstain from work until necessary measures are put into practice. The worker shall be entitled to payment during this period of abstention from work and his/her rights arising under the employment contract and other acts shall be reserved. In the event of serious, imminent and unavoidable danger, workers shall leave their workstation or dangerous area and proceed to a place of safety without any necessity to comply with the requirements mentioned above. Workers may not be placed at any disadvantage because of their action. Where the necessary measures are not taken despite the requests by workers, workers under labor contract might terminate their employment contract in accordance with the provisions of the act applicable to them. As for the workers under collective bargaining agreement, the abstention period as defined in this article shall be deemed as actual work time (The Occupational Health and Safety Act No. 6331, Article 13). In the survey, 58.8% of participants pointed out that they did not have any knowledge about this article that is quite important for the workers (see Table 5).

Table 5: *Questions Related to Participants' Knowledge about Occupational Health and Safety Act No. 6331*

	No		Yes	
	N	%	N	%
Do you have any knowledge about Occupational Health and Safety Act No. 6331?	35	11.2	50	88.8
Do you have any knowledge related to the right to avoidance of the dangerous work within the scope of the Occupational Health and Safety Act No. 6331?	35	41.2	50	58.8

Most of the participants disagree (27.1%) and strongly disagree (36.5%) with the proposition of "My priority is my work when I am exposed to a dangerous work?" while most of the participants agree (32.9%) and strongly agree (49.4%) with the proposition of "My priority is my health when I am exposed to a dangerous work?" (see Table 6). Hence it seems that participants think that their health comes first when they are exposed to a dangerous work.

Table 6: Participants' Answers about the Propositions related to the question of "What Participants Will Do When They Are Exposed to a Dangerous Work"

	Strongly Disagree		Disagree		Neutral		Agree		Strongly Agree	
	N	%	N	%	N	%	N	%	N	%
My priority is my work	31	36.5	23	27.1	9	10.6	13	15.3	9	10.6
My priority is my health	2	2.4	7	8.2	6	7.1	28	32.9	42	49.4
All kinds of measures are taken in our organization	13	15.3	11	12.9	16	18.8	35	41.2	10	11.8

As can be seen in Table 7, most of the participants who took occupational health and safety training previously always (47.6%) and often (34.5%) use personal protective equipment such as gloves, and mask while working.

Table 7: Frequency of Using Personal Protective Equipment While Working

		How often do you use personal protective equipment such as gloves, mask, shirt etc. while working?					
		Never	Rarely	Sometimes	Often	Always	Total
Did you take occupational health and safety training?	no	0	0	0	1	0	1
		0.0%	0.0%	0.0%	100.0%	0.0%	100.0%
	yes	1	3	11	29	40	84
		1.2%	3.6%	13.1%	34.5%	47.6%	100.0%
Total		1	3	11	30	40	85
		1.2%	3.5%	12.9%	35.3%	47.1%	100.0%

4 Conclusion

Importance of natural resources in lives of humans and society is a well-known fact. Considering 99% of the tools and equipment making human life functional are produced from natural resources especially minerals, it comes out that there is a close relationship between level of welfare and development of societies and mining activities.

Although mineral and mining sector is a heavy line of work that is hard, back-breaking and high risk bearing, and it requires knowledge, experience, proficiency and continuous control and inspection, it provides employment and income to the development of a country. Thus effective and productive usage of minerals is very important. Similarly, performances of the workers and performance-enhancing improvements in the sector are also important. These necessary improvements can only be possible by integrating corporate infrastructure, sectoral improvement and bureaucracy to each other.

Considering all these aspects together, determining the state of the mines becomes an obligation after the disaster happened in 2013 in Turkey. This study aims to determine which changes happened after occupational health and safety act and regulations were introduced. At the end of the study, we have observed that there are various improvements in workers' workplace and conditions after some changes have been made regarding occupational health and safety in mines with the changes made in act and regulations. However, it is necessary to make new revisions.

One of the important results that we obtain in our study is that although mine workers have knowledge about the occupational health and safety act introduced in 2012, they do not have enough knowledge about the right to avoidance of the work which is a benefit of the act. This situation indicates that workers have lack of knowledge about the act and they need to get training about this issue.

5 Suggestions

Our initial suggestion is that our perspective for occupational health and safety should change. At first we need to get away from "nothing happens to me" or "nothing happens just for doing once" perceptions. Giving up seeing occupational health and safety regulations as procedure is the first thing to do about this issue.

Safety standards of state's workplace and working conditions should be improved, mechanisms that make supervision and inspection more effective should be established, inspection for occupational safety should be conducted by the organizations that have independent accreditation and these organizations should be regarded as responsible for the results of the accidents due to lack of inspection.

Administrative and penal sanctions should be increased in the case of not providing occupational safety or deficiency of occupational safety, drills should be conducted carefully, firms should keep occupational safety report cards, statistical data about safety reports of firms should be made public, and firms and employers that cannot pass the limits should not be allowed to enter into public procurements, unionization activities should be supported, and technologic sufficiency standard should be introduced in labor-intensive sectors.

Employers should give priority to safety not production, they should include safety into their corporate strategy, they should employ alarm annunciation system and operate it, they should clearly define workers' job descriptions and responsibilities about workplace and occupational safety, they should train workers adequately to increase workers' cognitive awareness related to their work and occupational safety and raise their risk perception level and these trainings should be repeated at regular intervals, they should search causes and results of the accidents, they should include the results of these researches into the training, they should take necessary precautions that prevent similar accidents to happen again.

Plans should be prepared for emergencies and accordingly drills should be practiced. Communication culture should be created as such people report errors, mistakes and 119 violations. Suggestions for improving and developing the system should be rewarded. Although developments in technology bring significant solutions to the occupational accidents happening around world, statistics related to occupational accidents show that there are still a lot of things to do for occupational health and safety. Only acts, regulations and standards are not enough to prevent occupational accidents. In the studies, human mistakes are proportionately more as the leading cause among occupational accident causes. We suggest that qualifications, knowledge and education level of the workers for the job they do and improving their education level, increasing social and cultural activities, keeping morale and motivation high will be favorable in terms of safety efficiency. Occupational health and safety should be interiorized by employers and workers and social awareness should be created.

Inspection mechanism should be used actively to determine whether occupational health and safety rules are applied truly or not. Investments made for occupational health and safety should not be seen as an expenditure. On the contrary, they should be considered as investments made for the future. When rules for occupational health and safety are applied truly, rate of occupational accidents and illnesses will decrease. Finally, it is necessary to review contents of

"Occupational Health and Safety Basic Training" which become obligatory for all public and private sectors with Occupational Health and Safety Act No. 6331 and give more detailed information about the act to the workers.

References

Ernst & Young (2011). "The Mining Industry in the World and Turkey." Nederland: Ernst & Young.

Rossetti, M. D., R. R. Hill, B. Johansson, A. Dunkin and R. G. Ingalls (2009). "Using Simulation Analysis For Mining Project Risk Management." 2009 Winter Simulation Conference, 13–16 December 2009, Austin, TX.

TBMM (2010). "Mining Research Commission Report." Ankara, Turkey.

Cüneyt Koyuncu and Yüksel Okşak

Religion and Female Labor Force Participation

1 Introduction

Throughout history, inequality in women and men has shown itself in almost every field. The fact that man is physically stronger than females has triggered this disparity and has revealed a society structure in which man is dominant. However, special emphasis has been placed on equality between men and women in the last century. Hence, women's rights have started to be protected by law. Accordingly, it has been observed that women's participation to labor force has increased.

Female employment, i.e., female labor force participation (FLFP) rate, is calculated as the female labor force is divided by the economically active population. The fact that women's employment is secured by the law has certainly contributed positively to women's employment. However, different interpretations of laws in different societies, cultural differences, religion, etc. have effects on women's employment. Even though women have some rights in the law, encountering discrimination in business life (Foley et al., 1999), harassment (Bercovici, 2007), glass ceiling problem (Weyer, 2007), complying with certain forms in choosing a profession and a career (Winn, 2005), pregnancy, and marriage are frequent problems with women's employment.

In this study, the relationship between religion and women's employment is examined. Religions place some restrictions on their adherents. These restrictions may have an effect on the relationship between individuals and their family as well as the relationship between individuals and their relatives, neighbors, and society. Restrictions on adherents vary from religion to religion. Some religions provide women with a more liberal environment in a society while some other religions restrain the mobility of women in society. This calls for the question of whether religion can influence women's employment. Studies on women's employment are summarized in Table 1.

Table 1: Literature Summary

Author	Period/Countries	Results
Cooray et al. (2012)	191 Countries (1980–2005)	The impact of globalization, foreign direct investment and trade on women's labor force participation. It was found that globalization negatively affects women's labor participation.
H'madoun (2010)	48 Countries (2005)	The relationship between devoutness and women's labor force participation was examined.
Feldmann (2007)	80 Countries	The relationship between the Protestant religion and women's labor force participation was examined. It is concluded that female labor force participation rate and female employment rate are higher in Protestant countries.
Besamusca et al. (2015)	117 developing countries (2010)	It was found that female labor participation is higher in places where people are less religious, have maternity leave, and have higher pre-school enrollment rate.
Yalcinkaya Koyuncu et al. (2016)	110 countries (1985–2010)	A positive relationship between female labor participation rate and labor productivity was identified.
Lee and Lee (2014)	Japan (1971–2009)	The relationship between female labor force participation rate and fertility was examined for different age groups.

In the next section, data and methodology are introduced. Then empirical findings and estimation results are reported. The conclusions are given in the last section.

2 Data and methodology

In this study, we empirically investigate whether religion is important in FLFP. In other words, we try to identify that females of which religion are more prone to join labor force. The data used in the analyses are unbalanced data and cover the period of 1990–2010.

By using unbalanced panel data, we estimated the following multivariate fixed time effect model (FEM):

$$FLFP_{it} = (\beta_1 + \tau_t) + \beta_2 RELIG_{it} + \beta_3 AGRI_{it} + \beta_4 INDUST_{it} + \beta_5 URBPOP_{it}$$
$$+ \beta_6 INFL_{it} + \beta_7 BIRTH_{it} + \beta_8 ENRPRI_{it} + \beta_9 ENRSEC_{it}$$
$$+ \beta_{10} ENRTER_{it} + \beta_{11} CONSUMP_{it} + u_{it}$$

where *it* stands for the *i*-th country's observation value at time *t* for the particular variable. β_1 is the intercept term and τ_t represents time-specific effects that affect all countries in the same way (i.e., τ_t is variant across time but not across countries). u_{it} is idiosyncratic error term of the regression model.

Our dependent variable is the FLFP. It is taken from World Development Indicators (WDI) and measured as labor force participation rate, female (% of female population ages 15+) (modeled International Labor Organization's estimate).

The list of independent variables, their definitions, and the data sources are given in Table 2.

Table 2: List of Independent Variables

Variables	Definition	Source
RELIG	Percentage adherents of particular religion	World Religion Dataset of the Association of Religion Data Archives (ARDA)
AGRI	Employment in agriculture (% of total employment)	WDI
INDUST	Employment in industry (% of total employment)	WDI
URBPOP	Urban population growth (annual %)	WDI
INFL	Inflation, GDP deflator (annual %)	WDI
BIRTH	Fertility rate, total (births per woman)	WDI
ENRPRI	School enrollment, primary, female (% gross)	WDI
ENRSEC	School enrollment, secondary, female (% gross)	WDI
ENRTER	School enrollment, tertiary, female (% gross)	WDI
CONSUMP	Household final consumption expenditure per capita (constant 2010 US$)	WDI

Women are more inclined to prefer jobs possessing more flexible working hours or days because of interruptions in their life such as giving birth, child caring, and daily housework. Therefore, women may be more prone to work in agricultural sector than industrial sector since agricultural sector offers more flexible working periods than industrial sector. The expected sign for the coefficient of AGRI is positive whereas it is negative for INDUST.

An increase in urban population growth may force women to join labor force due to higher cost of living in urban area relative to rural area. Hence, we expect to have a positive sign for the coefficient of URBPOP variable.

Inflation in our model is proxy for the rate of increase of cost of living. If cost of living rises as a result of an increase in inflation, we anticipate women to participate in labor force more.

Giving birth and thus having children hold a significant portion in a woman's life and this type of interruptions discourage women to join labor force. The anticipated sign for the coefficient of BIRTH variable is negative.

Higher education level encourages women to take part in labor force and for that reason we expect to have a positive relation between ENRPRI, ENRSEC, and ENRTER variables and FLFP.

An increase in household consumption expenditure may compel women to participate in labor force. Therefore, a positive association between CONSUMP and FLFP variables is predicted.

3 Estimation results

This study reports only those estimation results in which we identified a statistically significant relationship between particular religion and FLFP.

Table 3 displays estimation results for Christianity. As seen from the table, there is a statistically significant positive impact of Protestant, Anglican, and Christianity in general on FLFP whereas there is a negative association between Roman Catholic and FLFP. The findings imply that societies with higher percentage of Protestant, Anglican, and Christian adherents experience higher level of FLFP while societies with higher percentage of Roman Catholic adherents experience lower level of FLFP. The other control variables take the expected signs whenever they are statistically significant.

Table 3: Estimation Results for Christianity

Religion =>	Protestant		Roman Catholic		Anglican		General	
	Coefficient	p-value	Coefficient	p-value	Coefficient	p-value	Coefficient	p-value
CONSTANT	21.3846	0.0603	13.3586	0.2657	14.2468	0.2346	13.7065	0.2562
AGRI	0.2763	0.0001	0.2471	0.0008	0.304	0	0.3025	0
INDUST	−0.1893	0.1583	−0.2653	0.0609	−0.202	0.1611	−0.2206	0.1278
URBPOP	0.2959	0.6594	−0.2436	0.7332	0.1004	0.8875	0.4879	0.5175
INFL	0.0081	0.6401	−0.0028	0.8774	0.0056	0.7603	0.0098	0.6007
BIRTH	−2.5056	0.0645	−0.826	0.5579	−1.2163	0.3879	−1.1246	0.4269
ENRPRI	0.2336	0.0008	0.3092	0	0.2493	0.0007	0.2264	0.0026
ENRSEC	−0.0144	0.7445	−0.0033	0.943	0.0036	0.9371	0.0073	0.8752
ENRTER	0.0889	0.0113	0.1211	0.001	0.1248	0.0007	0.1244	0.0008
CONSUMP	0.0002	0.0049	0.0004	0	0.0004	0	0.0004	0
RELIG	17.0882	0	−4.9494	0.0099	25.5376	0.0096	4.7622	0.0431
Num. of Observation	253		253		253		253	
Num. of Countries	87		87		87		87	
R-squared	0.4015		0.3293		0.3295		0.3221	
F-statistic	11.4078		8.3494		8.3554		8.0782	
Prob(F-statistic)	0		0		0		0	

Table 4 depicts estimation results for Islam. According to the findings, there is a statistically significant negative impact of Sunni, Shi'a, Alawite, and Islam in general on FLFP. The results reveal that societies with higher percentage of Sunni, Shi'a, Alawite, and Islam adherents experience lower level of FLFP. The remaining covariates get the anticipated signs whenever they are statistically significant.

Table 4: Estimation Results for Islam

Religion =>	Sunni		Shi'a		Alawite		General	
	Coefficient	p-value	Coefficient	p-value	Coefficient	p-value	Coefficient	p-value
CONSTANT	27.2441	0.0180	18.1829	0.1315	15.6021	0.1867	34.7747	0.0018
AGRI	0.2721	0.0001	0.2743	0.0002	0.3025	0.0000	0.2794	0.0000
INDUST	−0.2697	0.0434	−0.2745	0.0527	−0.2543	0.0685	−0.2321	0.0678
URBPOP	0.4790	0.4772	0.1626	0.8196	0.1754	0.8023	0.7467	0.2465
INFL	0.0117	0.5021	0.0231	0.2517	0.0097	0.5941	0.0398	0.0211
BIRTH	−0.2092	0.8754	−1.2928	0.3602	−1.2487	0.3687	0.2455	0.8471
ENRPRI	0.1613	0.0223	0.2359	0.0014	0.2612	0.0003	0.0725	0.2939
ENRSEC	0.0002	0.9956	0.0148	0.7523	−0.0103	0.8223	0.0136	0.7447
ENRTER	0.1052	0.0025	0.1153	0.0019	0.1351	0.0002	0.0846	0.0109

Religion =>	Sunni		Shi'a		Alawite		General	
	Coefficient	p-value	Coefficient	p-value	Coefficient	p-value	Coefficient	p-value
CONSUMP	0.0003	0.0001	0.0004	0.0000	0.0004	0.0000	0.0003	0.0002
RELIG	−16.4270	0.0000	−16.2449	0.0140	−138.7372	0.0003	−20.1168	0.0000
Num. of Observation	253		253		253		253	
Num. of Countries	87		87		87		87	
R-squared	0.4029		0.3276		0.3478		0.4590	
F-statistic	11.4748		8.2844		9.0658		14.4261	
Prob(F-statistic)	0.0000		0.0000		0.0000		0.0000	

Table 5 shows estimation results for other religions. The results hint that there is a statistically significant positive impact of Buddhism, Animist religion, and Nonreligious adherents on FLFP while there is a statistically significant negative impact of Hinduism, Sikh, and Jain religions on FLFP. According to the findings, societies with higher percentage of Buddhism, Animist religion, and Nonreligious adherents experience higher level of FLFP. On the other hand, societies with higher percentage of Hinduism, Sikh, and Jain adherents experience lower level of FLFP. The remaining independent variables possess the expected signs whenever they are statistically significant.

Table 5: Estimation Results for Other Religions

Religion =>	Buddhism		Hindu		Sikh	
	Coefficient	p-value	Coefficient	p-value	Coefficient	p-value
CONSTANT	13.3490	0.2625	13.6242	0.2603	14.3332	0.2350
AGRI	0.2340	0.0014	0.3010	0.0001	0.2963	0.0001
INDUST	−0.2858	0.0421	−0.2358	0.1021	−02671	0.0609
URBPOP	−0.7387	0.3190	−0.0551	0.9386	0.0008	0.9990
INFL	0.0048	0.7897	0.0018	0.9214	0.0020	0.9131
BIRTH	0.2072	0.8865	−0.9024	0.5250	−0.9726	0.4924
ENRPRI	0.2670	0.0003	0.2670	0.0003	0.2666	0.0003
ENRSEC	0.0057	0.9007	0.0029	0.9514	−0.0011	0.9808
ENRTER	0.1292	0.0004	0.1224	0.0010	0.1350	0.0003
CONSUMP	0.0004	0.0000	0.0005	0.0000	0.0005	0.0000
RELIG	12.5273	0.0017	−13.4460	0.0706	−617.2636	0.0573
Num. of Observation	253		253		253	
Num. of Countries	87		87		87	
R-squared	0.3383		0.3197		0.3207	
F-statistic	8.6940		7.9915		80277	
Prob(F-statistic)	0.0000		0.0000		0.0000	

Religion =>	Jain		Animist religions		Nonreligious	
	Coefficient	p-value	Coefficient	p-value	Coefficient	p-value
CONSTANT	12.9838	0.2807	32.9615	0.0052	17.6082	0.1397
AGRI	0.3151	0.0000	0.1782	0.0112	0.2797	0.0001
INDUST	−0.2464	0.0832	−0.3627	0.0073	−0.3512	0.0139
URBPOP	−0.1152	0.8713	−0.4489	0.5061	−0.0470	0.9468
INFL	0.0013	0.9423	0.0071	0.6828	0.0042	0.8170
BIRTH	−0.7080	0.6171	−2.7066	0.0475	−0.8010	0.5671
ENRPRI	0.2671	0.0003	0.1718	0.0149	0.2484	0.0007
ENRSEC	0.0019	0.9669	−0.0005	0.9917	5.33E-05	0.9991
ENRTER	0.1273	0.0005	0.1141	0.0010	0.1026	0.0059
CONSUMP	0.0005	0.0000	0.0004	0.0001	0.0005	0.0000
RELIG	−4163.4800	0.0151	97.0471	0.0000	16.2907	0.0016
Num. of Observation	253		253		253	
Num. of Countries	87		87		87	
R-squared	0.3272		0.3994		0.3386	
F-statistic	8.2710		11.3064		8.7052	
Prob(F-statistic)	0.0000		0.0000		0.0000	

4 Conclusion

Participation of females to labor force may vary across religions. This variation in female labor force among distinct religions may stem from the thought or practice of a particular religion. Hence this study investigated the relation between different religions and FLFP by using an unbalanced data covering the period of 1990–2010 and conducted empirical analyses in a multivariate FEM framework.

According to the empirical estimation results, there is a statistically significant positive impact of Protestant, Anglican, Christianity in general, Buddhism, Animist religion, and Non-religious adherents on FLFP whereas there is a statistically significant negative impact of Roman Catholic, Sunni, Shi'a, Alawite, Islam in general, Hinduism, Sikh, and Jain adherents on FLFP.

In other words, societies with higher percentage of Protestant, Anglican, Christian, Buddhism, Animist religion, and Non-religious adherents experience higher level of FLFP while societies with higher percentage of Roman Catholic, Sunni, Shi'a, Alawite, Islam, Hinduism, Sikh, and Jain adherents experience lower level of FLFP.

References

Bercovici, J. (2007). "The Workplace Romance and Sexual Favoritism: Creating a Dialogue Between Social Science and the Law of Sexual Harassment", *Southern California Interdisciplinary Law Journal*, 16: 183–214.

Besamusca, J., Tijdens, K., Keune, M., and Steinmetz, S. (2015). "Working Women Worldwide. Age Effects in Female Labor Force Participation in 117 Countries", *World Development*, 74: 123–141.

Cooray, A., Gaddis, I., and Wacker, K. M. (2012). "Globalization and Female Labor Force Participation in Developing Countries: An Empirical (Re-)Assessment", (ed.) Bent J. Christensen and C. Kowalczyk, *Globalization Strategies and Effects*, Berlin: Springer.

Feldmann, H. (2007). "Protestantism, Labor Force Participation, and Employment across Countries", *American Journal of Economics and Sociology*, 66(4): 795–816.

Foley, M., Maxwell, G. and McGillivray, D. (1999). "Women at Leisure and Work – Unequal Opportunities", *Equal Opportunities*, 18(1): 8–18.

H'madoun, M. (2010). "Religion and Labor Force Participation of Women", University of Antwerp, Faculty of Applied Economics Working Paper 2010007, Antwerp: University of Antwerp.

Lee, G. H., and Lee, S. P. (2014). "Childcare Availability, Fertility and Female Labor Force Participation in Japan", *Journal of the Japanese and International Economies*, 32: 71–85.

Koyuncu, J. Y., Yılmaz, R., and Ünver, M. (2016). "The Relationship Between Female Labor Force Participation and Labor Productivity: Panel Data Analysis", *Eskişehir Osmangazi Üniversitesi IIBF Dergisi*, 11(2): 237–249.

Weyer, B. (2007). "Twenty Years Later: Explaining the Persistence of the Glass Ceiling for Women Leaders", *Women in Management Review*, 22(6): 482–496.

Winn, J. (2005). "Women Entrepreneurs: Can We Remove the Barriers?", *International Entrepreneurship and Management Journal*, 1(3): 381–397.

Eda Özen and Tufan Sarıtaş

The Impact of Religion on Corruption: Empirical Evidence

1 Introduction

The issue of corruption has been frequently mentioned in academic writing over the past few decades. Accordingly, governments have developed anti-corruption policies and programs to fight against corruption due to its negative effects on economic growth and public spending. Khan (2006: 216) argues that reduction in the high level of corruption in developing countries leads to increase in the growth rate of these countries.

There are many definitions of corruption. The World Bank defines corruption as "the use of public power for personal interests." Corruption isn't a problem specific to the public sphere. Corruption also occurs in the private sector, especially in the procurement and recruitment departments of companies. The use of public power doesn't always happen for the benefit of individuals; the use of public power can be for the benefit of certain groups such as a party, class, family, and friends. Tanzi (1998: 8) reports that incomes and benefits received from corruption are transferred to finance political parties in many countries.

The reactions to corruption vary from country to country. Developed countries and underdeveloped countries react differently against corruption. The reactions against corruptions are also different within the same income groups of countries. Reactions of a government against corruption incidences also differ from country to country (Pellegrini and Gerlagh, 2007). The different attitudes toward corruption in different countries are related to the ethnic, cultural, and religious structure as well as the level of development of these countries.

2 The relationship between religion and corruption

The word "religion" comes from Latin word "religio," which means "something strictly bound by." Therefore, when an individual connects with God through religion, he/she must live in the moral stance prescribed by God. Religions advise people to adopt a moral attitude. For example, a person can't be defined as a good Muslim if he/she lacks moral norms (Qur'an: Şura, 42/37-43; Mü'minun, 23/2-8; Tekvir, 81/14; İnfitar, 82/5; Kahf, 18/47,49; Bakara, 2284; İsra, 17/36; Tekasür, 102/8; Dehr, 76/9; Mü'minun, 23/71; A'raf, 7/33, 157; Kasas, 28/47).

Similarly, "Ten Commandments" in Judaism advise some moral principles for people (Torah: Exit 20, Test 5). There are also ethical and moral principles in the Christian Bible. For example, in the Bible, virtues such as humility (Matta, 18:10-11; 23:11-12), honesty (Matta, 5:6; Letter to Hebrews, 1:9), being compassionate (Matta, 5:7), controlling anger (Letter to Ephesus from Petros, 4:31-32; Matta, 5:22), and being patient (Petros' First Letter, 2:19-20) are praised and people are encouraged to gain these moral qualities.

Religion and social contract are the sources of morality. Historically, bad and wrong behaviors of people are corrected by religion. However, the emergence of nation-state and the secularization of the state excluded the state from the public sphere. Hence, the moral void in the society is filled by the law which is the second source of morality. Thus, morality started to be shaped by the law in modern times (Berg, 1993; Midgley, 1993).

Graph 1 presents the level of corruption in countries where more than 70% of the population has a particular religion between the years 2002 and 2015. The positive numbers on the vertical axis indicate the increase in the corruption level, whereas the negative numbers indicate the decrease in the corruption level. There are 89 countries in the Christian country group, 37 countries in the Muslim country group, and 2 countries in the Hinduism country group (India and Nepal), whereas there is 1 country in the Shinto country group (Japan) and 1 country in the Judaism group (Israel).

Graph 1 shows that corruption level is the lowest in Shintoist countries. Corruption level is higher in Islamic and Hinduism countries than in Christian and Jewish countries. Because the religions don't approve immoral acts such as corruption, the ranks may indicate that religions are not understood sufficiently by the individuals and/or their principles are not followed by adherents in these countries.

Graph 1: Corruption level by country groups with dominant religion

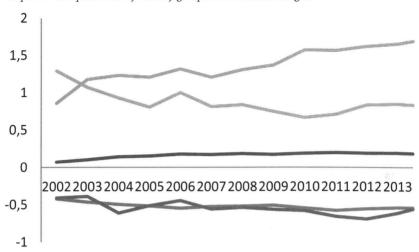

Source: The World Factbook data, https://www.cia.gov/library/publications/the-world-factbook/.

3 Literature review on the determinants of corruption

Many possible social, economic, and cultural determinants of corruption have been suggested by the empirical literature on the determinants of corruption. The results vary according to the sample of countries and the period under study. The results of empirical studies also reveal the causes of corruption. The study of Kaufmann (1998: 79) points out the possible causes of corruption as follows: poverty, ineffective economic policies, inadequate competition, inequality in income distribution, rich natural resources, high ethnic/religious/cultural diversity, inefficiency in the economy, inefficiency of the bureaucratic system, problems experienced in civil and political liberties, and low level of wages in the public sector. A summary of literature review of the empirical studies on corruption is presented in Table 1.

Table 1: A Summary of the Literature on Corruption

Author(s)	Period/Countries	Empirical Findings
Mauro (1995)	68 countries for the period 1980–1983; 57 countries for the period 1971–1979	A negative relation between growth and corruption was identified.
Tanzi and Davoodi (1997)	For the 1982–1995 period, the first group of countries covering 49 countries and the second group of countries covering 95 countries	A negative relationship between public revenues and corruption and a negative relationship between the quality of infrastructure facilities and corruption was determined.
Elliot (1997)	83 countries	A positive relationship between corruption and the size of the government in the economy was found.
Rijkeghem and Weder (1997)	25 countries	A negative relationship between public sector wage level and corruption was detected.
Mo (2001)	54 countries for the 1970–1985 period	A negative relationship between growth and corruption was identified.
Paldam (2001)	100 countries for 1998	It was found that tribal religions reduce corruption.
Toatu (2004)	Pacific Island countries	A negative relation between growth and corruption was observed.
Drury et al. (2006)	More than 100 countries for the period 1982–1997	There was no statistically significant relationship between growth and corruption in countries with democratic regimes. Growth was negatively affected by corruption in countries with undemocratic regimes.
Koyuncu and Bhattacharyya (2008)	25 OECD countries for the period 1975–1993	There was a negative relationship between investments and corruption, whereas there was no relationship between growth and corruption.
Koyuncu and Yılmaz (2009)	100 countries for the period 1980–1990/1990–1995/1990–2000	A positive relationship between deforestation and corruption was determined.
Koyuncu et al. (2010)	Transition economies	A negative relationship between privatization and corruption was identified.
Shadabi (2013)	174 countries for 2010	Islam and Christianity had no effect on corruption and that religion in general is not the cause of corruption.

In the empirical literature, corruption has been associated with many variables and various results were obtained. Empirical findings indicate that corruption negatively affects growth and investment level, whereas there is a positive relationship between corruption and deforestation. However, empirical findings on the relationship between religion and corruption are inconclusive and ambiguous.

4 Data and methodology

In this study, we investigate the association between religion and corruption level in an economy by using three different corruption indicators. The study attempts to reveal religions in which corrupt practices are more widespread. The data used in analyses are unbalanced data and cover the period of 2000–2010. In order to conduct our empirical analyses, we estimated the following multivariate random effect model:

$$CORRUPTION_{it} = \alpha + \beta_1 RELIGION + \beta_2 FDI_{it} + \beta_3 OPENNESS_{it}$$
$$+ \beta_4 INFLATION_{it} + \beta_5 DEMOCRACY_{it} + \varepsilon_i + u_{it}$$

where it subscript stands for the i-th country's observation value at time t for the particular variable; ε_i is a stochastic term, which is constant through the time and characterizes the country-specific factors not considered in the regression; and u_{it} is error term of the regression.

Our dependent variable is corruption. Three different corruption variables are used in order to see how robust our empirical results are. Results may vary depending on which corruption variable is used in the models. If the results remain valid across different corruption variables, it will be an indication of their robustness. The list of dependent variables, their definitions, and the data sources are given in Table 2.

Table 2: List of Dependent Variables

Variables	Definition	Source
CORRUPTION1	CORRUPTION1 = −1* (Control of corruption)	Worldwide Governance Indicators, www.govindicators.org
CORRUPTION2	CORRUPTION2 = −1* (Corruption perception index)	Transparency International, https://www.transparency.org/research/cpi/cpi_early/0/
CORRUPTION3	CORRUPTION3 = −1* (Freedom from corruption)	Index of Economic Freedom, http://www.heritage.org/index/explore?view=by-region-country-year

CORRUPTION1 reflects the level of corruption in a country. It is computed by multiplying control of corruption variable of Worldwide Governance Indicators with minus one. The control of corruption captures perceptions of the extent to which public power is exercised for private gain, including both petty and grand forms of corruption, as well as "capture" of the state by elites and private interests. Estimate gives the country's score on the aggregate indicator, in units of a standard normal distribution, i.e., ranging from approximately −2.5 to 2.5 (Ünver and Yalçınkaya, 2016: 635). Scores closer to 2.5 mean lower level of corruption and scores closer to −2.5 mean higher level of corruption. Because CORRUPTION1 variable is calculated by multiplying control of corruption variable with minus one, its higher scores indicate higher level of corruption and lower scores indicate lower level of corruption.

CORRUPTION2 shows the level of corruption in a country. It is computed by multiplying corruption perception index variable of Transparency International with minus one. Because CORRUPTION2 variable is calculated by multiplying corruption perception index variable with minus one, its higher scores indicate higher level of corruption and lower score indicates lower level of corruption.

CORRUPTION3 indicates the level of corruption in a country. It is computed by multiplying freedom from corruption variable of Index of Economic Freedom with minus one. Because CORRUPTION3 variable is calculated by multiplying freedom from corruption variable with minus one, its higher scores indicate higher level of corruption and lower score indicates lower level of corruption.

Our explanatory variables were chosen in light of previous studies found in the literature, the availability of the data. The data of religions from World Religion Dataset of the Association of Religion Data Archives (ARDA) are measured as percentage adherents of particular religion.

We also introduced four more explanatory variables peculiar to corruption into our analysis to see how robust our finding is. Definition and data source of other independent variables besides poverty variables are given in Table 3.

Table 3: List of Independent Variables

Variables	Definition	Source
OPENNESS	Trade (% of GDP)	WDI
DEMOCRACY	Democracy level (scaled between 0 and 10)	http://www.systemicpeace.org/inscrdata.html
INFLATION	Inflation, GDP deflator (annual %)	WDI
FDI	Foreign direct investment (inward, US dollars at current prices and current exchange rates in millions)	UNCTAD

The following paragraphs further describe the independent variables and discuss their expected signs.

In addition to RELIGION variable, we introduced four more determinants of corruption into our models to analyze the impact of poverty level on corruption: openness degree of an economy (OPENNESS), democracy level of a country (DEMOCRACY), inflation level of an economy (INFLATION), and foreign direct investment level of an economy (FDI).

OPENNESS reflects the degree of openness of an economy. It is measured as percentage ratio of trade in gross domestic product (GDP). Higher degrees of openness in an economy are related to lower levels of corruption. Thus, we expect to have a negative relationship between OPENNESS and corruption.

INFLATION reflects three things, namely degree of uncertainty in an economy, political instability, and economic instability. Corrupt practices can be performed more easily in countries having higher degree uncertainty and instability because accountability and transparency are lower in such an environment. Hence, a positive relationship between INFLATION and corruption is expected.

FDI represents inward foreign direct investment in an economy. FDI prefers to invest in economies having higher transparency and strong institutions. Thus, we expect to have a negative coefficient for FDI variable.

DEMOCRACY shows the level of democracy in a country. The political economy literature agrees on that higher democracy results in lower corrupt practices. Therefore, we anticipate having a negative coefficient for DEMOCRACY variable.

5 Estimation results

In this study, we report only those estimation results in which we identified a statistically significant relationship between religion and corruption for all the three corruption indicators.

Table 4 depicts the results for Protestants. It shows that there is a highly statistically significant negative association between Protestants and corruption. According to the finding, societies with higher percentage of Protestant adherents experience lower level of corruption. FDI, OPENNESS, and DEMOCRACY variables take the expected signs and are statistically significant in all models. INFLATION variable gets the anticipated sign and is statistically significant in just one model.

Table 4: Estimation Results for Christianity: Protestants

Dependent Variables =>	CORRUPTION1	P-value	CORRUPTION2	P-value	CORRUPTION3	P-value
CONSTANT	0.8166	0.0000	−2.6393	0.0000	−23.37944	0.0000
FDI	−2.79E−06	0.0141	−3.66E−06	0.0215	−5.05E−05	0.0383
OPENNESS	−0.0023	0.0121	−0.0054	0.0027	−0.066771	0.0003
INFLATION	0.0026	0.2607	−0.0026	0.2032	0.043766	0.0982
DEMOCRACY	−0.0744	0.0000	−0.1142	0.0000	−1.213074	0.0000
RELIGION	−0.8931	0.0047	−1.7479	0.0041	−28.7862	0.0000
No. of Observations	287		358		412	
No. of Countries	148		148		150	
R-squared	0.1841		0.1149		0.1357	
F-statistic	12.6836		9.1442		12.7483	
Prob(F-statistic)	0.0000		0.0000		0.0000	

Table 5 depicts the results for Eastern Orthodox. According to the estimation results, there is a statistically significant positive association between Eastern Orthodox and corruption. The finding reveals that societies with higher percentage of Eastern Orthodox adherents experience higher corrupt practices. Among the control variables, only FDI, OPENNESS, and DEMOCRACY variables take the expected signs and are statistically significant and this significance is valid in all models.

Table 5: Estimation Results for Christianity: Eastern Orthodox

Dependent Variables =>	CORRUPTION1	P-value	CORRUPTION2	P-value	CORRUPTION3	P-value
CONSTANT	0.6898	0.0000	−2.8469	0.0000	−26.2851	0.0000
FDI	−2.77E−06	0.0143	−3.76E−06	0.0173	−5.27E−05	0.0300
OPENNESS	−0.0021	0.0210	−0.0055	0.0021	−0.0655	0.0004
INFLATION	0.0029	0.1969	−0.0026	0.1868	0.0424	0.1092
DEMOCRACY	−0.0804	0.0000	−0.1278	0.0000	−1.4637	0.0000
RELIGION	0.5424	0.0515	1.3799	0.0208	13.5941	0.0276
No. of Observations	291		363		418	
No. of Countries	150		150		152	
R-squared	0.1713		0.1077		0.1095	
F-statistic	11.7835		8.6183		10.1376	
Prob(F-statistic)	0.0000		0.0000		0.0000	

Table 6 displays the results for Anglicans. According to the estimation results, there is a statistically significant negative association between Anglicans and corruption. The finding indicates that societies with higher percentage of Anglican adherents experience lower level of corruption. Among the control variables, only FDI, OPENNESS, and DEMOCRACY variables take the expected signs and are statistically significant and this significance is valid in all models.

Table 6: Estimation Results for Christianity: Anglican

Dependent Variables =>	CORRUPTION1	P-value	CORRUPTION2	P-value	CORRUPTION3	P-value
CONSTANT	0.7491	0.0000	−2.7104	0.0000	−24.8619	0.0000
FDI	−2.58E−06	0.0230	−3.59E−06	0.0238	−5.06E−05	0.0394
OPENNESS	−0.0022	0.0181	−0.0055	0.0020	−0.0666	0.0004
INFLATION	0.0027	0.2231	−0.0027	0.1850	0.0427	0.1097
DEMOCRACY	−0.0766	0.0000	−0.1200	0.0000	−1.3868	0.0000
RELIGION	−2.0190	0.0765	−3.9067	0.0887	−42.8619	0.0802
No. of Observation	291		363		418	
No. of Countries	150		150		152	
R-squared	0.0000		0.1005		0.1057	
F-statistic	11.4808		7.9825		9.7423	
Prob(F-statistic)	0.0000		0.0000		0.0000	

Table 7 reports the results for Sunni Muslims. The estimation result implies that there is a statistically significant positive association between Sunni Muslims and corruption. The finding indicates that societies with higher percentage of Sunni Muslim adherents experience higher level of corruption. FDI, OPENNESS, and DEMOCRACY variables take the anticipated signs and are statistically significant in all models. INFLATION variable gets the anticipated sign and is statistically significant in just one model.

Table 7: Estimation Results for Islam: Sunni

Dependent Variables =>	CORRUPTION1	P-value	CORRUPTION2	P-value	CORRUPTION3	P-value
CONSTANT	0.5328	0.0002	−3.1986	0.0000	−29.7741	0.0000
FDI	−2.67E−06	0.0187	−3.55E−06	0.0250	−5.06E−05	0.0392
OPENNESS	−0.0019	0.0368	0.0051	0.0045	−0.0615	0.0010
INFLATION	0.0024	0.2920	−0.0025	0.2178	0.0466	0.0818
DEMOCRACY	−0.0679	0.0000	−0.1005	0.0001	−1.1494	0.0001

Dependent Variables =>	CORRUPTION1	P-value	CORRUPTION2	P-value	CORRUPTION3	P-value
RELIGION	0.5243	0.0068	1.2656	0.0035	11.026	0.0135
No. of Observations	291		363		418	
No. of Countries	150		150		152	
R-squared	0.1789		0.1124		0.1104	
F-statistic	12.4264		9.0417		10.2324	
Prob(F-statistic)	0.0000		0.0000		0.0000	

Table 8 reports the results for Islam in general. The estimation result implies that there is a statistically significant positive association between Islam and corruption. The result hints that societies with higher percentage of Muslim adherents experience higher level of corruption. FDI, OPENNESS, and DEMOCRACY variables get the anticipated signs and are statistically significant in all models. INFLATION variable takes the anticipated sign and is statistically significant in just one model.

Table 8: Estimation Results for Islam: General

Dependent Variables =>	CORRUPTION1	P-value	CORRUPTION2	P-value	CORRUPTION3	P-value
CONSTANT	0.5065	0.0007	−3.2655	0.0000	−29.7125	0.0000
FDI	−2.64E−06	0.0191	−3.55E−06	0.0240	−5.11E−05	0.0369
OPENNESS	−0.0019	0.0401	−0.0050	0.0050	−0.0624	0.0008
INFLATION	0.0023	0.2979	−0.0026	0.2003	0.0458	0.0865
DEMOCRACY	−0.0661	0.0000	−0.0967	0.0002	−1.1484	0.0865
RELIGION	0.5065	0.0007	1.1706	0.0033	9.1123	0.0252
No. of Observations	291		363		418	
No. of Countries	150		150		152	
R-squared	0.1765		0.1115		0.1086	
F-statistic	12.2219		8.9666		10.0449	
Prob(F-statistic)	0.0000		0.0000		0.0000	

Table 9 reports the results for Shinto. The estimation result implies that there is a statistically significant negative association between Shinto and corruption. The result hints that societies with higher percentage of Shinto adherents experience lower corrupt practices. FDI, OPENNESS, and DEMOCRACY variables take the anticipated signs and are statistically significant in all models.

Table 9:   Estimation Results for Other Religions: Shinto

Dependent Variables =>	CORRUPTION1	P-value	CORRUPTION2	P-value	CORRUPTION3	P-value
CONSTANT	0.7368	0.0000	−2.736	0.0000	−25.2929	0.0000
FDI	−2.83E−06	0.0121	−3.82E−06	0.0152	−5.47E−05	0.0250
OPENNESS	−0.0022	0.0154	−0.0057	0.0014	−0.0674	0.0003
INFLATION	0.0027	0.2379	−0.0027	0.1730	0.0425	0.1098
DEMOCRACY	−0.0773	0.0000	−0.1198	0.0000	−1.3798	0.0000
RELIGION	−1.5651	0.0816	−4.8077	0.0145	−36.8848	0.0681
No. of Observations	291		363		418	
No. of Countries	150		150		152	
R-squared	0.1688		0.1068		0.1056	
F-statistic	11.5824		8.5404		9.7329	
Prob(F-statistic)	0.0000		0.0000		0.0000	

Table 10 depicts the results for nonreligious. The estimation finding shows that there is a statistically significant negative association between nonreligious and corruption. The result implies that societies with higher percentage of nonreligious adherents experience lower level of corruption. FDI, OPENNESS, and DEMOCRACY variables take the anticipated signs and are statistically significant in all models.

Table 10:   Estimation Results for Other Religions: Nonreligious

Dependent Variables =>	CORRUPTION1	P-value	CORRUPTION2	P-value	CORRUPTION3	P-value
CONSTANT	0.7691	0.0000	−2.6915	0.0000	−24.5597	0.0000
FDI	−2.49E−06	0.0291	−3.77E−06	0.0179	−5.07E−05	0.0382
OPENNESS	−0.0019	0.0361	−0.0052	0.0040	−0.0624	0.0008
INFLATION	0.0033	0.1497	−0.0028	0.1651	0.0409	0.1242
DEMOCRACY	−0.0731	0.0000	−0.1181	0.0000	−1.3038	0.0000
RELIGION	−1.3256	0.0013	−1.7035	0.0257	−25.0199	0.0087
No. of Observations	291		363		418	
No. of Countries	150		150		152	
R-squared	0.1896		0.1065		0.1142	
F-statistic	13.3424		0.0940		10.6278	
Prob(F-statistic)	0.0000		0.0000		0.0000	

6 Conclusion

This study investigates the relation between religion and corruption level in a country by using three distinct corruption indicators. The data used in analyses are unbalanced data and cover the years between 2000 and 2010 in the largest sample. The main finding of the study is that societies with higher percentage of Protestant, Anglican, Shinto, and nonreligious adherents experience lower level of corruption, whereas societies with higher percentage of Eastern Orthodox, Sunni, and Muslim adherents experience higher corrupt practices. This result does not alter when we added other determinants peculiar to corruption into our models. Moreover, our results are robust in the sense that our primary finding remains valid no matter which proxy is used for corruption in the models.

References

Berg, J. (1993). "How Could Ethics Depend on Ethics", A Companion to Ethics (Ed. by P. Singer), Basil Blackwell, Cambridge, 525–533.

Drury, A.C., Krieckhaus, J. and Lusztig, M. (2006). "Corruption, Democracy and Economic Growth", International Political Science Review, 27(2): 121–136.

Elliot, K.A. (1997). "Corruption as an International Policy Problem: Overview and Recommendations", Corruption and Global Economy (Ed. by K.A. Elliot), Peterson Institute for International Economics, Washington, DC, 175–233.

Kaufmann, D. (1998). "Revisiting Anti-Corruption Strategies: Tilt Towards Incentive-Driven Approaches?", Corruption and Integrity Improvement Initiatives in Developing Countries, United Nations Development Programme and OECD Development Centre Publication, New York, 63–82.

Khan, M.H. (2006). "Determinants of Corruption in Developing Countries: The Limits of Conventional Economic Analysis", International Handbook on the Economics of Corruption (Ed. by S. Rose-Ackerman), Edward Elgar Publishing, New York, 216–246.

Koyuncu, C. and Bhattacharyya, G. (2008). "Predicting Corrupt Practices in the Public Sector for 23 OECD Countries", Applied Econometrics and International Development, 7(1): 15–36.

Koyuncu, C., Öztürkler, H. and Yılmaz, R. (2010). "Privatization and Corruption in Transition Economies: A Panel Study", Journal of Economic Policy Reform, 13(3): 277–284.

Koyuncu, C. and Yılmaz, R. (2009). "The Impact of Corruption on Deforestation: A Cross-Country Evidence", Journal of Developing Areas, 42(2): 213–222.

Mauro, P. (1995). "Corruption and Growth", The Quarterly Journal of Economics, 110(3): 681–712.

Midgley, M. (1993). "The Origin of Ethics", A Companion to Ethics (Ed. by P. Singer), Basil Blackwell, Cambridge, 3–13.

Mo, P.H. (2001). "Corruption and Economic Growth", Journal of Comparative Economics, 29(1): 66–79.

Paldam, M. (2001). "Corruption and Religion: Adding to the Economic Model", Kyklos, 54(2–3): 383–413.

Pellegrini, L. and Gerlagh, R. (2007). "Causes of Corruption: A Survey of Cross-country Analyses and Extended Results", Economics of Governance, 9(3): 245–263.

Rıjkeghem, C.V. and Weder, B. (1997). "Corruption and the Rate of Temptation: Do Low Wages in the Civil Service Cause Corruption?", IMF Working Paper No. 97/73, International Monetary Fund, 1–56.

Shadabi, L. (2013). "The Impact of Religion on Corruption", The Journal of Business Inquiry, 12, 102–117.

Tanzi, V. (1998). "Corruption Around the World Causes, Consequences, Scope, and Cures", IMF Working Paper No. 98/63, International Monetary Fund, Washington DC.

Tanzi, V. and Davoodi, H. (1997). "Corruption, Public Investment, and Growth", IMF Working Paper No. 97/139, International Monetary Fund, Washington DC.

Toatu, T. (2004). "Corruption, Public Investment and Economic Growth: Evidence from Pacific Island Countries", PIAS-DG Governance Program Working Paper, University of South Pacific, Suva.

Ünver, M. and Yalçınkaya, K.J. (2016). "The Impact of Poverty on Corruption", Journal of Economics Library, 3(4): 632–642.

Julide Yalcinkaya Koyuncu and Mustafa Ünver

Does Corruption Deteriorate Labor Productivity?: Panel Evidence

1 Introduction

Corruption has many adverse effects on the economy, especially on the economic growth. This has stimulated academic studies on corruption. The empirical relationship between corruption and economic growth has been studied extensively in the literature (Dridi, 2013; Aghion, Akcigit, Cagé and Kerr, 2016). Corruption can also affect other variables. One of the variables that corruption can affect is labor productivity. In theoretical and empirical research, many variables have been associated with labor productivity (Yildirim, Koyuncu and Koyuncu, 2009; Koyuncu, Yilmaz and Unver, 2016). This chapter aims to explain the effect of corruption on the labor productivity by using data for 61 countries for 2000–2011 periods. This relationship was examined by using 3 different corruption indicators and 13 different labor productivity indicators. As such this study is the most comprehensive analysis on the subject in the literature. Similar studies examining this relationship do not have such a large sample (Del Mar Salinas-Jimenez and Salinas-Jimenez, 2011; Saastamoinen and Kuosmanen, 2014; De Rosa, Gooroochurn and Görg, 2015).

The remainder of the chapter is organized as follows: Section 2 examines theoretical and empirical literature on the relationship between corruption and the productivity, whereas Section 3 outlines the data and methodology. Section 4 provides the empirical results and Section 5 concludes.

2 Theoretical and empirical context

Corruption is often defined as the use of public power to generate personal benefits (Ghura, 1998: 3). At the same time, corruption motivates people to deal with bureaucratic procedures and illegal actions in government policies. Therefore, corruption is a natural reaction of the market to corrupt government policies (Aidt, 2003: 633). On the other hand, corruption is defined as an indicator of how the authorities provide private–public services in the context of receiving bribery. Existence of bribery actions indicates that there is the negation of the rule of law and individuals can't obtain their rights. In this context, if bribery affects the presentation of services, individuals will not be able to obtain the services they deserve (Welzel, Inglehart and Kligemann, 2003: 357). Corruption, therefore, is one of the most important problems of the governments because this problem can lead to the depletion of limited resources, inefficient bureaucracy, and lower growth and development. In addition, corruption creates problems in the trade sector by increasing input prices (Schulze and Frank, 2003: 143). In this context, it is more likely that corruption will arise in an economy where profits are determined by the government rather than the market, there are active government interventions, and the size of the public sector keeps increasing (Del Monte and Papagni, 2007: 380).

Most of the literature on corruption focuses on the determinants of corruption (Tanzi, 1998; Frechette, 2001; Schulze and Frank, 2003; Sosa, 2004; Voyer and Beamish, 2004; Koyuncu and Bhattacharyya, 2007; Koyuncu and Yilmaz, 2009; Koyuncu, Ozturkler and Yilmaz, 2010; Morris and Klesner, 2010; Koyuncu and Yilmaz, 2013; Koyuncu and Unver, 2016; Topal and Keyifli, 2016; Topal and Unver, 2016; Unver and Koyuncu, 2016; Unver and Koyuncu, 2017). Corruption can also affect other variables. The impact of corruption on public investment, capital, labor force, and total factor productivity has been studied by researchers (Tanzi and Davoodi, 1998; De Rosa, Gooroochurn and Görg, 2010; Mohammadi Khyareh, 2017). One of the variables that corruption can affect is the productivity performance of the economy. Productivity and efficiency is a key factor for the performance of economies. The main goal of countries is to reduce productivity disparity among them because the most important determinant of economic growth in the long run is productivity growth (Van Reenen, 2013: 113). This study focuses on the impact of corruption on productivity.

Labor productivity is a measure of performance that compares the number of hours worked and the amount of goods and services produced. Mathematically, it is a real output per working hour. Economic growth is realized as long as real output increases more than working hours (Sprague, 2017: 2).

In this context, it can be important whether labor productivity affecting growth is affected by corruption. Researchers and policy makers emphasize corporate honesty for sustainable growth. For example, despite the perception that corruption is low in the OECD (Organisation for Economic Co-operation and Development) area, it negatively affects productivity and hence growth. In this context, anti-corruption practices are essential for productivity, technological progress, and long-term growth (Del Mar Salinas-Jimenez and Salinas-Jimenez, 2007: 914).

Hence, social institutions are a fundamental component of the social infrastructure that is effective in increasing labor productivity. Although governments are the most effective providers of social infrastructure that protects against economic deviations, governments from the other side are the primary institutions that constitute economic deviations in practice. Examples of these public deviations are expropriation, unjust taxation, and corruption (Hall and Jones, 1999: 84).

In the literature, there are empirical studies on the relationship between corruption and labor productivity indicators. Del Mar Salinas-Jimenez and Salinas-Jimenez (2011) investigated the effect of corruption on productivity for 56 developed and developing countries. They found a statistically significant and negative relationship between corruption and total factor productivity. Similarly, De Rosa, Gooroochurn and Görg (2015) examined the effect of corruption on firm productivity for a cross-section data from 28 transition and developed economies in 2009. Their results indicate that corruption negatively affects productivity.

3 Data and methodology

This study examines the impact of corruption on labor productivity by using 13 different productivity indicators. Our unbalanced panel data contain 61 countries and cover the period of 2000–2011 in the widest sense. In order to conduct our empirical analyses, we estimated the following multivariate fixed time effect model (FEM):

$$PROD_{it} = (\beta_1 + \tau_t) + \beta_2 CORRUPT_{it} + \beta_3 CAPSTOCK_{it} + \beta_4 ENROL_{it} + \beta_5 AWH_{it} + u_{it}$$

and we also estimated the following multivariate random time effect model (REM):

$$PROD_{it} = \beta_1 + \beta_2 CORRUPT_{it} + \beta_3 CAPSTOCK_{it} + \beta_4 ENROL_{it} + \beta_5 AWH_{it} + (\tau_t + u_{it})$$

where subscript it denotes the ith country's observation value at time t for the variable. The coefficient β_1 measures the intercept term and τ_t indicates time-specific effects that influence all countries in the same way (i.e., τ_t is variant across time but not across countries). u_{it} is idiosyncratic error term of the regression model.

Thirteen distinct productivity indicators are used to represent labor productivity (PROD) in the analyses. The main result of analyses may vary across the productivity indicators in the sense of the sign taken and significance level of the relevant coefficient; however, if the finding of analyses remains valid across those 13 separate productivity indicators, then this will mean an indicator of the robustness of the result. The list of 13 productivity indicators and their data definitions from various sources are shown in Table 1. Table 2 provides the list of corruption indicators, whereas Table 3 presents the list of independent variables used in the study.

Table 1: List of Productivity Indicators

Indicator	Definition	Source
CTFP	Total factor productivity level at current PPPs	Penn World Table
CWTFP	Welfare-relevant total factor productivity levels at current PPPs	Penn World Table
LPROD1	Labor productivity per person employed in 1990 US$ (converted at Geary–Khamis PPPs)	The Conference Board
LPROD2	Labor productivity per person employed in 2014 US$ (converted to 2014 price level with updated 2011 PPPs)	The Conference Board
LPROD3	Labor productivity per hour worked in 1990 US$ (converted at Geary–Khamis PPPs)	The Conference Board
LPROD4	Labor productivity per hour worked in 2014 US$ (converted to 2014 price level with updated 2011 PPPs)	The Conference Board
PCVALADCUR	{Gross value added at factor cost (current US$)}/{total population}	WDI WDI
MANVLADPLCUR	{Manufacturing, value added (current US$)}/{employment in manufacturing (thousands of persons) × 1,000}	WDI ILO
AGRVLADPLCUR	{Agriculture, value added (current US$)}/ {(employment in agriculture (% of total employment)/100) × (persons employed (in thousands of persons) × 1,000)}	WDI WDI The Conference Board
INDVLADPLCUR	{Industry, value added (current US$)}/ {(employment in industry (% of total employment)/100) × (persons employed (in thousands of persons) × 1,000)}	WDI WDI The Conference Board
SERVLADPLCUR	{Services, etc., value added (current US$)}/{(employment in services (% of total employment)/100) × (persons employed (in thousands of persons) × 1,000)}	WDI WDI The Conference Board
PLVALADCUR	{Gross value added at factor cost (current US$)}/{persons employed (in thousands of persons) × 1,000}	WDI The Conference Board
GDPPEREMP	GDP per person employed (constant 1990 PPP US$)	WDI

Table 2: List of Corruption Indicators

Variable	Definition	Source
CORRUPTION1	CORRUPTION1 = −1* (control of corruption)	Worldwide Governance Indicators (WGI), www.govindicators.org
CORRUPTION2	CORRUPTION2 = −1* (corruption perception index) (CPI)	Transparency International (TI), https://www.transparency.org/ research/cpi/cpi_early/0/
CORRUPTION3	CORRUPTION3 = −1* (freedom from corruption)	Index of Economic Freedom, http://www.heritage.org/index/ explore?view=by-region-country-year

Table 3: List of Independent Variables

Variable	Definition	Source
AWH	Annual hours worked per worker	The Conference Board Total Economy Database
ENROL	School enrollment, tertiary (% gross)	WDI
CAPSTOCK	Capital stock at current PPPs (in million 2005 US$)	Penn World Table

We expect corruption and annual working hours to affect labor productivity negatively while anticipated effect of school enrollment and capital stock on labor productivity is positive.

4 Empirical results

In all analyses, Hausman test is included for choosing between FEM and REM, and decision is made at 1% significance level. Table 4 displays multivariate estimation results for CORRUPTION1. As seen from the table, CORRUPTION1 variable is highly statistically significant and has the expected negative sign across all 13 models. The remaining independent variables get the expected signs and are statistically significant whenever they are statistically significant. Table 5 depicts multivariate estimation results for CORRUPTION2. According to the estimation results, CORRUPTION2 variable gets the anticipated negative sign and is highly statistically significant across all 13 models. The other control variables take the anticipated signs and are statistically significant whenever they are statistically significant except ENROL variable in Model 8. Table 6 shows multivariate estimation results for CORRUPTION3. As results indicate, CORRUPTION3 variable possesses the anticipated negative sign and is highly statistically significant in all models. The other control variables get the expected signs and are statistically significant whenever they are statistically significant except ENROL variable in Model 8.

Table 4: Multivariate Estimation Results for CORRUPTION1

	LPROD1 Model 1	LPROD2 Model 2	LPROD3 Model 3	LPROD4 Model 4	CTFP Model 5	CWTFP Model 6	GDPPEREMP Model 7	PCVALADCUR Model 8	PLVALADCUR Model 9	AGRVLADPICUR Model 10	INDVLADPICUR Model 11	MANVLADPICUR Model 12	SERVLADPICUR Model 13
C	19172.2	67745.1	29.007	72.207	0.7761	0.6979	23211.9	41241.8	74549.1	54005.8	104627.6000	60599.1	81320.9
Prob.	0.0000	0.0000	0.0000	0.0000	0.0000	0.0000	0.0000	0.0000	0.0000	0.0000	0.0000	0.0001	0.0000
CORRUPTION1	−10487.3	−18719.3	−5.827	−10.515	−0.1552	−0.1116	−9761.7	−11716.4	−21753.1	−7052.7	−26653.3300	−24751.9	−21602.0
Prob.	0.0000	0.0000	0.0000	0.0000	0.0000	0.0000	0.0000	0.0000	0.0000	0.0000	0.0000	0.0000	0.0000
CAPSTOCK	0.0004	0.0005	2.59E-07	3.35E-07	1.25E-09	1.68E-09	0.0004	0.0005	0.0010	0.0004	0.0006	0.0015	0.0008
Prob.	0.0000	0.0000	0.0000	0.0000	0.2366	0.0518	0.0000	0.0000	0.0000	0.0032	0.0038	0.0000	0.0000
ENROL	157.41	173.54	0.0606	0.0466	3.67E-05	0.0007	160.65	−34.599	13.382	217.9	25.0415	−29.81	−34.26
Prob.	0.0000	0.0000	0.0000	0.0430	0.9263	0.0309	0.0000	0.1704	0.7670	0.0000	0.7490	0.6837	0.4170
AWH	−2.371	−16.99	−0.0102	−0.0262	−7.74E-05	−6.24E-05	−4.473	−15.52	−27.210	−24.94	−40.9411	−20.02	−28.99
Prob.	0.1466	0.0000	0.0000	0.0000	0.0270	0.0291	0.0069	0.0000	0.0000	0.0000	0.0000	0.0035	0.0000
No. of Obs.	527	527	527	524	493	493	527	468	468	482	485	293	485
No. of Countries	60	60	60	59	56	56	60	55	55	59	59	48	59
R-square	0.7468	0.6847	0.7972	0.7340	0.5051	0.4725	0.7353	0.6795	0.7073	0.3512	0.5726	0.6154	0.7346
F-statistic	384.8946	283.33	512.94	357.98	124.49	109.27	362.46	74.056	84.37	64.54	48.5364	115.19	100.29
Prob(F-statistic)	0.0000	0.0000	0.0000	0.0000	0.0000	0.0000	0.0000	0.0000	0.0000	0.0000	0.0000	0.0000	0.0000
Hausman Stat.	0.6087	1.7239	1.3517	2.4003	5.0133	3.2304	0.4685	44.424	56.19	8.264	36.1035	11.184	47.047
Prob(Hausman Stat.)	0.9621	0.7864	0.8525	0.6626	0.2859	0.5200	0.9765	0.0000	0.0000	0.0824	0.0000	0.0246	0.0000
Selected Model	REM	REM	REM	REM	REM	REM	REM	FEM	FEM	REM	FEM	REM	FEM

Table 5: Multivariate Estimation Results for CORRUPTION2

	LPROD1	LPROD2	LPROD3	LPROD4	CTFP	CWTFP	GDPPEREMP	PCVALADCUR	PIVALADCUR	AGRVLADPLCUR	INDVLADPLCUR	MANVLADPLCUR	SERVLADPLCUR
	Model 1	Model 2	Model 3	Model 4	Model 5	Model 6	Model 7	Model 8	Model 9	Model 10	Model 11	Model 12	Model 13
C	4230.11	42599.3	19.810	56.163	0.5247	0.5214	8820.2	18504.2	34166.9	45350.1	49707.1	25864.8	41112.6
Prob.	0.2412	0.0000	0.0000	0.0000	0.0000	0.0000	0.0152	0.0002	0.0002	0.0000	0.0005	0.0738	0.0000
CORRUPTION2	-4575.8	-8888.2	-2.5870	-4.644	-0.068	-0.0493	-4318.8	-5052.40	-9204.3	-2479.0	-11051.8	-9832.0	-8804.6
Prob.	0.0000	0.0000	0.0000	0.0000	0.0000	0.0000	0.0000	0.0000	0.0000	0.0000	0.0000	0.0000	0.0000
CAPSTOCK	0.0003	0.0004	2.40E-07	2.99E-07	6.75E-10	1.43E-09	0.0004	0.0005	0.0010	0.0004	0.0005	0.0010	0.0007
Prob.	0.0000	0.0000	0.0000	0.0000	0.5080	0.0957	0.0000	0.0000	0.0000	0.0062	0.0069	0.0027	0.0000
ENROL	153.6	166.92	0.0575	0.0405	0.0002	0.0009	153.8	-40.187	13.96	242.52	67.390	-65.18	-2.3403
Prob.	0.0000	0.0000	0.0000	0.0652	0.5834	0.0050	0.0000	0.0853	0.7411	0.0000	0.3353	0.3331	0.9530
AWH	-4.139	-20.78	-0.0108	-0.027	-9.68E-05	-8.04E-05	-5.910	-14.53	-26.25	-26.06	-37.400	-21.37	-27.91
Prob.	0.0053	0.0000	0.0000	0.0000	0.0030	0.0034	0.0001	0.0000	0.0000	0.0000	0.0000	0.0004	0.0000
No. of Obs.	612	612	612	609	580	580	612	539	539	565	568	353	568
No. of Countries	61	61	61	60	57	57	61	56	56	58	58	47	58
R-square	0.7475	0.6751	0.8030	0.7310	0.5132	0.4704	0.7398	0.6839	0.7053	0.3272	0.574	0.6441	0.7153
F-statistic	449.24	315.39	618.8	410.43	151.51	127.70	431.43	75.421	83.428	68.095	49.62	40.659	92.463
Prob(F-statistic)	0.0000	0.0000	0.0000	0.0000	0.0000	0.0000	0.0000	0.0000	0.0000	0.0000	0.0000	0.0000	0.0000
Hausman Stat.	0.4570	1.5483	1.3789	2.4021	5.7869	1.6828	0.3575	64.886	91.23	9.7832	57.007	28.632	101.95
Prob(Hausman Stat.)	0.9775	0.8180	0.8478	0.6622	0.2156	0.7938	0.9858	0.0000	0.0000	0.0442	0.0000	0.0000	0.0000
Selected Model	REM	REM	REM	REM	REM	REM	REM	FEM	FEM	REM	FEM	FEM	FEM

Table 6: Multivariate Estimation Results for CORRUPTION3

	LPROD1	LPROD2	LPROD3	LPROD4	CTFP	CWTFP	GDPPEREMP	PCVALADCUR	PLVALADCUR	AGRVLADPLCUR	INDVLADPLCUR	MANVLADPLCUR	SERVLADPLCUR
	Model 1	Model 2	Model 3	Model 4	Model 5	Model 6	Model 7	Model 8	Model 9	Model 10	Model 11	Model 12	Model 13
C	4583.12	41020.3	19.800	54.962	0.5424	0.5383	9196.8	16876.4	31134.4	43525.5	48511.5	27930.2200	40693.0700
Prob.	0.2079	0.0000	0.0000	0.0000	0.0000	0.0000	0.0114	0.0006	0.0005	0.0000	0.0005	0.0467	0.0000
CORRUPTION3	-452.18	-806.95	-0.255	-0.462	-0.0067	-0.0048	-424.79	-502.27	-916.14	-251.58	-1087.5	-958.6584	-863.9952
Prob.	0.0000	0.0000	0.0000	0.0000	0.0000	0.0000	0.0000	0.0000	0.0000	0.0000	0.0000	0.0000	0.0000
CAPSTOCK	0.0004	0.0004	2.35E-07	2.89E-07	4.52E-10	1.17E-09	0.0003	0.0004	0.0010	0.0003	0.0005	0.0008	0.0007
Prob.	0.0000	0.0001	0.0000	0.0000	0.0000	0.1832	0.0000	0.0000	0.0000	0.0087	0.0082	0.0056	0.0000
ENROL	146.13	156.51	0.0547	0.0380	7.27E-05	0.0006	149.90	-45.75	-2.159	233.11	66.66	-71.9675	2.1361
Prob.	0.0000	0.0000	0.0000	0.0793	0.8435	0.0263	0.0000	0.0451	0.958	0.0000	0.3305	0.2744	0.9563
AWH	-3.8024	-19.34	-0.0106	-0.026	-9.56E-05	-7.80E-05	-5.670	-13.35	-23.87	-24.78	-36.10	-21.1521	-27.2767
Prob.	0.0115	0.0000	0.0000	0.0000	0.0036	0.0054	0.0002	0.0000	0.0000	0.0000	0.0000	0.0003	0.0000
No. of Obs.	626	626	626	623	593	593	626	553	553	579	582	361	582
No. of Countries	61	61	61	60	57	57	61	56	56	58	58	47	58
R-square	0.7361	0.6644	0.7964	0.7250	0.4951	0.4421	0.7315	0.6869	0.7063	0.3206	0.5715	0.6468	0.7135
F-statistic	433.04	307.398	607.40	407.47	144.17	116.49	423.00	78.56	86.128	67.723	50.340	42.1360	93.9774
Prob(F-statistic)	0.0000	0.0000	0.0000	0.0000	0.0000	0.0000	0.0000	0.0000	0.0000	0.0000	0.0000	0.0000	0.0000
Hausman Stat.	1.7890	2.4739	2.3663	2.9995	10.040	4.6693	2.5476	92.40	106.21	6.3278	49.814	61.2508	72.4594
Prob(Hausman)	0.745	0.6493	0.6687	0.5579	0.0398	0.3229	0.6361	0.0000	0.0000	0.1760	0.0000	0.0000	0.0000
Selected Model	REM	REM	REM	REM	REM	REM	REM	FEM	FEM	REM	FEM	FEM	FEM

5 Conclusion and Discussion

Various aspects and outcomes of corruption had been studied in the literature. Another outcome of corruption may be on labor productivity. Therefore, in this chapter, we explore the effect of corruption on labor productivity. We utilized 3 distinct corruption indicators and 13 different proxies for labor productivity. The data used in analyses employ unbalanced panel data for 61 countries over the period 2000–2011. According to the estimation results, we identified an inverse statistically significant association between corruption and labor productivity. In other words, countries with higher corrupt practices experience lower level of labor productivity. This finding remains valid across 13 different indicators of labor productivity and for 3 distinct proxies of corruption and hence our finding is valid and robust.

References

Aghion, P., Akcigit, U., Cagé, J. and Kerr, W. R. (2016). "Taxation, Corruption, and Growth." European Economic Review, 86: 24–51.

Aidt, T. S. (2003). "Economic Analysis of Corruption: A Survey." The Economic Journal, 113(491): 632–652.

De Rosa, D., Gooroochurn, N. and Görg, H. (2010). "Corruption and Productivity: Firm-level Evidence from the BEEPS Survey." Policy Research Working Paper No. 5348, The World Bank, Washington DC.

De Rosa, D., Gooroochurn, N. and Görg, H. (2015). "Corruption and Productivity: Firm-level Evidence." Jahrbücher für Nationalökonomie und Statistik, 235(2): 115–138.

Del Mar Salinas-Jiménez, M. and Salinas-Jiménez, J. (2007). "Corruption, Efficiency and Productivity in OECD Countries." Journal of Policy Modeling, 29(6): 903–915.

Del Mar Salinas-Jiménez, M. and Salinas-Jiménez, J. (2011). "Corruption and Total Factor Productivity: Level or Growth Effects?" Portuguese Economic Journal, 10(2): 109–128.

Del Monte, A. and Papagni, E. (2007). "The Determinants of Corruption in Italy: Regional Panel Data Analysis." European Journal of Political Economy, 23(2): 379–396.

Dridi, M. (2013). "Corruption and Economic Growth: The Transmission Channels." Journal of Business Studies Quarterly, 4(4): 121–152.

Frechette, G. R. (2001). "An Empirical Investigation of the Determinants of Corruption: Rent, Competition, and Income Revisited." Canadian Economic Association 2001 Meeting, May 31-June 3, Kingston.

Ghura, M. D. (1998). "Tax Revenue in Sub-Saharan Africa: Effects of Economic Policies and Corruption." IMF Working Papers No. 98/135, International Monetary Fund, Washington DC.

Hall, R. E. and Jones, C. I. (1999). "Why Do Some Countries Produce So Much More Output Per Worker than Others?" The Quarterly Journal of Economics, 114(1): 83–116.

Koyuncu, C. and Bhattacharyya, G. (2007). "Predicting Corrupt Practices in the Public Sector for 23 OECD Countries." Applied Econometrics and International Development, 7(1): 15–36.

Koyuncu, C., Ozturkler, H. and Yilmaz, R. (2010). "Privatization and Corruption in Transition Economies: A Panel Study." Journal of Economic Policy Reform, 13(3), 277–284.

Koyuncu, C. and Unver, M. (2016). "Information and Communication Technologies (ICTs) and Corruption Level: Empirical Evidence from Panel Data Analysis." 2nd International Osmaneli Social Sciences Congress, 12–14 October, Bilecik, Turkey.

Koyuncu, C. and Yilmaz, R. (2009). "The Impact of Corruption on Deforestation: A Cross-country Evidence." The Journal of Developing Areas, 42(2): 213–222.

Koyuncu, C. and Yilmaz, R. (2013). "Deforestation, Corruption, and Private Ownership in the Forest Sector." Quality & Quantity, 47(1), 227–236.

Koyuncu, J. Y., Yilmaz, R. and Unver, M. (2016). "The Relationship between Female Labor Force Participation and Labor Productivity: Panel Data Analysis." Eskişehir Osmangazi Üniversitesi İİBF Dergisi, 11(2): 237–249.

Mohammadi Khyareh, M. (2017). "Institutions and Entrepreneurship: The Mediating Role of Corruption." World Journal of Entrepreneurship, Management and Sustainable Development, 13(3): 1–25.

Morris, S. D. and Klesner, J. L. (2010). "Corruption and Trust: Theoretical Considerations and Evidence from Mexico." Comparative Political Studies, 43(10): 1258–1285.

Saastamoinen, A. and Kuosmanen, T. (2014). "Is Corruption Grease, Grit or a Gamble? Corruption Increases Variance of Productivity across Countries." Applied Economics, 46(23): 2833–2849.

Schulze, G. G. and Frank, B. (2003). "Deterrence versus Intrinsic Motivation: Experimental Evidence on the Determinants of Corruptibility." Economics of Governance, 4(2): 143–160.

Sosa, L. A. (2004). "Wages and Other Determinants of Corruption." Review of Development Economics, 8(4): 597–605.

Sprague, S. (2017). "Below Trend: The U.S. Productivity Slowdown since the Great Recession." Beyond the Numbers, 6(2). Bureau of Labor Statistics, Washington, DC.

Tanzi, V. (1998). "Corruption around the World: Causes, Consequences, Scope, and Cures." Staff Papers, 45(4): 559–594.

Tanzi, V. and Davoodi, H. (1998). "Corruption, Public Investment, and Growth." In: Shibata H. and Ihori T. (eds), The Welfare State, Public Investment, and Growth (pp. 41–60). Springer, Japan.

Topal, M. H. and Keyifli, N. (2016). "Yolsuzluk ve Kamu Borçları: OECD Ülkeleri İçin Ampirik Bir Kanıt." 2. Uluslararası Osmaneli Sosyal Bilimler Kongresi, 12–14 Ekim, Bilecik, Turkey.

Topal, M. H. and Unver, M. (2016). "Yolsuzluğun Belirleyicileri: Kırılgan Ekonomiler İçin Panel Eş-bütünleşme Analizi." Balkan ve Yakın Doğu Sosyal Bilimler Dergisi, 2(2): 58–68.

Unver, M. and Koyuncu, J. Y. (2016). "The Impact of Poverty on Corruption." Journal of Economics Library, 3(4): 632.

Unver, M. and Koyuncu, J. Y. (2017). "Do Corrupt Countries Emit more CO_2?: Panel Evidence." 4th International Balkan and Near Eastern Social Sciences Congress Series, 8–9 April, Russe, Bulgaria.

Van Reenen, J. (2013). "Productivity under the 1997–2010 Labour Government." Oxford Review of Economic Policy, 29(1): 113–141.

Voyer, P. A. and Beamish, P. W. (2004). "The Effect of Corruption on Japanese Foreign Direct Investment." Journal of Business Ethics, 50(3): 211–224.

Welzel, C., Inglehart, R. and Kligemann, H. D. (2003). "The Theory of Human Development: A Cross-Cultural Analysis." European Journal of Political Research, 42(3): 341–379.

Yildirim, K., Koyuncu, C. and Koyuncu, J. (2009). "Does Temperature Affect Labor Productivity: Cross-Country Evidence." Applied Econometrics and International Development, 9(1): 29–39.

Süleyman Emre Özcan

Renewable Energy Potential of Turkey

1 Introduction

Energy is an input that has a vital importance for all emerging economies. At the heart of many of the wars in the past, the attraction of energy sources has been dominant. Today, the situation is not very different. Turkey has to make energy planning very carefully to look at the future safely, accelerate economic development, and increase prosperity. It is vital that the required energy should be provided safely, uninterruptedly, and inexpensively, and it should be provided by protecting nature. The aim of this study is to determine the state of renewable energy potential of Turkey.

2 A brief history of energy

The word *energy* is derived from the word "energos" in ancient Greek, which means "hard working," and "ergon," which means "work." Energy is the capacity of a system to do work. Energy is as important as life because humankind can sustain life through energy. Sun, wind, and water are the energy sources used until 150–200 years ago (Malanima, 2014: 5). In the past, solar energy was used for warming and enlightenment while wind power was used in ships and water power was used in mills. James Watt's invention of steam engine in 1776 contributed substantially to the Industrial Revolution (Smil, 2004: 555). Coal gained importance with steam engine. In 1779, internal combustion engines started to gain importance. The discovery of crude oil by Colonel Edwin Drake in 1859 led to the first gasoline-powered car and aircraft. The 1880s revealed the need for electricity and hydroelectric power plants (MÜSİAD, 2006: 42).

Increasing energy demand after the Great Depression and the use of petroleum products as an embargo weapon necessitated new energy sources (Pamir, 2008: 96). The search for new energy sources gained momentum after the discovery of Marie Curie's radioactivity, and nuclear fusion has begun to be used in power plants. The recognition of the hazards of nuclear reactors and the rise in reactor costs have led to the notion of "energy efficiency" and popularity of natural gas as a much cleaner energy (Pamir, 2008: 96–97). Although natural gas has been used since the year 500 B.C., it is seen as an alternative energy source after the developments in the long-line pipe and welding technology during World War II (Beşergil, 2007: 133).

Throughout history, different forms of energy have been used. Initially, solid fuel was used, later liquid fuel was used, and then gas was used. It is argued that the thermal value obtained per unit volume and mass was the dominant reason for transfer from one energy form to another. Another reason for this transfer was the price of the source rather than the exhaustion risk of the source (MÜSİAD, 2006: 42).

3 Energy resources

Energy sources can be classified as primary and secondary or renewable (inexhaustible) and nonrenewable (consumable). Primary sources (coal, crude oil, natural gas, nuclear, biomass, hydraulics, sun, wind, wave, tide) are usually found in pure form in nature. Secondary sources (electricity, gasoline, diesel, secondary coal, coke, petroleum coke, air gas, liquefied petroleum gas (LPG)) are derived from the transformation of primary energy sources (Koç and Şenel, 2013: 33).

Nonrenewable energy sources are sources that do not form or replenish when they are consumed. In fact, there is no renewable source of energy on the earth, but they are called in this way because it requires a very long time for the formation of resources. Nonrenewable resources can be classified as fossil (coal, oil, natural gas) and nuclear (uranium and thorium). Renewable energy sources are energy sources that can exist the same in the next day through nature's own evolution. These resources continue their existence with the world and are environment friendly. These resources are the sun (water, wind, sunrays, biomass), the earth (geothermal energy generated by core heat), and the moon (lunar tide) (Önal and Yarbay, 2010: 79).

As of the end of 2014, the world's primary energy consumption was equivalent to 12,928.4 million tons of oil; 87% of this was oil, coal, and natural gas, which are nonrenewable fossil resources. The share of renewable energy is only 2%. The situation in Turkey is not very different: 91% of the primary energy consumption equivalent to 125.3 million tons of oil is composed of natural gas, coal, and oil. While hydroelectricity accounts for 7%, renewable energy accounts for only 2% (BP, 2015: 40–41).

As can be seen from Table 1, Turkey's primary energy consumption is constantly increasing. A very small proportion of this is made up of renewable resources. This demonstrates the importance of finding new energy sources and reducing the dependence on nonrenewable sources. Inevitable energy sources such as hydraulics, solar, biomass, wind, geothermal, wave, and tide will be important sources in future. Therefore, the future of Turkey will be determined in parallel with the development of renewable energy sources.

Table 1: Turkey's Primary Energy Consumption (Equivalent to Million Tons of Petroleum)

Year	2004	2005	2006	2007	2008	2009	2010	2011	2012	2013	2014
Consumption	83.7	86.7	96.9	103.7	103.2	104.2	111	118.4	123.6	122	125.3

Source: BP (2015: 40).

4 Renewable energy sources

4.1 Solar energy

Solar energy, a clean and inexhaustible source of energy for the earth, is the energy of radiation emitted by the helium transformation (fusion) of hydrogen gas in the solar core. Solar energy is a renewable energy source that has a constant solar intensity of 1.370 W/m^2 outside the earth's atmosphere and a value of 0–1,100 W/m^2 on the earth. The sun sends energy that is equivalent to an average of 200 billion tons of coal to the earth every year (Varınca and Gönüllü, 2006: 271).

Solar energy is used in heating and cooling, hot water supply, heating of swimming pools and greenhouses, drying agricultural products, sun quarries, deriving salt and fresh water from sea water, solar batteries, transportation and communication vehicles, signaling and automation, and in electricity generation (Varınca and Gönüllü, 2006: 271).

Solar energy has many environmental benefits compared to fossil-based sources. Use of solar energy reduces carbon dioxide emissions, maintains the quality of water resources, requires less power transfer lines, reduces external energy dependency, regulates energy market prices, and enables the use of electricity in rural areas (Gekas et al., 2002: 1570). There are two basic usages of the solar energy as a source of energy: solar collectors (concentrating solar power) and solar cells (photovoltaic systems). In solar collectors, the heat from the sun is used directly or electricity is generated by sending it to steam turbines. In solar batteries, semiconductor materials convert solar rays (photons) directly to electrical energy. As of the end of 2013, 97.6% of the installed capacity was photovoltaic and 2.4% was using solar collector systems. Photovoltaic systems are growing very rapidly. The capacity of 200 gigawatts, as of July 2015, is expected to reach 400 gigawatts by the end of 2019. The driving force behind the growth of photovoltaic systems is Germany, China, Japan, America, and India (Shahan, 2015).

The average annual global solar energy potential is 2,500 $kW-h/m^2$. The part of the African continent on the equatorial line, the deserts in this area, the southern parts of Australia, and southern part of South Africa are the most suitable and rich areas for solar energy.

Turkey, situated between 36° and 42° north latitudes, is in a favorable position in terms of solar energy potential. Southeastern Anatolia and the Mediterranean regions have an average solar energy potential of 1,800–2,000 kW-h/m². As we move southward, the solar energy per square meter increases. The available suitable fields cover a total area of 11,000 km² (TMMOB, 2012: 180). Turkey has an average annual total sunshine duration of 2,640 hours and a total of 7.2 hours per day. The longest sunshine per month takes place in July with 365 hours. The average total radiation intensity is 1,311 kW-h/m² per year (total of 3.6 kW-h/m² per day). On a daily basis, July has the longest sunrise time with 11.31 hours. Turkey has very high solar energy potential with 110 days. An average of 1,100 kW-h electricity per year can be produced if necessary investments can be made in Turkey (Dinçer, 2011: 10).

Turkey's thermal solar energy potential (concentrated solar power/CSP) is estimated to be 380 billion kW-h per year based on the calculation done by taking into consideration the areas whose slope is lower than 3°, the annual sunshine duration is higher than 1,650 kW-h/m², which is suitable for establishing solar energy power plant (TMMOB, 2012: 176–177). Use of solar energy potential will decrease external dependency of Turkey since the gross solar energy potential of Turkey is equivalent to 87.5 million tons of oil.

As of 2016, there was 290 megawatts installed power in 313 active solar power plants (313 MWe power) in Turkey. With this installed power, annual electricity generation is about 458 gigawatts. The target for 2023 is to reach at least 3,000 megawatts of licensed photovoltaic power by increasing the installed power 10-fold (ETKB, 2016).

4.2 Wind power

Wind power is a source that is local, not dependable on external factors, foreign exchange saving, and unexhausted; does not lead to acid rain and greenhouse effect; has no adverse effects on natural vegetation and human health; and has rapid technological development (Güler, 2005, 162). The source of wind energy is solar radiation, which warms different parts of the earth at different rates. Heat and humidity differences lead to air movements by creating pressure differences. Wind energy was first used by the Egyptians and Chinese for propulsion of ships for transportation purposes, for grinding cereals, and for mechanical works on windmills (Seyidoğulları, 2013: 23).

It is estimated that windmills, the oldest known wind power machines, were built near Alexandria 3,000 years ago. The mills seen in Egypt, Iran, and the Far East were transferred to Europe through the Crusades. The first wind turbine for generating electricity was built by Dane Paul La Cour in 1891, but did not find much use in the shadow of fossil fuels. While technological development in wind turbines continued with Smidth wind turbines in 1942 and the Gedser wind turbines in 1957, the increase in fossil fuel prices in the 1970s brought wind energy usage for electricity generation in the agenda (Şenel and Koç, 2015: 47–48). Although wind power has positive aspects such as being able to be produced in a short time, potential to create employment, lack of risk of increase in prices, and lack of transportation problem, it has some drawbacks such as noise, visual pollution, bird deaths, and creating interference in radio–TV receivers (Güler, 2005: 162).

The kinetic energy of the wind is transformed into electric energy with the help of wind turbines. However, factors such as the speed of the wind, direction, and the frequency of blowing are important for obtaining energy economically. Economically, the minimum wind speed for electricity generation should be 5–6 m/s, i.e., 18–19 km/h (Hayli, 2001: 8).

According to the International Energy Agency, the world technical wind potential was 53,000 TWh per year as of July 2014. North America, Eastern Europe, and Russia had 66% of this potential. The world's total installed wind power was 336,327 megawatts as of July 2014. The installed power of China, the USA, Germany, Spain, and India, which is one of the leaders of wind turbine technology, corresponds to 72% of the world total installed power (Şenel and Koç, 2015: 48–49).

Turkey has a significant wind potential because of its latitude, surface area, and climate characteristics. Turkey has an average annual wind speed of 2.54 m/s and a wind power density of 24 W/m². The Electrical Power Resources Survey Administration and the General Directorate of Meteorological Affairs work together in determining the wind potential of Turkey. Wind atlases prepared by measurements of meteorological stations are the main source of data regarding site selection for wind power plants (Hayli, 2001: 8).

The first studies on wind energy in Turkey were carried out at Ankara University in the 1960s and at the Ege University, the Middle East Technical University, and the TÜBİTAK Marmara Research Center in the 1970s. In 1992, the European Wind Energy Association's Turkey branch was opened and the Turkish Wind Atlas was started to be established with the data from the General Directorate of State Meteorology Affairs (Hayli, 2001: 23).

According to this atlas, the Aegean and Marmara coasts have the highest potential. The first serious step regarding the use of the wind potential of Turkey was the opening of the Çeşme – Germiyan wind power plant on February 21, 1998. The second power plant, Çeşme – Alaçatı Wind Power Plant, was established on November 28, 1998 on a build–operate–transfer model (Hayli, 2001: 26–27). The total installed capacity of 124 wind power plants in Turkey is 4,540.9 megawatt. In 2014, a total of 8,366,804,300 kW-h electricity was produced in these plants.

Given the distribution of wind power plants in terms of installed power, the Aegean region ranks first with 1,486.45 megawatt production. The Aegean region is followed by Marmara with 1,359.15 megawatts and the Mediterranean region with 543 megawatts (TREİR, 2015: 13).

The total capacity of the total 39 wind power plants under construction in Turkey is 1,210.2 megawatts (TREİR, 2015: 17). When all the power plants licensed by the Energy Market Regulatory Authority will be in operation, the wind power will reach 9,590.04 megawatts. These figures are quite low compared to the potential of Turkey.

4.3 Geothermal energy

Geothermal energy is obtained from hot water, steam, dry steam, and hot dry rocks. Geothermal resources mostly occur near active fracture systems and volcanic and magmatic units (Kılıç and Kılıç, 2013: 46). Geothermal energy is used in either direct or indirect way. Heating (greenhouse and house heating), hot water supply, carbon dioxide and dry ice production, heat pumps, industrial processes, and health tourism are the areas where geothermal energy is used directly. Geothermal energy is indirectly used in electricity production (Külekçi, 2009: 86–87).

Geothermal energy is mainly used as heat energy and its usage goes back to ancient times. The Romans used it as natural hot water for heating and health purposes in thermal baths. It was first used in the USA in 1891 to provide heat to homes. Overheated water steam are extracted from the earth by drilling of geothermal resources and electricity is generated by sending the hot water steam to the power plants. The electricity was produced for the first from geothermal power in Larderello, Italy, in 1904. The second industrial producer after Italy was the Wairakei plant with the production of 200 MW power in New Zealand. In 1960, the first successful geothermal power plant was built in California geysers. With the power plants established in 1967 in Russia and 1981 in America, new technologies were started to be used and the use of geothermal energy became widespread (Çukurçayır and Sağır, 2008: 267; Çentez, 2016).

The advantages of geothermal energy are the following: it is an indigenous, clean, and sustainable source of energy; it can be used for the production of electricity and heat energy; and its operating costs are low. High investment costs, low prevalence, and environmental risks are the disadvantages of geo-thermal energy.

The geothermal energy capacity of the world was 12,635 MWe in 2015. In 2020, total geothermal energy use is estimated to reach 21,443 MWe of electrical power. In the world, the top five countries of electricity generation from geothermal energy are the USA, the Philippines, Indonesia, Mexico, and Italy. The top five countries for geothermal heat and hot spring applications are China, the USA, Sweden, Turkey, and Japan.

Turkey has a very high geothermal potential because it is located on the Alpine–Himalayan belt. This potential is approximately 31,500 MWe; 79% of these potential areas are in Western Anatolia, 8.5% in Central Anatolia, 7.5% in Marmara region, 4.5% in Eastern Anatolia, and 0.5% are located in other regions. Also, 94% geothermal resources in Turkey are at low and medium temperatures and can be used directly, while 6% are suitable for electricity gen-eration (ETKB, 2015).

The studies show that there are more than 227 geothermal areas on economi-cally useful scale and there are about 2,000 mineral water sources at temperature ranging from 20° to 278° in Turkey (Mertoğlu et al., 2015: 1). The total power of 21 geothermal power plants established in Turkey is 63,510 MWe. The potential geothermal energy to be produced is estimated to be 2,000 MWe (16 billion kW-h per year). In 2014, total 2,251,793,602 kW-h of electricity was produced by the geothermal power plants in Turkey. Geothermal resources account for only 0.87% of total installed capacity in Turkey. However, with the new laws and in-centives numbered 6094, total geothermal electricity potential is planned to reach 4,500 MWe (ETKB, 2015).

The data indicate that Turkey does not use its potential despite its high geother-mal sources. When all geothermal potential is used in Turkey, 5 million homes can be heated, 30 million m² greenhouse can be heated, and 400 thermal facili-ties with 1 million bed and 250 thousand employment capacity can be operated (EİE, 2016).

4.4 Hydraulic energy (hydroelectric energy)

Hydraulic energy is the energy obtained by converting the potential energy of water into kinetic energy. Electrical energy obtained by turning the turbines by dropping the water collected in a dam on the turbines in the power plants is called hydroelectricity (Ürker and Çobanoğlu, 2012: 66–67). Although hydro-electric power plants (HPPs) in operation do not cause harm to the environ-ment, but they have negative effects such as damaging the integrity of rivers, decreasing biodiversity, and creating soil erosion in the process of construction (Önal and Yarbay, 2010: 82).

The world's annual gross hydropower potential is 40,150,000 gigawatts. Technically feasible part of this potential is calculated as 8,905,000 gigawatts (Gökdemir et al., 2012: 18). As of the end of 2011, the world's hydroelectricity capacity was 936 gigawatts with 11,000 HPPs in 160 countries. China is the highest producer of hydroelectric power. Brazil is the second while Turkey is the eighth in the rank.

Turkey is located in the middle climate zone, and climate and precipitation vary considerably from region to region and season to season. The average annual rainfall of 643 mm/m² in Turkey corresponds to an average of 501 billion m³ of water. Gross overland water potential is 433 billion kilowatts per year with 193 billion m³ of water in 26 hydropower basins. The economic potential is 127 billion kW-h (Uluatam, 2011: 64).

The first dam in Turkey was built by the Hittites in 1300 B.C. Some of the two hydraulic structures that the Urartians built in Van 1,000 years ago are still in use today. Until the end of World War II, there was no dam for energy production in Turkey. With the establishment of General Directorate of State Hydraulic Works in 1954, hydroelectric capacity reached 412 megawatts, and 44% of total electricity production was obtained from these dams. Although HPPs were built by various governmental institutions between 1950 and 1969, all dams were constructed and controlled by one authority with the establishment of Turkish Electricity Authority in 1970 (Gökdemir et al., 2012: 20). With the legislation number 3096 passed in 1984, private sector has been given the opportunity to build HPP with build–operate–transfer model. With the "Electricity Market Law" number 4628 dated February 20, 2001, free entry was allowed in all areas of energy services and the supervision was left to Energy Market Regulatory Authority (TMMOB, 2012: 121). The installed capacity of 65 HPPs constructed by General Directorate of State Hydraulic Works between 1956 and 2014 was 12,396.45 megawatt and the average annual energy production was 43,294.55 gigawatts. As of 2015, the installed power was 25,917.80 megawatts and the electricity production was 69,222 gigawatts (see Table 2). The share of the existing 561 HPPs in total installed power was 35.30% (EÜAŞ, 2014: 36–37).

Table 2: Hydroelectricity Consumption of Turkey (Equivalent to Million Tons of Petroleum)

Year	2004	2005	2006	2007	2008	2009	2010	2011	2012	2013	2014
Turkey	10.4	9	10	8.1	7.5	8.1	11.7	11.8	13.1	13.4	9.1
World	635.2	661.3	689	700.4	139.9	737.4	783.9	795.5	833.8	861.6	879

Source: BP (2015: 36).

Examined data indicate that Turkey has not used technical water power potential enough. Turkey needs to work hard to reach its 2023 targets in the field of hydropower.

4.5 Biomass energy

The energy acquired by photosynthesis is the basis of biomass energy. Trees, forest wastes, corn, wheat, grasses, moss, fruit, and vegetable residues from houses; algae in the sea; animal feces; fertilizers; and industrial wastes are biomass (Topal and Arslan, 2008: 242). Because the amount of carbon dioxide released in the atmosphere after the burning of biomass is equal to oxygen released in the atmosphere by photosynthesis, harmful emission does not occur. Biomass energy can be classified into two groups, classical and modern. The classical biomass energy is obtained by simple burning of turf and wood. Various fuels such as biodiesel and ethanol obtained from energy plants, energy forests, and wood industry wastes are called modern biomass energy. Biomass is either directly burned or indirectly used to produce biofuels (biogas, biodiesel, bioethanol) by increasing the quality of biomass in various processes (Topal and Arslan, 2008: 243).

Turkey started producing biodiesel and bioethanol in the year 2000 and more than 200 biodiesel plants were established. However, because there are not enough raw materials, only one plant has survived. In the bioethanol field, three facilities with a capacity of 149.5 million liter are in production. Researches on biogas started in the Ministry of Agriculture in 1980 but have not been maintained. Following the biogas and electricity production researches from city garbage, a 22.6 megawatt plant was established in Ankara (TMMOB, 2012: 187–188).

As of 2015, the total installed capacity of 69 biogas and biomass power plants in Turkey was 344.7 megawatts. Electricity is generated at an annual capacity of 1,568 gigawatts at 67 power plants (ETKB, 2015).

Turkey has high economic value in terms of energy forestry. There are fast-growing and indigenous trees such as poplar, aspen, alder, coral, oak, ash, peanut pine, larch, cedar, and cypress in Turkey. Approximately 15% of the area suitable for energy forestry in Turkey is utilized, while the remaining 85% of the potential area is kept idle (Topal and Arslan, 2008: 244).

Turkey is a very rich country in terms of biomass energy although it is not used enough. It also has enough manpower to utilize these resources more effectively. The state should support manpower.

4.6 Tide energy (wave energy)

The waves occur as a result of winds blowing on the sea surface. The power of the waves is 10–15 times more than other renewable energies. It is calculated that 1% of the wave power in the oceans is more than the world energy demand. Sea wave energy, sea temperature gradient energy, sea current energy (in the straits), and tidal energy are types of sea energy. For Turkey, energy that can be emphasized is sea wave energy. Contrary to the claim that the Black Sea is wavier than the other seas, the wave energy in the Aegean and Mediterranean is more than other seas in Turkey. The best place for producing wave energy in Turkey is the seas between Dalaman and Finike (Izmir–Antalya). Researches indicate that the wave intensity in Kalkan, one of the best sources of wave power, is between 6.6 and 7.6 kW-h/m. For the majority of the year, the wave height reaches 1.21 meters and the wave periods reach 6.09 seconds. The coastline of Turkey (excluding Marmara) is 8,210 km long. One-fifth of this area can be used for obtaining wave energy. From this part, 10 TWh energy can be obtained annually, which is 12.5% of the hydroelectric potential of Turkey (Sağlam and Uyar, 2005: 1–5; Çakır, 2010: 289).

5 Conclusion

Energy is an input that has vital importance for all economies in the world. As mentioned earlier, nonrenewable resources will be depleted in the near future. Therefore, the future will very much depend on renewable energy sources. Turkey has all the renewable resources mentioned earlier due to its location. However, the examined data indicate that Turkey can use only a fraction of its high potential. Turkey is an external energy–dependent country. When Turkey will start utilizing its potential, it will overcome external dependence and strengthen its future position. So it is important that government, together with scientists, should work intensively to utilize Turkey's renewable energy potential more effectively.

References

Beşergil, B. (2007). Ham petrolden Petrokimyasallara El Kitabı, Gazi Kitabevi, Ankara.

BP. (2015). BP Statistical Review of World Energy, British Petroleum, London.

Çakır, M. T. (2010). "Türkiye'nin Rüzgâr Enerji Potansiyeli ve AB Ülkeleri İçindeki Yeri", Politeknik Dergisi, Cilt 13, Sayı 4.

Çentez, M. (2016). "Yer Altından Gelen Enerji: Jeotermal", http://www.elektrikport. com/sektor-rehberi/yer-altindan-gelen-enerji-jeotermal/2856#ad-image-0 Accessed on 09.02.2016

Çukurçayır, M. A. and Sağır, H. (2008). "Enerji Sorunu, Çevre ve Alternatif Enerji Kaynakları", Selçuk Üniversitesi Sosyal Bilimler Enstitüsü Dergisi, 20.

Dinçer, F. (20119. "Türkiye'de Güneş Enerjisinden Elektrik Üretimi Potansiyeli-Ekonomik Analizi ve AB Ülkeleri ile Karşılaştırmalı Değerlendirme", KSU Mühendislik Dergisi, 14(1): 8–17.

EİE (2016), Elektrik İşleri Etüt İdaresi Genel Müdürlüğü Web Sitesi. http://www. eie.gov.tr

Enerji ve Tabii Kaynaklar Bakanlığı/ETKB. (2015). "Dünya ve Ülkemiz Tabii Kaynaklar Görünümü", Strateji Geliştirme Başkanlığı, Sayı 10, Ankara.

ETKB (2016), T.C. Enerji ve Tabii Kaynaklar Bakanlığı Web Sitesi. http://www. enerji.gov.tr

EÜAŞ (2014). Elektrik Üretim A.Ş, Yıllık Rapor 2014. Elektrik Üretim A.Ş., Ankara.

Gekas, V., Frantzeskaki, N., and Tsoutsos, T.T. (2002). "Environmental Impact Assessment of Solar Energy Systems Results From A Life Cycle Analysis", Proceedings of the International Conference ICPRE, "Protection and Restoration of the Environment VI", Skiathos, July 1–5.

Gökdemir, M., Kömürcü, M. İ. and Evcimen, T.U. (2012). "Türkiye'de Hidroelektrik ve HES Uygulamalarına Genel Bakış", Türkiye Mühendislik Haberleri, TMH-471-2012/1.

Güler, Ö. (2005). "Dünyada ve Türkiye' de Rüzgâr Enerjisi", V. Enerji Sempozyumu, Ankara, 21–23 Aralık .

Hayli, S. (2001). "Rüzgâr Enerjisinin Önemi, Dünya'da ve Türkiye'deki Durumu", Fırat Üniversitesi Sosyal Bilimler Dergisi, Cilt 11, Sayı 1.

Kılıç, F. Ç. and Kılıç, M. K. (2013). "Jeotermal Enerji ve Türkiye", Mühendis ve Makine, Cilt 54, Sayı 639.

Koç, E. and Şenel, M. C. (2013). "Dünyada ve Türkiye'de Enerji Durumu, Genel Değerlendirme" Mühendis ve Makine, Cilt 54, Sayı 639.

Külekçi, Ö. C. (2009). "Yenilenebilir Enerji Kaynakları Arasında Jeotermal Enerjinin Yeri ve Türkiye Açısından Önemi", Ankara Üniversitesi Çevre Bilimleri Dergisi, Cilt 1, Sayı 2.

Malanima, P. (2014). "Energy in History", The Basic Environmental History, Editors M. Agnoletti and S. Neri Serneri, Springer, New York.

Mertoğlu O., Şimşek, Ş., and Başarır, N. (2015). "Geothermal Country Update Report of Turkey (2010–2015), Proceedings of the World Geothermal Congress 2015, Melbourne, Australia, 19–25 April.

MÜSİAD (2006). "Türkiye'nin Enerji Ekonomisi ve Petrolün Geleceği", Müsiad Araştırma Raporları: 49, Editörler: İbrahim Öztürk ve Sohbet Karbuz, Şubat, Müstakil Sanayici ve İşadamları Derneği, İstanbul.

Önal, E. and Yarbay, R. Z. (2010). "Türkiye'de Yenilenebilir Enerji Kaynakları Potansiyeli ve Geleceği", İstanbul Üniversitesi Fen Bilimleri Dergisi, Yıl: 9, Sayı: 18, Güz.

Pamir, N. (2008). "Cumhuriyetten Günümüze Türkiye'de Enerji Politikaları", Çeşitli Yönleriyle Cumhuriyetin 85. Yılında Türkiye Ekonomisi, Editör Gülen Elmas Arslan, Ankara.

Sağlam, M. and Uyar, T.S. (2005). "Dalga Enerjisi ve Türkiye'nin Dalga Enerjisi Teknik Potansiyeli", III. Yenilenebilir Enerji Kaynakları Sempozyumu (YEKSEM), 19–21 Ekim 2005, Mersin.

Şenel, M. C. and Koç, E. (2015). "Dünyada ve Türkiye'de Rüzgâr Enerjisi Durumu – Genel Değerlendirme", Mühendis ve Makine Dergisi, cilt 56, Sayı 663.

Seyidoğulları, H. S. (2013). "Sürdürülebilir Kalkınma için Yenilenebilir Enerji", Planlama Dergisi, 23(1): 19–25.

Shahan, Z. (2015). "Global Solar Power Capacity About to Hit 200 GW", Clean Technica, http://cleantechnica.com/2015/07/11/global-solar-power-capacity-about-to-hit-200-gw/ (10.02.2015).

Smil, V. (2004). "World History and Energy", Encyclopedia of Energy, Volume 6, Elsevier, Amsterdam.

TMMOB, Makine Mühendisleri Odası (2012). Türkiye'nin Enerji Görünümü, Yayın No: MMO/588, Nisan.

Topal, M. and Arslan, I. E. (2008). "Biokütle Enerjisi ve Türkiye", VII: Ulusal Temiz Enerji Sempozyumu, UTES 2008, İstanbul, 17–19 Aralık.

TREİR. (2015). Türkiye Rüzgâr Enerjisi İstatistik Raporu, Türkiye Rüzgâr Enerjisi Birliği (TÜREB), Ankara.

Uluatam, E. (2011). Türkiye'de Hidroelektrik Politikaları ve Yatırımlarına Bakış, Ekonomi Forum, 62, Aralık.

Ürker, O. and Çobanoğlu, N. (2012). "Türkiye'de Hidroelektrik Santrallerinin Durumu (HES'ler) ve Çevre Politikaları Bağlamında Değerlendirilmesi", Ankara, 3(2).

Varınca, K.B. and Gönüllü, M.T. (2006). "Türkiye'de Güneş Potansiyeli ve Bu Potansiyelin Kullanım Derecesi, Yöntemi ve Yaygınlığı Üzerine Bir Araştırma", UGHEK 2006, I. Ulusal Güneş ve Hidrojen Enerjisi Kongresi, Eskişehir, ESOGÜ, 21–23 Haziran.

Nagihan Birinci and Murat Can Genç

The Relationship between Fiscal Devaluation and Foreign Trade in Turkey: A Toda and Yamamoto Causality Approach

1 Introduction

The goal of reaching higher levels of prosperity forces countries to display high growth rate performance. In today's world, countries are able to achieve this goal by giving deficits in their balance of payments due to the globalization of trade and finance. This situation carries "fight against balance of payments deficits" on the agenda of economic policies.

Foreign trade imbalances have become one of the most debated and major economic problems which the global economy faces over recent years. Many economists and politicians have agreed that sustaining trade imbalances are one of the current economic problems and a threat to the maximization of welfare of the society.

The foreign trade deficit arises from the fact that the foreign currency outflows are higher than the foreign exchange inflows. It leads to a decrease in the foreign exchange reserves that countries utilize in their international payments or to net foreign borrowing. However, there is a limit to both the foreign exchange reserves and the foreign borrowing of the countries, and it is not possible to permanently close the external deficits by these tools (Kaya, 2015: 163). However, in terms of closing foreign trade deficits, it may not be possible to increase production and employment through public borrowing because the debt reaches unsustainable dimensions in the long run, especially in advanced industrialized countries. In the most advanced industrialized countries (G7), the expansionary monetary policy has reached its boundaries because the interest rates of the Central Bank are close to zero in such countries. Moreover, the steady increase in money supply can lead to increased inflation and the risk of growing speculative bubbles (Petersen, 2015: 2–3).

In countries where the fixed exchange rate system is adopted, external deficits are tried to be handled by controlling domestic demand, import restrictions, or devaluation in medium and long term. The most preferred policy among these policies is devaluation because of its direct effect and faster delivery. The exchange rate devaluation is an official lowering of the exchange value of a country's currency relative to other currencies in countries where the fixed exchange rate system is adopted in order to close the balance of payments imbalances. Under the flexible exchange rate system, there is an automatic mechanism that restores the trade balance in relation to supply and demand under free market conditions. However, in the fixed exchange rate system, trade balance can't be achieved by foreign exchange rate changes because there is no automatic mechanism to restore foreign trade imbalances (Kaya, 2015: 163).

Devaluation reduces the price of exported goods in terms of foreign currency, while increasing the price of imported goods in national currency. With devaluation, it is aimed to increase foreign exchange income by encouraging exports from one side and to increase foreign exchange savings by reducing the domestic demand of import goods from the other side. However, it is dependent on the Marshall–Lerner condition ($e_m + e_x \geq 1$) that the devaluation can bring about an improvement in the current account balance. This means that under the assumption that supply elasticities are infinite, the sum of domestic demand elasticity for import goods (e_m) and foreign demand elasticity for exports (e_x) should be greater than 1. The greater the sum of elasticities than 1, the greater the effect of exchange rate adjustments on trade balance (Karagöz and Dogan, 2005: 220).

Especially after the establishment of the EU's Economic and Monetary Union, the external imbalance among member countries has begun to attract great attention. In these countries, due to disappearance of exchange rate risk and country risk premium, capital has flowed into neighboring countries and the decrease in competitiveness led to the growth of trade balance deficits (Hohberger and Kraus, 2015: 3). Before joining the EU Monetary Union, governments were able to carry out an independent monetary and exchange rate policy. When the countries' competitiveness weakened and their growth slowed down, devaluation of the exchange rate was widely used for fixing external imbalances. However, with the adoption of the common currency of the EU, these countries have not been able to devalue exchange rates and attention has been shifted to the substitute for devaluation (European Commission, 2013: 9). At this point, the concept of fiscal devaluation (FD) has come to the agenda. The ability to realize the same effect as the monetary devaluation by means of fiscal policy tools has made FD important today among both scientists and policy makers (Vdovchenko and Zubritskiy, 2014: 3).

In this study, the relationship between FD and exports and imports in Turkey for the period of 1985–2014 was examined by Toda and Yamamoto causality test. In Sections 2 and 3, the concept of FD and the studies that reveal the effects of fiscal devaluation on foreign trade are discussed. The data set, the econometric method used in the study, and the econometric findings are given in Sections 4 and 5. The final section concludes.

2 The concept of fiscal devaluation

A country that has a control over the exchange rate can devalue its currency if its growth rate is weak and its competitiveness weakens. Because this policy option does not apply to countries that are members of the Monetary Union, they must consider alternative policies for external imbalances (European Commission, 2013: 13). For countries in the euro area, the potential way to remove external imbalances is to use a fiscal policy tool that can create the same effect as devaluation under certain circumstances (Engler et al., 2014: 5). This fiscal policy tool is called FD, which is a tax reform that can create the same effect as devaluation (European Commission, 2013: 13).

Fiscal devaluation is a policy tool that aims to increase economic growth and competitiveness by reducing the gross labor cost and simultaneously increasing the tax burden on consumption. Therefore, it depends on reducing the income tax burden and increasing the value added tax (VAT) and other consumption taxes (Milošević and Babin, 2015). The general practice is that the deduction for employer social security contributions (ESSCs) is financed by an increase in the VAT rate (European Commission, 2013: 9). In other words, the simultaneous implementation of these two policies is called fiscal devaluation. According to this strategy, while employers' social security premium liabilities are reduced, indirect taxes are increased in the domestic market. Thus, even if the nominal wages do not change, real wages will be reduced, and export-oriented sectors will be in a more advantageous position compared to the internal market-oriented sectors.

Fiscal devaluation is based on the reorganization of the tax system by shifting the tax burden from the ESSCs toward the consumption tax. It is expected that such a reform would create the same effect as the effect created by the devaluation of the exchange rate (Langot et al., 2014: 2). The reduction in social security contributions reduces the unit labor cost and the relative price of domestic goods, and this reduction in contributions is financed through an increase in consumption tax. Because the consumption tax is a tax based on destination, it increases price of domestic goods and after-tax price of import goods equally, but does not affect the price of export goods. In general, the combination of lower unit labor costs and higher consumption tax reduces the price of exported goods and increases the after-tax relative price of imported goods (Gomes et al., 2014: 4). In this respect, FD can make exports cheaper and imports more expensive, hence contributes to the reduction of external imbalances by increasing demand for domestic goods (Langot et al., 2014: 2). Thus, the effect of exchange rate devaluation can be realized with increase in consumption tax and reduction in social security contributions.

3 The implementation of fiscal devaluation and literature review

Although the concept of FD is considered as a new concept, it has a fairly long history. Keynes stated in 1931 that the effect of the monetary devaluation in the countries where the gold standard was used and therefore the exchange rate devaluation was not the case could be achieved by ad valorem custom tax to be levied on all import goods and the same size export subsidy. Thus, while the cost of imports will increase, exportation will be advantageous. This theory is called "Keynesian fiscal devaluation theory" (Engler et al., 2014: 5–6; Vdovchenko and Zubritskiy, 2014: 3). However, the new debate about the feasibility and potential effects of FD has begun with the establishment of the EU Monetary Union and the remarkable liberalization of world trade (Vdovchenko and Zubritskiy, 2014: 4).

FD has not yet been adequately analyzed in the theoretical literature. However, some European countries have some kind of fiscal devaluation experience. The first examples of this practice are Italy (three devaluations in 1970s), Denmark (1988), Sweden (1993), Ireland (2002), and Germany (2007). Since the beginning of the world economic crisis in 2008, it has been implemented in Spain and France (2010), Holland (2012), and France (2014). In addition, FD played an important role in the European Commission's proposals for tax changes in Belgium, France, Germany, Italy, Latvia, and Spain between 2011 and 2014 (Milošević and Babin, 2015). For example, in 2007, Germany increased its standard VAT rate from 16% to 19% and simultaneously reduced the employer social security contribution to 1.8%. Hungary reduced the employer social security contribution by 5% in 2009 and simultaneously increased the VAT rate by 5%. In France, the standard VAT rate is increased from 19.6% to 20% and the medium VAT rate is increased from 7% to 10% (Koske, 2013: 7).

The implementation of FD can be beneficial for both countries that are members of the Monetary Union and countries with high public debt in foreign currency, which can contribute to improving the trade balance by increasing the competitiveness of the economy. The FD can lead to economic growth and export growth by increasing price competition through two channels: (a) smaller gross labor costs allow price decrease of the final product and (b) VAT is levied on importers and reimbursed to exporters. Lower gross cost per workforce allows companies to invest in new technology and equipment, especially in capital-intensive sectors. In the labor-intensive sectors, FD can provide jobs for the new workforce without pressure on general corporate costs (Milošević and Babin, 2015).

In general, it is argued that FD is an instrument that can be used to increase economic growth without increasing public debt and the money supply and devaluing the exchange rate. The success of this tool depends on global conditions, especially the reactions of countries' export partners (Petersen, 2015: 3). The simulations indicate that if the FD is implemented unilaterally, it may be the most appropriate option to increase the GDP of the country; on the other hand, it will be less effective or completely ineffective if trade partners implement the same policy (Milošević and Babin, 2015). Moreover, FD is essentially a policy tool for countries that cannot devalue their exchange rates. In this context, the empirical literature examining the effects of FD on foreign trade is presented in the following paragraphs.

Mooij and Keen (2012) identified the impact of FD on net exports by panel data analysis for the 30 Organisation for Economic Co-operation and Development (OECD) countries for the period of 1965–2009. The impact of FD was examined by separating the sample into two groups: one belonging to the eurozone and one not included in the eurozone. The difference between coefficients of the VAT rates and the ESSCs were taken as an indicator of FD. The findings from the Panel Generalized Method of Moments (GMM) estimates show that the FD has boosted net exports in the eurozone in the short term.

Eiras (2013) investigated the impact of FD on the current account deficit by analyzing panel data for the period of 1999–2010 for the 17 euro region countries. The following variables were taken as an indicator of FD: (a) tax rate on implicit ESSCs (% GDP)/tax rate implicit consumption tax (% GDP); (b) ESSCs (% GDP)/consumption tax (% GDP); (c) ESSCs/employee social security contribution (% GDP); (d) ESSCs (% GDP)/corporate tax (% GDP); and (e) ESSCs (% GDP)/personal income tax (% GDP). Coefficients of all FD indicators were found to be negative as expected and statistically significant. Thus, it is determined that FD has a positive effect on the current account deficit and reduces it.

Vdovychenko and Zubritskiy (2014) examined the relationship between FD and trade balance by using time series analysis for Ukraine in 2001–2013 quarterly. The difference between VAT and ESSCs was used as a FD indicator in the study. The findings of the Granger and Hsiao causality tests revealed a one-way causality relationship from the trade balance to the FD. Therefore, the effect of FD on trade balance isn't determined in the study.

Hurduzeu et al. (2015) examined the effect of the FD on the current account deficit by using the panel fixed effect method for the period of 2000–2012 for

28 EU countries. The ratio of tax on labor (% GDP) to consumption tax (% GDP) is used as an FD indicator in the study. The findings from regression estimates show that a 1-unit decrease in the ratio of tax on labor to consumption tax would increase the current deficit by 2.4%. Ultimately, FD will have a positive impact on the current account deficit by contributing to competitiveness.

When the studies are overviewed, it is observed that there is a limited literature empirically revealing the effects of FD on foreign trade. In addition, the study that examines the effects of FD on foreign trade for Turkey has not been determined in the literature. Therefore, this study aims to contribute to this gap in the literature.

4 Econometric method and data set

In this study, the relation between fiscal devaluation (FD) and export (EX) and the relation between FD and import (IM) are examined by the Toda and Yamamoto causality (1995) test for the period of 1985–2014 in Turkey. The FD is calculated by subtracting the share of employer social security contributions in GDP (ESSC/GDP) from the share of value added tax in GDP (VAT/GDP). EX and IM series are obtained from World Development Indicators (WDI) online database and VAT/GDP and ESSC/GDP series are obtained from OECD income statistics online database. Δ symbol indicates that the difference of the series is taken.

Relationships between FD and EX and IM were determined by the Toda and Yamamoto causality test. Causality test is performed by estimating the Vector Autoregression (VAR) $_{(k+dmax)}$ system with the Seemingly Unrelated Regressions (SUR). First, the values of k in the system (the optimal lag length of the VAR system consisting of level values of the series) and d_{max} (the maximum order of integration for the variables in the VAR system) have to be determined. The existence and direction of the causality relations is determined by the Modified Wald (MWALD) test. Hence, the causality test was employed through the VAR systems presented as follows:

$$lnEX_t = \pi_0 + \sum_{i=1}^{k} \gamma_{1i} lnEX_{t-i} + \sum_{i=k+1}^{k+d_{max}} \mu_{1i} lnEX_{t-i} + \sum_{i=1}^{k} \vartheta_{1i} FD_{t-i} + \sum_{i=k+1}^{k+d_{max}} \beta_{1i} FD_{t-i} + \sum_{i=1}^{k} \rho_{1i} lnIM_{t-i} + \sum_{i=k+1}^{k+d_{max}} \delta_{1i} lnIM_{t-i} + \varepsilon_{1t} \tag{1}$$

$$lnIM_t = \pi_0 + \sum_{i=1}^{k} \gamma_{2i} lnEX_{t-i} + \sum_{i=k+1}^{k+d_{max}} \mu_{2i} lnEX_{t-i} + \sum_{i=1}^{k} \vartheta_{2i} FD_{t-i} + \sum_{i=k+1}^{k+d_{max}} \beta_{2i} FD_{t-i} + \sum_{i=1}^{k} \rho_{2i} lnIM_{t-i} + \sum_{i=k+1}^{k+d_{max}} \delta_{2i} lnIM_{t-i} + \varepsilon_{2t} \tag{2}$$

$$lnFD_t = \pi_0 + \sum_{i=1}^{k} \gamma_{3i} lnEX_{t-i} + \sum_{i=k+1}^{k+d_{max}} \mu_{3i} lnEX_{t-i} + \sum_{i=1}^{k} \vartheta_{3i} FD_{t-i}$$
$$+ \sum_{i=k+1}^{k+d_{max}} \beta_{3i} FD_{t-i} + \sum_{i=1}^{k} \rho_{3i} lnIM_{t-i} + \sum_{i=k+1}^{k+d_{max}} \delta_{3i} lnIM_{t-i} + \varepsilon_{3t} \qquad (3)$$

Causality relations between EX, IM, and FD were examined through multivariate VAR($k+d_{max}$) system (1), (2), and (3). Causality relations from the FD to the EX and IM are examined through the null hypotheses of no-causality which are formed as, $i = 1 \dots k$, respectively. The causality relations from EX to IM and FD are examined through the null hypotheses of no-causality which are formed as $= 0$ and, $i = 1 \dots k$, respectively. The causality relations from IM to EX and FD are examined through the null hypotheses of no-causality which are formed as and, $i = 1 \dots k$, respectively. If the null hypotheses tested by the MWALD test are rejected, the existence and direction of causality relations is decided by accepting the alternative hypothesis indicating the existence of causality relations.

5 Econometric findings

It is employed the augmented Dickey–Fuller (ADF) unit root test to determine the maximum order of the integration for the series of EX, IM, and FD. The ADF test results are presented in Table 1. The ADF test indicates that EX, IM, and FD series have a unit root in both models with a constant and models with a constant and trend for their level values. When the first difference of the series is taken and whether they are stationary or not is examined, it is determined that the series are stationary at the 1% significance level and first difference in both constant and constant–trend models. The results of ADF test indicate that the maximum order of integration (d_{max}) for these series is one. On the other hand the optimal lag length of the VAR system (k) is determined as 1 according to the Akaike Information Criteria (AIC). Therefore, the VAR ($k + d_{max} = 2$) system is estimated by the SUR method.

Table 1: ADF Unit Root Test Results

Variables	Constant	Constant–Trend
lnEX	−0.821602 (0)	−3.216575 (5)
lnIM	−0.729298 (0)	−3.161022 (0)
FD	−1.720265 (0)	−1.462723 (0)
ΔlnEX	−5.627286[a] (0)	−5.714585[a] (0)
ΔlnIM	−6.647321[a] (0)	−6.549495[a] (0)
ΔFD	−6.292068[a] (0)	−4.624912[a] (1)

Note: Values in parentheses indicate the optimal lag length determined according to the AIC criteria by taking the maximum lag length 7. Superscript letter a means that the relevant statistic is significant at the 1% significance level.

The null hypotheses are tested by the MWALD test, and the results of the MWALD test are shown in Table 2.

Table 2: Results of Toda and Yamamoto Causality Test

VAR ($k + d_{max}$ = 2) k = 1, d_{max} = 1			
Null Hypothesis	**MWALD Test χ^2 statistic**	**Significance Value**	**Direction and Sign of Causality**
lnEX doesn't cause FD	4.859300	0.0275	lnEX → FD
lnEX doesn't cause lnIM	0.204594	0.6510	lnEX Ø lnIM
lnIM doesn't cause lnEX	4.719703	0.0298	lnIM → lnEX
lnIM doesn't cause FD	8.03E−05	0.9929	lnIM Ø FD
FD doesn't cause lnEX	4.087108	0.0432	FD → lnEX
FD doesn't cause lnIM	0.007765	0.9298	FD Ø lnIM

Note: → and Ø show the direction of causality and the absence of causality, respectively.

As seen from Table 2, null hypotheses indicating that there is no causality relationship from FD to EX, from EX to FD, and from IM to EX are rejected at a statistically 5% significance level. On the other hand, null hypotheses indicating that there is no causality relationship from EX to IM, from IM to FD, and from FD to IM are not rejected at the 10% significance level. Therefore, the findings indicate that there is two-way causality relationship between FD and EX, and there is one-way causality from IM to EX. We conclude that FD can be used as a policy tool to close foreign trade deficits in Turkey because empirical findings show that FD increases EX while it isn't effective on IM. On the other hand, the finding of causality from EX to IM reveals that Turkey's EX is dependent on her IM.

6 Conclusion and suggestions

Foreign trade imbalances are one of the main economic problems that the global economy has faced and intensively debated. In countries that implement a fixed exchange rate system, devaluation of foreign exchange is a commonly used method in closing foreign trade deficits. Countries can fix their foreign trade imbalances by devaluating their exchange rates when their competitiveness diminishes and growth rates slow down. However, after the establishment of the EU Monetary Union, it became impossible for the member countries of the Union to carry out an independent monetary and exchange rate policy and alternative policies to the exchange rate devaluation started to be implemented. At this point, the concept of fiscal devaluation, which means that the effect created by exchange rate devaluation is realized by means of tax policy, started to be discussed.

Although the fiscal devaluation is described as a new concept, Keynes suggested a similar proposal in the 1930s as a result of the countries adopting the gold standard failed to devalue their exchange rate. In this context, he stated that the effect created by the monetary devaluation can be achieved with the ad varolem custom duty tax to be placed on all import goods and the same size export subsidies. The new debate about the feasibility and potential effects of fiscal devaluation has begun with the creation of the EU Monetary Union and the remarkable liberalization of world trade.

Fiscal devaluation is the way of affecting trade and relative prices by the increase in consumption tax and the reduction of ESSCs in an open economy. Thus, the effect of exchange rate devaluation is realized with financial instruments. This policy is an alternative policy to exchange rate devaluation in countries that implement the fixed exchange rate system while it is a policy closing the foreign trade deficits in countries that implement flexible exchange rate system. To the best of our knowledge, this is the first study on the relationship between fiscal devaluation and foreign trade in Turkey.

In this study, the relationship between fiscal devaluation and exports and imports in Turkey for the period of 1985–2014 was examined by Toda and Yamamoto causality test. Causality tests indicate that there is a two-way causality relationship between fiscal devaluation and export and there is no causality relationship between fiscal devaluation and import in Turkey. Thus, our empirical results suggest that fiscal devaluation can be used as a policy tool to close foreign trade deficits in Turkey.

References

Eiras, A. C. V. (2013). "Is Fiscal Devaluation a Way Out?", U. Porto FEP Economia E Gestão, Master Dissertation in Economics, https://repositorio-aberto.up.pt/bitstream/10216/69836/2/25486.pdf.

Engler, P., Ganelli, G., Tervala, J. and Voigts, S. (2014). "Fiscal Devaluation in a Monetary Union", IMF Working Paper, WP/14/201, https://helda.helsinki.fi/bitstream/handle/10138/144095/Fiscal_devaluation_IMF_WP_2014.pdf?sequence=1.

European Commission (2013). "Study on the Impacts of Fiscal Devaluation", European Commission Taxation Papers, Working Paper No. 36, The Hague, Netherlands.

Gomes, S., Jacquinot, P. and Pisani, M. (2014). "Fiscal Devaluation in the Euro Area: A Model-Based Analysis", European Central Bank Working Paper Series No. 1725, https://www.ecb.europa.eu/pub/pdf/scpwps/ecbwp1725.pdf?a2b06e8889fe274c5a5ad3afd6affbee.

Hohberger, S. and Kraus, L. (2015). "Is Fisal Devaluation Welfare Enhancing? A Model-Based Analysis", Universität Bayreuth Discussion Paper 01-15, http://www.fiwi.uni-bayreuth.de/de/download/WP_01-15.pdf.

Hurduzeu, G., Lazar, M. I. and Popescu, M. E. (2015). "An Assessment of Enhanced Competitiveness through Fiscal Devaluation", *Procedia Economics and Finance*, 22: 262–267.

Karagöz, M. and Doğan, Ç. (2005). "Döviz Kuru Dış Ticaret İlişkisi: Türkiye Örneği", *Fırat Üniversitesi Sosyal Bilimler Dergisi*, 15(2): 219–228.

Kaya, A. (2015). "Parasal Devalüasyona Alternatif Bir Öneri: Mali Devalüasyon", *Vergi Sorunları Dergisi*, 319: 162–175.

Koske, I. (2013). "Fiscal Devaluation-Can it Help to Boost Competitiveness?", OECD Economics Department Working Papers No. 1089, OECD Publishing, Paris.

Langot, F., Patureau, L. and Sopraseuth, T. (2014). "Fiscal Devaluation and Structural Gaps", http://lise.patureau.free.fr/Papiers/Recherche/fileoid_fiscaldev.pdf.

Milošević, M. and Babin, M. (2015). "Potentials and Structure of Fiscal Devaluation in Serbia", 63(3), http://ojs.ius.bg.ac.rs/index.php/anali/article/view/153/340.

Mooij, R. and Keen, M. (2012). "Fiscal Devaluation and Fiscal Consolidation: The VAT in Troubled Times", IMF Working Paper, WP/12/85, https://www.imf.org/external/pubs/ft/wp/2012/wp1285.pdf.

Petersen, T. (2015). "Fiscal Devaluation – A Route to More Growth?", Future Social Market Economy, Bertelsmann Stiftung, https://ged-project.de/wp-content/uploads/2015/06/Impulse-2015-04-Fiscal-devaluation-.pdf.

Toda, H. Y. and Yamamoto, T. (1995). "Statistical Inference in Vector Autoregressions with Possibly Integrated Processes". *Journal of Econometrics*, 66(1-2): 225–250.

Vdovychenko, A. and Zubritskiy, A. (2014). "The Ukrainian Case of Fiscal Devaluation in Small Open Economies", Munich Personal RePEc Archive (MPRA), Research Institute of Financial Law, MPRA Paper No. 69329, https://mpra.ub.uni-muenchen.de/69329/1/MPRA_paper_69329.pdf.

Muhammed Benli

Asymmetric Effect of Exchange Rates on Exports: An Empirical Analysis of Exports from Turkey to the USA

1 Introduction

Since the pioneering study by Magee (1973), there has been a large volume of studies exploring the long-run relationship between exchange rates and international trade. Following the collapse of the Bretton Woods system in the 1970s, the 1997 Asian financial crisis and more recently the 2008 global financial crisis, defining the link between exchange rates and international trade, has continued to be a hot topic. Historical experiences of developed and developing countries and emerging economies suggest that changes in exchange rate typically have substantial effects on trade (IMF, 2015).

The earlier theoretical and empirical studies mostly focused on the effect of exchange rate volatility on trade flows. The rationale of examining this effect is that the exchange rate fluctuations induce increased uncertainty to traders, which may influence the volume of trade and economic activity. However, both the theory and the empirical evidence exhibit ambiguity regarding the effect of the exchange rate volatility on trade flows (Bahmani-Oskooee and Hegerty, 2007).

In the last decade, the attention of researchers has moved toward the impact of the changes in the exchange rates on international export and import flows. The conventional wisdom predicts that currency devaluation (depreciation) lowers the foreign currency price of exports and increases the prices of imports in domestic currency, which probably increases the quantity of exports and leads to fewer imports resulting in an improvement in the domestic country's trade balance. This conjecture is based on the elasticity approach incorporating the so-called Bickerdike–Robinson–Meltzer (BRM) model (Bickerdike, 1920; Robinson, 1947; and Metzler, 1948) and the Marshall–Lerner (ML) condition (Marshall, 1923; Lerner, 1944). The BRM model has been recognized in the literature as providing a sufficient condition (the BRM condition) for a trade balance improvement when exchange rates devalue (depreciate). On the other hand, the ML condition, which is a particular solution of the BRM model, states that the positive effect of a devaluation (depreciation) on trade balance depends on whether the absolute values of the sum of the demand elasticities for exports and imports exceed unity.

Because the empirical evidence in support of the elasticity approach has been inconsistent, the literature shifted to the J-curve and the S-curve phenomena. The idea behind the J-curve phenomenon is the lagged response of consumers and producers to the changes in exchange rates (Junz and Rhomberg, 1973; Magee, 1973), whereby in response to devaluation, the trade balance worsens in the short run but improves over time toward the ML condition. On the other hand, the S-curve hypothesis (Backus et al., 1994) suggests that the past values of the trade balance are negatively correlated with the current exchange rate, but the cross-correlation between the current exchange rate and future values of the trade balance could be positive (Bahmani-Oskooee and Fariditavana, 2015).

Previous empirical studies investigating the effects of currency depreciation on the trade balance assumed a linear relationship between these variables (Bahmanki-Oskooee and Fariditavana, 2015). The assumption of linear relationship has been questioned by recent studies of Verheyen (2013), Bahmanki-Oskooee and Fariditavana (2015, 2016), and Bahmani-Oskooee, Halicioglu, and Mohammadian (in press). Using bilateral trade balance models of the USA with each of her six largest trading partners, Bahmanki-Oskooee and Fariditavana (2015) find that introducing nonlinear adjustment process provides more evidence in support of the J-curve. They also suggest that the effects of exchange rate changes on the trade balance are asymmetric in most cases. Bahmani-Oskooee et al. (in press) use data on Britain's trade balances with her eight trading partners and examine whether pound appreciations affect trade differently than do pound depreciations. They present no evidence of a long-run relationship in the case of the UK–Spain and the UK–Norway trade balance models while they find empirical evidence for the presence of long-run asymmetries of exchange rates in the case of the UK–Germany, the UK–Italy, the UK–Korea, and the UK–Japan trade balance models. Verheyen (2013), adopting the nonlinear autoregressive distributed lag (NARDL) approach of Shin et al. (2011), shows that there is a nonlinear relationship between exchange rate movements and exports in the long run. Particularly, using bilateral export data for 12 European countries and the USA, he argues that exports respond stronger to euro depreciations than to euro appreciations in the long run. To sum up, there is growing evidence showing that ignoring the nonlinear effect of the exchange rate on trade is too restrictive. The main idea behind examining the asymmetric effects of exchange rate changes is that exporters and importers react differently to depreciation than to appreciation (Bahmani-Oskooee et al., in press).

Following Verheyen (2013), the purpose of this study is to identify whether exports respond to exchange rates in a linear or a nonlinear way in the long run.

Particularly, using the NARDL model recently advanced by Shin et al. (2011), the presence of a nonlinear pattern between the changes in US Dollar/Turkish Lira (USD/TRY) exchange rate and bilateral exports from Turkey to the USA is investigated. The estimated NARDL model affirms the presence of nonlinear effect of exchange rate changes on exports. In particular, it is found that Turkish exporters seem to benefit more from Turkish Lira depreciation than from Turkish Lira appreciation in the long run. In other words, exports respond positively to an increase in USD/TRY exchange rate but they don't respond to declines in the exchange rate.

2 Econometric methodology

The model used in this study is based on the export demand function suggested by the literature:

$$X_t = f(Y_t, E_t, P_t)$$

X = US exports from Turkey

Y = US demand for exports

E = dollar/Turkish Lira parity

P = relative export prices

For our purpose, the NARDL model recently advanced by Shin et al. (2011) is used to jointly examine the long- and short-run asymmetries between dollar/euro parity and Turkey's exports to the USA.

The standard linear autoregressive distributed lag (ARDL) (p,q) cointegration model (Pesaran and Shin, 1999; Pesaran, Shin and Smith, 2001) with two series y_t and x_t ($t = 1, 2, ..., T$) has the following form:

$$\Delta y_t = \alpha + \omega y_{t-1} + \theta x_{t-1} + \delta z_t + \sum_{i=0}^{p-1}(\varphi_i \Delta y_{t-1}) + \sum_{i=0}^{q-1}(\gamma_i \Delta x_{t-1}) + u_t \ (1)$$

where z_t is a vector of deterministic regressors (trends, seasonals, and other exogenous influences with fixed lags) and u_t is an independent and identically distributed stochastic process.

The ARDL model in Equation (1) implies symmetric adjustment in the long and the short run. It becomes, therefore, inappropriate when the links between y_t and x_t are nonlinear (asymmetric). To account for this issue, Shin, Yu, and Greenwood-Nimmo (2011) introduced the NARDL model in which x_t is decomposed into positive and negative partial sums:

$$x_t = x_0 + x_t^+ + x_t^- \ (2)$$

where

$$x_t^+ = \sum\nolimits_{i=1}^{t} \Delta x_i^+ = \sum\nolimits_i^t \max(\Delta x_i^+, 0), \ x_t^- = \sum\nolimits_{i=1}^{t} \Delta x_i^- = \sum\nolimits_i^t \min(\Delta x_i^-, 0) \ (3)$$

Then the long-run equilibrium relationship can be expressed as follows:

$$y_t = \beta^+ x_t^+ + \beta^- x_t^- + v_t \ (4)$$

where β^+ and β^- are the asymmetric long-run parameters associated with positive and negative changes in x_t, respectively. As shown in Shin et al. (2011), combining Equations (4) and (1), we can obtain the following asymmetric error correction model that is known as the NARDL (p,q) model:

$$\Delta y_t = \alpha + \omega y_{t-1} + \theta^+ x_{t-1}^+ + \theta^- x_{t-1}^+ + \delta z_t + \sum\nolimits_{i=1}^{p-1} (\varphi_i \Delta y_{t-1})$$
$$+ \sum\nolimits_{i=0}^{q-1} (\gamma_i^+ \Delta x_{t-1}^+ + \gamma_i^- \Delta x_{t-1}^-) + u_t \qquad (5)$$

where $\theta^+ = -\frac{\omega}{\beta^+}$ and $\theta^- = -\frac{\omega}{\beta^-}$ are the long-run effects associated with positive and negative changes in x on y, whereas the short-run impacts of changes in x on y are measured by $\sum\nolimits_{i=0}^{q-1} \gamma_i^+$ and $\sum\nolimits_{i=0}^{q-1} \gamma_i^-$. Hence, in this setting, the NARDL model enables us to capture asymmetric long-run as well as short-run effects of changes in underlying exogenous variables on dependent variable.

In the economic literature, the empirical studies on nonlinear cointegration have primarily relied on regime-switching-type models. However, the NARDL approach has a number of advantages over the existing class of regime-switching techniques (Greenwood-Nimmo et al., 2011). First, the NARDL (p,q) model can be estimated simply by the standard Ordinary Least Squares (OLS). Second, the test for an asymmetric (nonlinear) cointegration relationship between the variables can be easily carried out by means of bounds-testing procedure advanced by Pesaran et al. (2001) and Shin et al. (2011), based on a modified F-test (denoted as F_{PSS}), which remains valid irrespective of whether the regressors are I(0), I(1), or mutually cointegrated. Third, long- and short-run asymmetries can be estimated using standard Wald tests. In particular, the associated joint null hypothesis for the long-run symmetry is $\theta^+ = \theta^-$, whereas for short-run symmetry, the joint null hypotheses are $\sum\nolimits_{i=0}^{q-1} \gamma_i^+ = \sum\nolimits_{i=0}^{q-1} \gamma_i^-$ (Greenwood-Nimmo et al., 2011).

3 Data

To investigate the exchange rate nonlinearities in Turkey's exports to the USA, this study uses monthly data over the period Jan. 2000 to Dec. 2016. The nominal export data series are based on the Foreign Trade Statistics (FTS) collected by the

Turkish Statistical Institute (TURKSTAT) and consist of bilateral exports from Turkey to the USA in Turkish Lira. The real export series are constructed by deflating nominal export series with export value index (2010 = 100) provided by the TURKSTAT. The US demand for Turkish exports is proxied by the US Industrial Production Index (2010 = 100) collected from the Federal Reserve Economic Data (FRED) and relative prices are calculated as the ratio of export value index to the US export prices (2010 = 100) provided by the Netherlands Bureau for Economic Policy Analysis. Finally, USD/TRY parity is obtained from the FRED. An increase of the exchange rate series corresponds to a depreciation of Turkey's currency.

The data series are seasonally adjusted and transformed into natural log prior to the analysis. However, in this analysis, exchange rate series will not be incorporated in logs because of the decomposition of exchange rate series into positive and negative partial sums, so that the log of a negative number is not defined. Nonetheless, because the exchange rate series float around one, a one unit change in exchange rate series roughly corresponds to a one unit percentage change.

4 Empirical findings

The empirical analysis is started by conducting unit root tests for the variables at level and first difference using the ADF and Kwiatkowski–Phillips–Schmidt–Shin (KPSS) tests because the cointegration test procedure requires that no I(2) variables are involved in the model. The results are presented in Table 1 and the findings of the ADF and KPSS tests confirm the stationarity of all the variables at first difference, indicating that the variables are I(1). Therefore, it is proceeded the cointegration test for the nonlinear specification.

Table 1: Unit Root Test Results (ADF and KPSS)

Variable	Deterministic Component	k	ADF	KPSS
exports	C	5	−0.815	1.64
	C/T	5	−1.334	0.498
Δexports	C	12	−3.830***	0.176***
	C/T	12	−3.829**	0.166***
parity	C	2	0.81	4.67
	C/T	2	−0.288	0.993
Δparity	C	1	−9.251***	0.337***
	C/T	1	−9.328***	0.187***
demand	C	8	−2.047	0.782
	C/T	5	−3.351*	0.211*

Variable	Deterministic Component	k	ADF	KPSS
Δdemand	C	7	−3.853***	0.068***
	C/T	7	−3.851**	0.063***
relative	C	2	−1.772	3.31
	C/T	2	−1.32	1.35
Δrelative	C	1	−9.380***	0.22***
	C/T	1	−9.462	0.0602***

Notes: ***, **, and * denote significance at the 1%, 5%, and 10% levels, respectively. k denotes the optimal lag structure of the ADF test, based on the AIC.

Table 2 reports the results. When the model is specified in a nonlinear fashion, there is strong evidence in favor of cointegration. Therefore, it can be argued that focusing on linear cointegration is too restrictive.

Table 2: Bounds Test for Nonlinear Cointegration

Model Specification	F-Statistics	95% Lower Bound	95% Upper Bound	Conclusion
Nonlinear	13.06	3.79	4.85	Cointegration

Note: The critical values are from Pesaran et al. (2001) Case III.

Applying the general to specific procedure to determine the lag length in each case, we arrive at the final model specification and the results are reported in Table 3. The long-run coefficients of export demand and relative price are positive and negative, respectively, and both are significant at 1% significance level. The results suggest that, holding the other variables constant, a 1% increase in the US demand for exports from Turkey is related to the increase in the exports by approximately 1.54%, whereas a 1% increase in relative prices is related to the decline in the exports by approximately 1.14%. The results also suggest an asymmetric long- and short-run relation between exports and USD/TRY parity. In the long run, depreciation of domestic currency has a positive impact on exports indicated by positive and statistically significant coefficient at 1% significance level, whereas appreciation of domestic currency is found to be insignificant. Therefore, our findings indicate an incomplete pass-through effect of the exchange rate to the exports from Turkey to the USA. In other words, exports respond to depreciations, but do not respond to appreciations.

Table 3: Final Specification of the NARDL Model (Dependent Variable: Δexports)

Variable	Coeff.	Std. Dev.
constant	6.988***	1.815
exports$_{(t-1)}$	−0.489***	0.079
NomExRate_pos$_{(t-1)}$	0.452***	0.091
NomExRate_neg$_{(t-1)}$	−0.217	0.138
Δexports$_{(t-1)}$	−0.185*	0.070
Δexports$_{(t-7)}$	−0.143**	0.059
Δexports$_{(t-11)}$	−0.145**	0.059
Δ NomExRate _pos$_t$	0.631***	0.183
Δ NomExRate _neg$_{(t-1)}$	0.863*	0.316
Δ NomExRate _neg$_{(t-7)}$	0.651**	0.310
Δ NomExRate _neg$_{(t-9)}$	0.772**	0.315
Exp_Demand	1.538***	0.379
Rel_price	−1.142***	0.272
F_{PSS}	13.06	
$L^{+}_{NomExRate}$	0.925***	
$L^{-}_{NomExRate}$	0.444	
$W^{LR}_{NomExRate}$	21.67***	
$W^{SR}_{NomExRate}$	7.678***	

Note: *, **and ***denote significance at the 1%, 5% and 10% levels, respectively.

5 Conclusion

In this study, the effect of exchange rate changes on exports is empirically examined. In particular, the presence of a nonlinear pattern between the changes in USD/TRY exchange rate and bilateral exports from Turkey to the USA is examined. To do so, the NARDL model recently advanced by Shin et al. (2011) is used. This approach enables us not only to test the short- and long-run nonlinearities simultaneously through positive and negative partial sum decompositions of the exchange rate but also to quantify the respective response of exports to positive and negative changes in the exchange rate from the asymmetric dynamic multipliers.

The estimated NARDL model affirms the presence of nonlinear effect of exchange rate changes on exports. In particular, it is found that Turkish exporters seem to benefit more from Turkish Lira depreciation than that of Turkish Lira appreciation in the long run. In other words, exports respond positively to an increase in USD/TRY exchange rate (depreciation of Turkish Lira) but they don't respond to declines in the exchange rate (appreciation of Turkish Lira).

References

Backus, D.K., Kehoe, P.J., and Kydland, F.E. (1994). Dynamics of the Trade Balance and the Terms of Trade: The J-Curve? *The American Economic Review*, 84, 84–103.

Bahmani-Oskooee, M., and Hegerty, S.W. (2007). Exchange Rate Volatility and Trade Flows: A Review Article, *Journal of Economic Studies*, 34(3), 211–255.

Bahmani-Oskooee, M., Fariditavana, H. (2015). Nonlinear ARDL Approach, Asymmetric Effects, and the J-curve. *Journal of Economic Studies*, 42(3), 519–530.

Bahmani-Oskooee, M. and Fariditavana, H. (2016). Nonlinear ARDL Approach and the J-Curve Phenomenon, *Open Economies Review*, 27, 51–70.

Bahmani-Oskooee, M., Halicioglu, F., and Mohammadian, A. (in press). On the Asymmetric Effects of Changes on Domestic Production in Turkey, *Economic Change and Restructuring*, doi:10.1007/s10644-017-9201-x.

Bickerdike, C. F. (1920). The Instability of Foreign Exchanges, *The Economic Journal*, 30, 118–122.

Greenwood-Nimmo, M. J., Shin, Y., and Van Treeck, T. (2011). The Nonlinear ARDL Model with Multiple Unknown Threshold Decompositions: An Application to the Phillips Curve in Canada, Leeds University Business School, Mimeo.

IMF (International Monetary Fund). (2015). *World Economic Outlook Database*, October, Washington.

Junz, H., and Rhomberg, R. R. (1973). Price Competitiveness in Export Trade among Industrial Countries, *Papers and Proceedings of American Economic Review*, 63, 412–418.

Lerner, A. P. (1944). *The Economics of Control: Principles of Welfare Economics*, The Macmillan Company, New York.

Magee, S. P. (1973). Currency Contracts, Pass-Through and Devaluation, *Brooking Papers on Economic Activity*, 1, 303–325.

Marshall, A. (1923). *Money, Credit and Commerce*, Macmillan, London.

Metzler, L. (1948). *A Survey of Contemporary Economics*, Vol. I, Richard D. Irwin, INC, Homewood, IL.

Pesaran, H. and Shin, Y. (1999). An Autoregressive Distributed Lag Modelling approach to cointegration analysis", In S. Strom (Ed.), Econometrics and Economic Theory in the 20th Century: The Ragnar Frisch Centennial Symposium, Cambridge University Press.

Pesaran, M. H., Shin, Y., and Smith, R. J. (2001). Bounds Testing Approaches to the Analysis of Level Relationships, *Journal of Applied Econometrics*, 16, 289–326.

Robinson, J. (1947). *Essays in the Theory of Employment*, Basil Blackwell, Oxford.

Shin, Y., Yu, B., and Greenwood-Nimmo, M. (2011). Modeling asymmetric cointegration and dynamic multipliers in an ARDL framework. In William C. Horrace and Robin C. Sickles (Eds.), Festschrift in Honor of Peter Schmidt. Springer Science & Business Media, New York (NY).

Verheyen, F. (2013). Interest Rate Pass-Through in the EMU: New Evidence Using Nonlinear ARDL Framework. *Economics Bulletin*, 33, 729–739.

Adil Akinci

The Relationship between Public Investment Expenditures and Private Investment Expenditures in Turkey

1 Introduction

Public investment expenditures and private investment expenditures are among the main determinants of economic growth and development. Public investment and private investment expenditures need to be constantly increased to ensure sustainable economic growth. Although public investment expenditures and private investment expenditures have a significant influence on economic growth and development, public expenditures may result in inappropriate outcomes due to the crowding out of public expenditures. However, public expenditures may result in outcomes that are above expectations due to the crowding in of public expenditures. This study examines econometrically whether there is any exclusion or withdrawal effect between public investment expenditures during the period 2006:Q1 to 2016:Q2 in Turkey. The period of econometric analysis has been started since 2006 due to the enactment of the Public Financial Management and Control Law No. 5018 in 2006 and the restructuring of the financial structure of the public expenditure with this law. Yavuz (2005), Kuştepeli (2005), Günaydın (2006), Başar and Temurlenk (2007), Altunç and Şentürk (2010), Başar et al. (2011), Cural et al. (2012), Tülümce and Buyrukoğlu (2013), Şen and Kaya (2014), Yılancı and Aydın (2016), and Çelik (2016) are the main studies for Turkey on the subject.

2 Data and methodology

The period under study is between 2006:Q1 and 2016:Q2. The period of econometric analysis has been started since 2006 due to the enactment of the Public Financial Management and Control Law No. 5018 in 2006. The data set includes the quarterly data. The gross domestic product (GDP) is the dependent variable in the study, whereas public sector total fixed capital investments (public) and private sector total fixed capital investments (private) were used as independent variables. The series of the variables are seasonally adjusted, and calendar effects are corrected in the series. The series of the variables are made stationary by taking logarithm of them. The data for the variables are obtained from the Turkish Statistical Institute (TURKSTAT).

In order to apply the co-integration tests developed by Engel and Granger (1987), Johansen (1988), and Johansen and Juselius (1990), which are used extensively in investigating the long-term relationships between variables, it is necessary that the series should be nonstationary and become stationary when first difference is applied. In other words, the degree of integration of variables must be the same. Pesaran et al. (2001) developed the Boundary Test Approach to remove these constraints. This test can investigate long-term relationships between variables, regardless of the degree of integration of variables (Kıran and Güriş, 2011).

3 Unit root test

The Augmented Dickey–Fuller (ADF) test and the Phillips–Perron (PP) test were conducted to determine whether the time series has a unit root.

According to the results of the ADF and PP unit root tests in Table 1, it is understood that the variables "gdp" and "private" are I (1) and the variable "public" is I (0). In other words, variables are stationary at different levels. Co-integration analysis is used to reveal the relationships between the variables in the study. The difference in stationarity levels of the variables is of great importance in determining the method to be applied in the analysis. The Autoregressive Distributed Lag (ARDL) test is used in the study because the series are stationary at I (0) and I (1).

Table 1: Unit Root Test Results

Variable		ADF		PP	
		Trend with Constant	Constant	Trend with Constant	Constant
gdp		−2.7862	−0.3718	−2.0880	−0.4678
Δgdp		−4.6300*	−4.6662*	−4.5753*	−4.6199*
private		−2.7169	−1.8308	−2.0273	−1.5752
Δprivate		−3.4858**	−3.4989**	−3.4429**	−3.4584**
public		−3.9854**	−1.0652	−3.3529	−0.9740
Δpublic		−4.5619*	−4.5334*	−7.6130*	−7.6530*
Critical Values	1%	−4.2050	−3.6055	−4.1985	−3.6009
	5%	−3.5266	−2.9369	−3.5236	−2.9350
	10%	−3.1946	−2.6068	−3.1929	−2.6058

Notes: *Variable is stationary at 1% and **variable is stationary at 5%. "Δ" indicates the difference operator, i.e., the first difference.

4 Co-integration test

The most important step in conducting the boundary test is to determine the appropriate lag lengths. Due to the use of quarterly data, models were estimated up to four lags, and the calculated information criteria and the existence of auto-correlation were examined.

According to the results in Table 2 and the Akaike information criterion (AIC) and Hannan–Quinn (HQ) criterion, the optimal lag length is the fourth lag length in which autocorrelation is not present and lag length is minimum. After determining the appropriate delay length, the investigation of the co-integration relation is required. In order to determine the existence of co-integration relation, the F-test is calculated by the Boundary test. The presence of a long-term relationship is decided by comparing the F-statistic with critical values.

Table 2: Determination of Lag Lengths

Number of Lag	AIC	SC	HQ	LM(1)	LM(4)
1	−5.1489	−4.7689	−5.0115	0.0962	0.0288
2	−5.3065	−4.7946	−5.1229	0.8123	0.0126
3	−5.4050	−4.7585	−5.1750	0.3667	0.0360
4	−5.5319	−4.7482	−5.2556	0.1131	0.1592

Since the calculated F-statistic is greater than Pearson's upper bound value at the 5% level of significance, it is concluded that there is a long-term relationship between the variables "gdp", "private" and "public" (see Table 3).

Table 3: Results of Boundary Test

Dependent Variable	"gdp"	
F-Statistic	4.4555	
Critical Values (k = 2)		
	Lower Bound	Upper Bound
5%	3.10	3.87

Since the co-integration relation is determined between the variables, the ARDL model is established in order to determine the long- and short-term relationships.

5 Autoregressive Distributed Lag model

Long- and short-term relationships between variables are determined by establishing the ARDL model. The model used to investigate the long-term relationship is ARDL (3,1,0). Only long-term coefficients are included in the model, and the significance of the coefficients is examined. The results obtained from the model are presented in Table 4.

Table 4: Results of ARDL (3,1,0) Model

Variables	Coefficient	t-Statistic	Probability
gdp(−1)	0.949938	6.430758	0.0000
gdp(−2)	−0.532116	−2.649800	0.0124
gdp(−3)	0.425398	3.276934	0.0025
private	0.269884	4.990848	0.0000
private(−1)	−0.197426	−3.534965	0.0013
public	0.045822	1.295753	0.2043
c	0.934485	1.309461	0.1997

Long-term coefficients were calculated by considering ARDL (3,1,0) model. Long-term coefficients are presented in Table 5. When the long-term results of ARDL are examined, there is a statistically significant relation between "private" and "gdp" as well as between "public" and "gdp". In the long term, the 1% increase in the "private" variable causes an increase of 0.48% in "gdp". The 1% increase in the "public" variable leads to an increase of 0.31% in "gdp".

Table 5: Long-Term Coefficients of ARDL (3,1,0) Model

Variables	Coefficient	t-Statistic	Probability
private	0.480080	2.357786	0.0249
public	0.312295	2.741650	0.0101
c	5.410177	2.230379	0.0331

After a long-term relationship is established, short-run relationships are examined by establishing an error correction model based on the ARDL (3,1,0) model. The results of error correction model are presented in Table 6. According to the results, the fact that the short-term error coefficient (−0.1602) is between −1 and 0 and statistically significant (Probability = 0.0001) indicates that the error correction model works. This parameter forces the variables closer to the long-term equilibrium value. Since the error-inducing parameter is meaningful, there is a causal relationship between the variables.

Table 6: Error Correction Model Based on ARDL (3,1,0) Model

Variables	Coefficient	t-Statistic	Probability
d(gdp(−1))	0.1018	0.1278	0.4317
d(gdp(−2))	−0.4178	0.1218	0.0017
d(private)	0.2722	0.0475	0.0000
d(public)	0.0320	0.0385	0.4115
ECT(−1)	−0.1602	0.0365	0.0001

6 Evaluation of empirical findings

As a result of the econometric analysis on the relationship between private investment expenditures and public investment expenditures with the ARDL model,
the existence of a long-term relationship between variables is detected by the fact
that the calculated F-statistic is greater than the critical value. When the long-term
coefficients are examined, it is seen that the independent variables are statistically
significant at the 5% significance level, the 1% increase in the private investment
expenditures will lead to a 0.48% increase in the long-term GDP, and the 1%
increase in the public investment expenditures will lead to an increase of 0.31%
in the GDP in the long run.

After determining the long-term relationships, the short-term coefficients are
calculated by the error correction model. The fact that the error correction term is
between 0 and −1 and statistically significant at the 5% significance level indicates
the validity of the established model. The error correction coefficient indicates
that 16% of the deviations from the long-term equilibrium are corrected every
quarter. When short-term coefficients are examined, it is determined that the 1%
increase in private investment expenditures will cause the GDP to increase by
0.27% in the short term, while the public investment expenditures do not have
statistically significant effect on the GDP in the short term.

7 Conclusion

Increasing public investment spending plays a very important role both in achieving economic growth target and in making economic growth sustainable. Due to
the increase in public investments, the demand for funds increases, and in this
case the amount of funds required for private investment expenditures decreases
or the interest rates increase due to the demand for increased fund usage of the
public sector. Therefore, private investment expenditures decrease due to the increase of the costs of investments. The effects of public investment expenditures
and private investment expenditures on GDP were examined, both crowding-out

and crowding-in effects were investigated, and it was tried to find out which of the investment expenditures was more effective in Turkey for the period of 2006:Q1 to 2016:Q2. Given the tight implementation of fiscal discipline practices in the public sector since 2002 in Turkey and the fact that there had been series of problems on public finance in the previous periods, this study reveals the financial implications of current public fiscal policy implementations.

The findings of the econometric analysis indicate that there is a long-term relationship between public investment expenditures and private investment expenditures, which points out that there is a crowding in between public investment expenditures and private investment expenditures. When we look at long- and short-term coefficients, it shows that private investment expenditures are more effective than GDP in terms of public investment expenditures. The fact that private investment expenditures are more effective on the GDP is a strong indication of the crowding-in effect of public investment expenditures and a strong indication of nonexistence of crowding-out effect of public investment expenditures.

The empirical fact of this study "the effect of private investment expenditures on GDP is higher than public investment expenditures" should be considered in the formulation of public fiscal policies. Applying policies that will not create crowding out and giving necessary support to private investment expenditures will provide significant contributions to economic growth and development.

References

Altunç, Ö. F. and Şentürk, B. (2010). "Türkiye'de Özel Yatırımlar ve Kamu Yatırımları Arasındaki İlişkinin Ampirik Analizi: Sınır Testi Yaklaşımı". *Maliye Dergisi*, 158, 531–546.

Başar, S., Polat, O. and Oltulular, S. (2011). "Crowding Out Effect of Government Spending on Private Investments in Turkey: A Cointegration Analysis". *Kafkas Üniversitesi Sosyal Bilimler Enstitüsü Dergisi*, 8, 11–20.

Başar, S. and Temurlenk, M. S. (2007). "Investigating Crowding-Out Effect of Government Spending for Turkey: A Structural VAR Approach". *Atatürk Üniversitesi İktisadi ve İdari Bilimler Dergisi*, 21(2), 95–104.

Çelik, N. (2016). "Yapısal Kırılmalar Altında Kamu-Özel Kesim Yatırım Harcamaları İlişkisi". *Yönetim ve Ekonomi Dergisi*, 23(4), 653–669.

Cural, M., Eriçok, R. E. and Yılancı, V. (2012). "Türkiye'de Kamu Yatırımlarının Özel Sektör Yatırımları Üzerindeki Etkisi: 1970–2009". *Anadolu Üniversitesi Sosyal Bilimler Dergisi*, 12(1), 73–88.

Engle, F. and Granger, C.W.J. (1987). "Co-Integration and Error Correction: Representation, Estimation, and Testing". *Econometrica*, 55(2), 251–276.

Günaydın, I. (2006). "Türkiye'de Kamu ve Özel Yatırımlar Arasındaki İlişki: Ampirik Bir Analiz". *Atatürk Üniversitesi İktisadi ve İdari Bilimler Dergisi*, 20(1): 177–195.

Johansen, S. (1988). "Statistical Analysis of Cointegration Vectors". *Journal of Economic Dynamics and Control*, 12(3), 231–254.

Johansen, S. and Juselius, K. (1990). "Maximum Likelihood Estimation and Inference on Cointegration– with Applications to the Demand for Money". *Oxford Bulletin of Economics and Statistics*, 52(2), 169–210.

Kıran, B. and Güriş, B. (2011). "Türkiye'de Ticari Ve Finansal Dışaaçıklığın Büyümeye Etkisi: 1992–2006 Dönemi Üzerine Bir İnceleme". *Anadolu Üniversitesi Sosyal Bilimler Dergisi*, 11(2), 69–80.

Kuştepeli, Y. (2005). "Effectiveness of Fiscal Spending: Crowding-Out and/or Crowding-In?". *Yönetim ve Ekonomi*, 12(1), 185–192.

Pesaran, M. H., Shin, Y. and Smith, R. J. (2001). "Bounds Testing Approaches to the Analysis of Level Relationships". *Journal of Applied Econometrics*, 16(3), 289–326.

Şen, H. and Kaya, A. (2014). "Crowding-Out or Crowding-In? Analyzing the Effects of Government Spending on Private Investment in Turkey". *Panoeconomicus*, 6, 631–651.

Tülümce, S. Y. and Buyrukoğlu, S. (2013). "Türkiye'de Kamu ve Özel Yatırımlar Arasındaki İlişkinin Ampirik Analizi: Dışlama Etkisi (1980–2010)". *Mali Çözüm Dergisi*, 119, 59–78.

Yavuz, N. Ç. (2005). "Türkiye'de Kamu Harcamalarının Özel Sektör Yatırım Harcamalarını Dışlama Etkisinin Testi (1980–2003)". *Marmara Üniversitesi, İİBF Dergisi*, 20(1), 269–284.

Yılancı, V. and Aydın, M. (2016). "Testing of the Crowding Out Effect for Turkey". *Global Journal on Humanities and Social Science*, 4, 216–220.

Guner Tuncer, Ersin Nail Sagdic, and Fazli Yildiz

The Topography of Social Security and Social Solidarity Expenditures in Turkey

1 Introduction

The geography of public finance deals with the geographical distribution of public expenditure, the regional diversity of the income burdens, and the connection of these two with each other. It focuses on suppliers, resources, and goods in the supply chain of public goods. There are three main objectives of public finance geography. The first objective is to determine whether there are different financial motives; the second, to identify the effects of geographical factors; and the third, to make policy recommendations to increase efficiency (Bennett, 1980). Knowledge of geographical patterns of regional financial capability and financial needs is a prerequisite for understanding the differences of public service provision and for evaluating strategies to combat social and economic problems caused by financial inequality in a region (Pacione, 2001).

The aim of this study is to analyze the public expenditure of the central government on the social security and social solidarity services in Turkey from the point of view of the geography of public finance. In this context, the study is centered on whether public finance geography has different financial patterns or not. Bennett (1980), Johnston (1980), Mas Ivars et al. (2003), McLean and McMillan (2003), Psycharis (2008), Monastiriotis and Psycharis (2009), Blažek and Mačešková (2010), and Lincaru et al. (2015) have examined the geographical motives of public expenditures in various countries. Studies of Sağbaş (2000), Saruç et al. (2007), Kaya (2009), Sağbaş and Kaya (2009), Dökmen and Tekbaş (2011), and Tuncer et al. (2015) are the main studies on Turkey in this area. Data and methodology, geographical visualizations, cartogram, and conclusion are provided in the following sections.

2 Data and methodology

After achieving political stability in 2002, the highest economic growth was witnessed in 2011 by 11.1% and the lowest economic growth (shrink) was observed in 2009 by–4.7% (TUIK, 2016). That is why, years of 2009 and 2011 are considered for analysis in the study. The data on social security and social solidarity expenditures were obtained from the General Directorate of Public Accounts of the Ministry of Finance. In the study, per capita values are calculated by dividing the data of the district by the population of the district.

Social security and social solidarity expenditures can be classified as invalidity pension, old-age pension, family and children, unemployment, housing assistance, widows' and orphans' pensions (survivorship), and research and development expenditures on the social security and social assistance (BUMKO, 2016). In the central government budget, social security and social solidarity expenditures consist of invalidity assistance services, old-age assistance services, family and child assistance services, services provided to those without social security, and unclassified social security and social assistance services. The data are provided on provincial bases. There are 81 provinces in Turkey. There are also data called the central data that consist of the amounts paid for the central accounting units of the ministries. Central data are not included in the analysis because they do not have a geographical location.

Public expenditures and gross domestic product (GDP) figures for 2009 and 2011 are as follows: Public expenditures made from central government budget were realized as approximately 314 billion TL in 2011 whereas they were approximately 268 billion TL in 2009. The 2009 GDP was approximately 999 billion TL whereas it was 1,394 billion TL in 2011. The central government budget public spending and GDP ratio was about 23% in 2011 whereas it was about 27% in 2009. Social security and social solidarity expenditures were realized as approximately 60 billion TL in 2011 whereas they were approximately 56 billion TL in 2009. The share of social security and social solidarity expenditures in public expenditures of the central government budget was approximately 21% in 2009 and 19% in 2011.

Geographic visualizations (geovisualizations) as well as cartograms and extreme positions have been presented in order to determine whether social security and social solidarity expenditures have different financial patterns. A cartogram is a geographic visualization method used for specifying outlier regions. Spatial units are represented in a circle. The area of the circle is presented in proportion to the value of the selected variable (Anselin, 2005). Analyses were performed using the GeoDa program.

3 Geographic visualizations and cartogram

The contents of the variables to be considered in the study are given below. The contents of each classification part of social security and social solidarity expenditures are as follows (BUMKO, 2016):

> Invalidity Benefit Expenditures: Expenditures to cover the loss of earnings resulting from the temporary absence of persons from work due to illness or injury, other than expenses

related to health services. These also include services provided by the Administration for Disabled Persons and payments for invalidity pensions, early retirement benefits, care payments, and social protection payments for disabled people under the age of retirement due to the loss of working power.

Old-Age Expenditures: These cover expenditures on nursing homes or elderly shelters to provide social protection for elderly people, spending on improving the occupational and social rehabilitation of the elderly, and payments on aged care.

Family and Child Benefit Expenditures: Payments to families needing care, pregnancy and childbirth allowances, maternity leave allowances, and payments for children (care, food, orphanages, etc.).

Expenditures Provided to Those without Social Security: These include payments to groups that are at risk of social exclusion (poor, immigrants, refugees, alcohol and drug addicts, etc.).

Unclassified Social Security and Social Solidarity Expenditures: Food, materials, and so on for the people affected by natural disasters, social protection benefits, and payments for other social protection services not included in the abovementioned categories.

In the analysis, first, quantile maps of subcategories of social security and social solidarity expenditures were created. As the colors evolve from the open to the dark, they show that districts have high values in the variant discussed.

It can be observed in Figure 1 that Invalidity Benefit Expenditures are intensified in Black Sea, Eastern Anatolia, and Southeast Anatolia regions.

Figure 1: Quantile map of Invalidity Benefit Expenditures

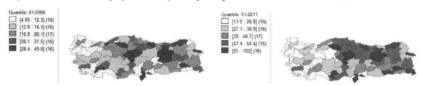

When Old-Age Expenditures are examined in Figure 2. It can be said that expenditures are concentrated on the western regions of Turkey in 2009, whereas this density decreased partly in 2011.

Figure 2: Quantile map of Old-Age Expenditures

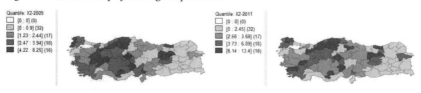

A significant regional concentration in Family and Child Benefit Expenditures is not observed in both 2009 and 2011, as shown in Figure 3. However, the Mediterranean and Southeastern Anatolian regions have lower values than other regions.

Figure 3: Quantile map of Family and Child Benefit Expenditures

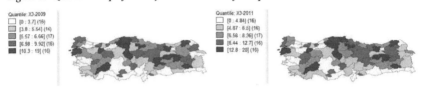

When the Expenditures Provided to Those without Social Security are examined, it can be observed in Figure 4 that the values in the Eastern Black Sea and East Anatolia regions in 2009 and 2011 are lower than those in other regions.

Figure 4: Quantile map of Expenditures Provided to Those without Social Security

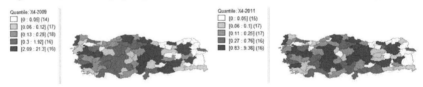

Unclassified Social Security and Social Solidarity Expenditures had a significant concentration in Eastern Black Sea and Eastern Anatolia regions in 2009, but the level of this concentration decreased in 2011 (see Figure 5).

Figure 5: Quantile map of Unclassified Social Security and Social Solidarity Expenditures

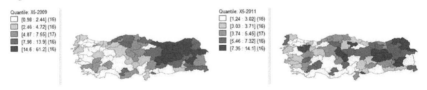

When we examine the cartograms of the Invalidity Benefit Expenditures, it can be noticed that there are three upper outlier regions, namely Artvin, Nevşehir, and Rize, in 2009 whereas the number of upper outlier regions are two (Artvin and Nevşehir) in 2011 (see Figure 6).

Figure 6: Cartogram of Invalidity Benefit Expenditures

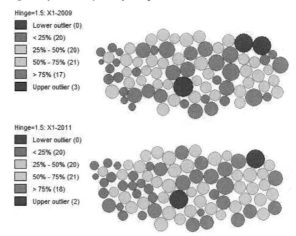

When we examined the cartogram of the Old-Age Expenditures in Figure 7, any upper outlier region can't be detected in 2009. However, Bolu and Yalova are detected as upper outlier regions in 2011.

Figure 7: Cartogram of Old-Age Expenditures

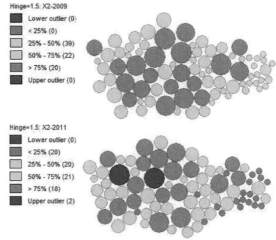

When we examined the cartograms of the Family and Child Benefit Expenditures, it can be observed in Figure 8 that there are seven provinces in the upper outlier in 2009. These are Artvin, Bilecik, Bingöl, Çankırı Gümüşhane, Kırşehir, and Tunceli. There is not any upper outlier region in 2011.

Figure 8: Cartogram of Family and Child Benefit Expenditures

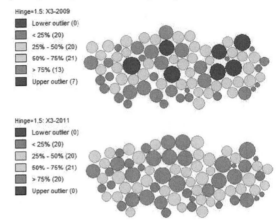

According to the 2009 cartogram of the Expenditures Provided to Those without Social Security, there are nine outlier regions, namely, Bitlis, Diyarbakır, Edirne, Erzurum, Kastamonu, Kütahya, Malatya, Tokat, and Trabzon. It can be noticed in Figure 9 that the number of outlier regions increased to 10 in 2011: Bitlis, Diyarbakir, Edirne, Erzurum, Kastamonu, Kütahya, Malatya, Sivas, Tokat, and Trabzon.

Figure 9: Cartogram of Expenditures Provided to Those without Social Security

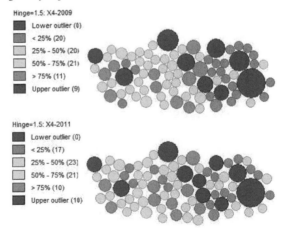

According to the cartograms of the Unclassified Social Security and Social Solidarity Expenditures, the number of outlier regions in 2009 is seven. These regions are Ağrı, Bingöl, Bitlis, Erzurum, Giresun, Ordu, and Tunceli. In 2011, the number of outlier regions decreased to three: Bitlis, Kars, and Tunceli (see Figure 10).

Figure 10: Cartogram of Unclassified Social Security and Social Solidarity Expenditures

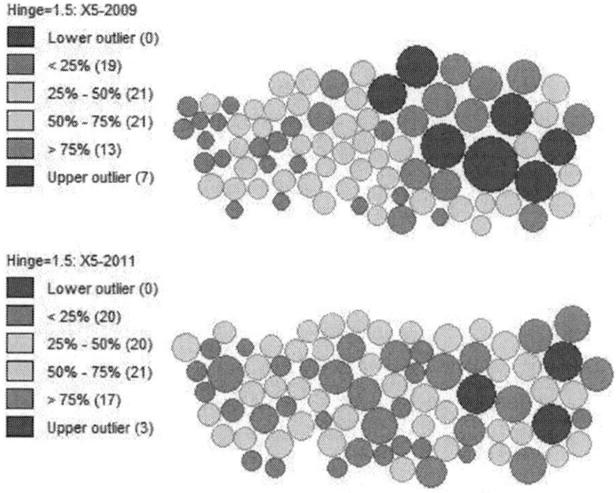

4 Conclusion

Nowadays, it is widely accepted that geographical assessments should be made for economic and financial events. Studies carried out in this area may be an important input for policy makers to make regional assessments.

In this study, the public expenditure of the central government on the social security and social solidarity services is analyzed from the regional point of view as such financial patterns for 81 provinces of Turkey are presented. This assessment was carried out for the years 2009 and 2011, the lowest and highest years of economic growth after 2002. Financial patterns are detected by geographical visualizations and cartograms.

It is observed that the regional concentration of Invalidity Benefit Expenditures has increased in 2011 compared to 2009. In the Old-Age Expenditures, the regional concentration has partly decreased. A significant regional concentration in the Family and Child Benefit Expenditures has not been observed both in 2009 and in 2011. Regarding the Expenditures Provided to Those without Social Security, the values of the Eastern Black Sea and Eastern Anatolia regions were lower than those of other regions in both 2009 and 2011. The concentration level in some regions has decreased in the Unclassified Social Security and Social Solidarity Expenditures.

Various results were also obtained in the study through cartograms. Lower outliers have not been observed in all cartograms. In the Invalidity Benefit Expenditures, Artvin, Nevşehir, and Rize were upper outlier regions in 2009, whereas Artvin and Nevşehir were the upper outlier regions in 2011. In 2009, there were no upper outliers in the Old-Age Expenditures, but in 2011 Bolu and Yalova were the outlier regions. Artvin, Bilecik, Bingöl, Çankırı Gümüşhane, Kırşehir, and Tunceli were outliers in 2009 in the Family and Child Benefit Expenditures, but in 2011 there were no outliers. In 2009, Bitlis, Diyarbakir, Kütahya, Malatya, Kastamonu, Kütahya, Malatya, Tokat, and Trabzon were outliers in the Expenditures Provided to Those without Social Security, whereas Bitlis, Diyarbakır, Edirne, Erzurum, Kastamonu, Kütahya, Malatya, Tokat, and Trabzon were outliers in 2011. In 2009, Ağrı, Bingöl, Bitlis, Erzurum, Giresun, Ordu, and Tunceli were the upper outlier regions in the Unclassified Social Security and Social Solidarity Expenditures whereas Bitlis, Kars, and Tunceli were the upper outliers in 2011.

With this study, an attempt has been made to contribute to the field of public finance geography by making an evaluation for social security and social solidarity expenditures, which are important public spending in Turkey. The study focuses on the purpose of determining whether there are different geographical financial patterns. The obtained financial patterns as a result of this study can be the basis for policy makers and researchers who can conduct further research.

References

Anselin, L. (2005). Exploring Spatial Data with GeoDa: A Workbook. Center for Spatially Integrated Social Science, Urbana, IL.

Bennett, R. J. (1980). The Geography of Public Finance Welfare under Fiscal Federalism and Local Government Finance. Methuen, New York.

Blažek, J. and Macešková, M. (2010). "Regional Analysis of Public Capital Expenditure: To Which Regions Is Public Capital Expenditure Channelled–to 'Rich' or to 'Poor' Ones?". Regional Studies, 44(6), 679–696.

BUMKO Bütçe ve Mali Kontrol Genel Müdürlüğü. (2016). 2017–2019 Dönemi Bütçe Çağrısı ve Bütçe Hazırlama Rehberi. http://www.bumko.gov.tr/Eklenti/10215,20172019butcecagrisi.pdf?0, Access Date: 21.12.2016.

Dökmen, G. and Tekbaş, A. (2011). "Türkiye'de Kamu Harcamaları ve Kamu Gelirlerinin Bölgesel Analizi". İstanbul Üniversitesi İktisat Fakültesi Maliye Araştırma Merkezi Konferansları, 56 Seri 2, 1–26.

Johnston R.J. (1980). The Geography of Federal Spending in the USA. John Wiley, New York.

Kaya, A. (2009). Türkiye'de Bölgesel Net Mali Yansıma. T.C. Maliye Bakanlığı Strateji Geliştirme Başkanlığı, Ankara.

Lincaru, C., Pirciog, S., Ciucă, V., Atanasiu, D. and Chiriac, B. (2015). "A Territorial Profile of Public Expenditures at LAU 2 Level, for 2007–2013 Period in Romania". The USV Annals of Economics and Public Administration, 15(1(21)), 204–213.

Mas Ivars, M., Pérez García, F. and Uriel Jiménez, E. (2003). El Stock de Capital en España su Distribución Territorial. Fundación BBVA, Bilbao.

McLean, I. and McMillan, A. (2003). "The Distribution of Public Expenditure across the UK Regions". Fiscal Studies, 24(1): 45–71.

Monastiriotis, V. and Psycharis, Y. (2009). Types of Public Investment and the Regions: A Spatial Economic Analysis of Government Spending on Greek Prefectures over the Period 1976–2005. III World Conference of Spatial Econometrics, 8–10 July, University of Barcelona, Spain (unpublished).

Pacione, M. (2001). "Geography of Public Finance: Planning for Fiscal Equity in a Metropolitan Region". Progress in Planning, 56(1): 1–59.

Psycharis, Y. (2008). Public Spending Patterns: The Regional Allocation of Public Investment in Greece by Political Period. GreeSE Paper 14, London School of Economics and Political Science.

Sağbaş, I. (2000). The Impact of Population Changes on Local Expenditures in Turkey. Yapı Kredi Economic Review, 11(1): 23–44.

Sağbaş, I. and Kaya, A. (2009). Türkiye'de Kamu Harcamalarının Bölgesel Dağılımının Analizi: Mekansal Ekonometri Yaklaşımı. 24. Türkiye Maliye Sempozyumu, Antalya, 19–23 Mayıs, 63–88.

Saruç, N. T., Sagbas, I. and Cigerci, I. (2007). The Geographical Distribution of Public Expenditures and Tax Revenues in the Turkish Case: A Convergence Analysis. Selected Proceedings of the Third International Conference on Business, Management and Economics, 13–17 June, Cesme-Izmir.

TUIK (2016). National Accounts Statistics. Turkish Statistical Institute, Ankara.

Tuncer, G., Yıldız, F. and Celebioglu, F. (2015). Kamu Maliyesi Coğrafyası. Academia Yayınevi, Kütahya.

Esin Benhür Aktürk

Ethical Leadership

1 Introduction

Conflicts in the human relations and the complexity of the social environment make tasks of leaders difficult and charge new tasks to the leaders in our time. These role models/leaders should have a system of beliefs and ethical values. Actions and achievements in the enterprise should be developed around this system. The leader needs to apply and learn leadership, fulfill his/her responsibilities, and make his/her decisions based on moral values. The responsibility to create an ethical climate within a firm adds new dimensions to the leadership approach. These new dimensions reveal the ethical leadership roles of the person who manages the firm. At a time full of unethical acts and scandals, they must be role models by fulfilling ethical leadership roles that demonstrate appropriate ethical principles to the staff.

Ethical leaders are seen as principled and honest decision-makers who are working hard to bring society and people in better position. Ethical leaders are people who know how to act ethically in their professional and personal lives. Some researchers refer to ethical leadership as ethics directors.

2 Leadership

Leadership is a concept that emerges regardless of culture, religion, or life structure. The concept of leadership is seen in every society. Although the word "leader" dates back to the 1300s, the concept of leadership has emerged as a new concept in the 19th century. Leadership means guidance and direction (Sertoğlu, 2010).

Leadership is to manage and motivate staff in a good way in order to achieve business success and to establish and provide trust, honesty, openness, and respect for the people in the business administration. The so-called leader is followed by the others; followers follow the leader willingly and lovingly. Leaders are sentimental. Followers respect and believe in them. The essence of leadership is charisma. Humility and sacrifice are qualities that are at the core of leadership (Kıngır and Şahin, 2005: 409).

The leader is the person who has the ability to lead the society, gives energy to the society with his/her work, creates a great synergy around him/her, and hence contributes to the society to reach its goals. The leader not only leads and teaches but also is a creative person who senses the needs and requirements of people who lead and organize them to reach these needs. Leadership is the skill of a person that influences the behavior and movement of people in the direction of specific goals. The basis for leadership is the ability of one person to influence others (Durmuş, 2015:12).

The legitimacy of a dishonest leader can be questioned because individual honesty must be a part of a leader, and a dishonest leader will not find anyone who pursues him/her. Forward vision, intelligence, courage, and characteristics such as honesty and accuracy prove the existence of leadership. Many studies focus on the qualities that the leader should have. The qualities of leadership are given in Table 1.

Table 1: Leadership Features

Ability to grasp the situation at a glance	Fast and accurate judgment ability	Scientific management knowledge and skill
Common sense	Ability to adapt to situation	Rigor in the task
Standing out capacity against unexpected events	Ability to create and use opportunities	The ability to ensure the physical and spiritual well-being of lower management
Spiritual courage	Material courage	Simple attitude
Risk resistance capacity	Body strength	Strong logic
Ability to apply innovations	Ability to make deal decisions	Ability to adapt to changes
Diligence	Intuition	Searcher
Ability to practice what he/she thinks	Knowledge and application skills at tactical, operational, and strategic level	The ability to motivate both himself/herself and lower management effectively
Calmness	Broad and logical imagination	Ability to distribute justice
Adventurer tendency	Mind strength	Creativity

Source: Sertoğlu (2010:57).

In general, we can talk about the existence of leadership in somewhere if people are affected by a single person in order to reach their goals. Leadership is related to the ability to influence. A person who does not have the power to influence can be a head or manager of a group. However, he/she must have the ability to influence others in order to become the leader of the group. Leadership is a process that requires the leader to perceive and overcome changes happening around him/her. The leader is the person who decides what to do against the changes (Yıldırım, 2010: 1).

3 Types of leadership

There is not a single definition of leadership. The studies on the leadership reveal the following leadership types.

3.1 Visionary leadership

The visionary leader is the person who explains the general situation and problems that help to develop ideas and thoughts to the followers. The visionary leader has impressive qualities. The visionary leader expresses the promising solutions for social necessities. Their vision emerges in light of past experiences, fundamental values, present possibilities, and cultural traditions. In order to unite their followers, visionary leaders should have thinking power, analyze the information very successfully, and come up with new ideas to combat against problems (Doğan, 2016).

3.2 Shared leadership

In the case of shared leadership, leadership responsibility is distributed among the members of group, team, or organization. In this leadership, every member of organization is responsible for leadership. Leadership comes up as a result of regular interactions and cooperation of team members. This leadership is a collaborative and relational leadership process in which responsibilities and tasks are shared. Therefore, leadership is carried out by more than one person instead of a single person in classic leadership. The success is not the success of a particular person but the success of the team. This leadership stems from four factors: nontransferable accountability based on results and defined roles, equality that includes the definition of the contributions of each individual, a partnership that involves mutual respect and trust between individuals, and personal commitment. In shared leadership, team members participate in decision-making and goal setting and accept responsibility as a result of these decisions. In this sense, the existing autonomy and accountability are distributed among all members of the organization (Bostancı, 2012: 1620).

3.3 Transformational leadership

Power is distributed in this type of leadership because leaders consider leadership as something that can be distributed. Transformational leaders develop conscious and collaborative action and behavior by identifying their own values and the values of the rest of the organization that will shape their decisions and actions. They observe the values of customers, sellers, shareholders, and the community. Transformational leaders entice their followers toward a vision rather than concrete objectives. Transformational leaders have a long-term vision, aiming to bring out all the skills and abilities of the lower management and raise their confidence and productivity (Tabak et al., 2009).

3.4 Charismatic leadership

The charismatic leadership influences and directs organizations, groups, and people with individual qualities such as persuasiveness, high self-confidence, and oratory power. Charismatic leader influences, motivates, and directs organizations and people with their individual qualities such as persuasiveness and high self-confidence. These leaders are the people who are trusted, believed, and taken as an example. At the same time, charismatic leaders attach importance and take account of the problems and demands of the members of the organization. They stimulate the members of the organization for the aims of the organization (Bulut, 2012).

3.5 Authentic leadership

In this type of leadership, the personal idea and thoughts of the leader and the behavior and goals of the organization must be harmonious. Followers trust and respect the charismatic leaders. Authentic leaders also adhere and pay attention to ethical principles. The authentic leader is reliable, honest, harmonious, and natural leader (Çelik, 2015: 296).

3.6 Servant leadership

The concept of servant leadership was first proposed by Robert K. Greeleaf in 1970 in his essay named "The Servant as Leader." The priority of this kind of leadership is to "serve" the followers. The servant leader puts the needs and demands of his followers over his/her own demands and requirements. The servant leader doesn't seek power, fame, or any other personal purpose. The servant leader thinks how his/her decisions will affect his/her followers. That is why he/she is sensitive. This type of leadership is not a taught method, but a result of natural feeling (Koçel, 2015: 685).

In servant leadership, the leader places the prosperity and happiness of followers in high regard. This behavior includes charismatic and transformational leadership qualities. While these leaders keep the achievements of those who follow him/her in the foreground, they do not overlook the happiness of humankind and society as well. They follow the win–win strategy (Bektaş, 2016: 49).

3.7 Cultural leadership

Cultural leadership aims to shape, protect, change, and integrate the structure of organization.

Existing culture is either preserved or maintained, or a new culture is being created (Yılmaz, 2006). The environment determines the type of leadership. Autocratic cultural environment creates autocratic leadership, whereas democratic and participatory cultural environments give a way to other types of leaderships compatible with them. The leader not only is influenced by the cultural environment but also influences the cultural environment. The starting point of interaction is culture (Erçetin, 2000: 18).

3.8 Emotional intelligence leadership

Emotional intelligence is a very important concept that comes not from birth but from experience. The main reason behind the failure of genius people in the society is the lack of emotional intelligence. With the help of emotional intelligence, a person can better recognize himself/herself, progress toward his/her goals in a determined manner, and share his/her emotions and feelings more sincerely with the rest of the people. In this way, he/she becomes more successful in family, business, and society. Managers with emotional intelligence leadership can better understand their staff, leverage emotions of their staff, and bring in a variety of attitudes and values to their staff (Goleman, 2016: 438).

4 The concept of ethical leadership

Ethical leadership is a concept that reveals that a moral issue is false or correct. It is necessary for the leaders to instill confidence in the communities in order to influence the mass of people and continue to be impressed for a long time. The subject of ethical leadership includes the concept of ethical leadership, its characteristics, and its importance for staff, firm, and society. The existence of ethical rules at the basis of a firm can prevent stress between employers, managers, and staff. The ethical leadership is the process of harmony of the ethical values with leadership ability. The ethical leader must put forth an attitude by accepting people's personal differences and their beliefs in a nonprejudicial manner. The ability of ethical leaders involves deciding which principles are compatible with ethical principles and creating a system model relevant to moral values. The ethical leader is the one who increases the energy of the institution, enables the firm to grow, and takes up a position explicitly. When establishing their team, it is extremely important for ethical leaders to give the opportunity to those who both give importance to ethical values and fulfill the aims of the institution (Akdoğan, 2016: 2). Other definitions of the concept of ethics are as follows:

- Ethics is the description of the wrong and right criteria for today and the past (Yatkın, 2013: 3).
- Ethics is a philosophy that investigates moral and ethical relationships, behavioral views, and forms of people (Yatkın, 2013: 3).
- Ethics, in the general sense, is related to morally wrong–right or bad–good (Sakarya and Kara, 2010: 57).
- Ethics is all the mental activities related to deciding on wrong and right, negotiating, and moving the capacity to imagine to the higher point (Yüksel, 2005: 42).
- Ethics refers to the behavior of the individual in moral terms (Kaplan, 2009: 244).
- Ethics is a philosophical science that investigates the values that affect the relationships, the qualities and basis of morally bad–good or wrong–right behaviors (İşgüden and Çabuk, 2006).

Ethical leaders have constructed the behavior so that followers and stakeholders can rely on it. Instead of marginalization and alienation, it provides a sense of partnership that promotes embracing and inclusion. Leaders serve as role models for lower management about ethically acceptable movements and how to solve and manage ethical and other problems. It is one of the leaders' roles to punish certain pattern behaviors and reward others to give personal and situational information about what is ethical.

Ethical leaders are honest, compassionate, and principled people who make fair and balanced decisions. Ethical leaders often help developing behavior of their followers by talking about ethics, creating ethical standards, rewarding ethical behaviors, and punishing unethical behaviors. Ethical leaders not only talk about ethical values but also become proactive role models for ethical conduct and do what they say (Kesimli, 2013: 5).

It is inevitable that there will be some problems everywhere where there is individual competition and individual relations in the advanced level. These problems bring about the behavior of what is "ethical" and not "ethical." Problems related to ethics have brought about the concept of ethical behavior. Leaders are always at the forefront with behaviors they have displayed as managers of ethical issues. Integrating skills and competencies into ethical behavior is a necessity in ethical leadership. Another element that needs to be emphasized is that leaders should firmly believe in the behaviors that should be applied by analyzing the corporate vision well. These attitudes are preconditional for prospective ethical leaders. The ethical leader is expected to have a "character" and "rightness"-based focus and respect the rights of employees (Bilgen, 2014: 4).

5 Conclusion

The term ethics derives from ancient Greek word "Ethos," meaning custom, habit, and morality. In the course of time, the studies and intellectual activities that try to find and understand the right and the good have led to the emergence of ethical philosophy that has become a discipline with universal value. The theory of moral principles, which criticizes the way of life of the society and sets new life criteria in order to create an ideal way of life by putting alternative achievements instead of existing achievements, is expressed as "ethics."

The leader encourages any kind of intraorganizational actions that motivate the movements of groups, help followers to reach a common goal, and express his/her experiences. Ethical leader is the person who decides on according to ethical principles, behave in an ethical way in his/her private and working life, is fair, contributes and adds value to people, and can influence the ethical status of the employees they lead (Bulut, 2012: 22).

Ethical leadership is not considered separately in leadership types. The fact that the leader has ethical values or complies with ethical values does not cause him/her to have a different profile of leadership. In fact, the situation explained here is more internal. Examination of the dependence of an individual's leadership on ethical criteria can be perceived as the ethical dimension of leadership. Although the leadership position is at the top of the hierarchy within the group, behaviors, attitudes, and the ethical understandings of the leader are similar to those of group. Thus, it is not expected that behaviors, attitudes, and the ethical understandings of the leader are completely free from those of group.

References

Akdoğan, S. (2016). Etik Liderlik Davranışlarının Örgütsel Performansa Etkileri. İstanbul: T.C. İstanbul Gelişim Üniversitesi Sosyal Bilimler Enstitüsü.

Bektaş, Ç. (2016). Liderlik Yaklaşımları ve Modern Liderden Beklentiler. Selçuk Üniversitesi Akşehir Meslek Yüksekokulu Sosyal Bilimler Dergisi, 2(7), 44–53.

Bilgen, A. (2014). "Çalışanların Etik Liderlik ve Etik İklim Algılamalarının Örgütsel Bağlılıklarına Etkisi: Özel ve Kamu Sektöründe Karşılaştırmalı Bir Uygulama", Yayınlanmamış Yüksek Lisans Tezi, Bahçeşehir Üniversitesi, Sosyal Bilimler Enstitüsü, İstanbul.

Bostancı, A. B. (2012). Paylaşılan Liderlik Algısı Ölçeği'nin Türkçe Uyarlaması. International Journal of Human Sciences, 9(2), 1619–1632.

Bulut, H. (2012). Etik Liderliğin ve Etik İklimin Çalıçanların Örgütsel Bağlılığına ve İş Performanslarına Etkisi. Kocaeli: Gebze Yüksek Teknoloji Enstitüsü Sosyal Bilimler Enstitüsü.

Çelik, V. (2015). Eğitimsel Liderlik. Ankara: Pegem Yayıncılık.

Doğan, S. (2016). Eğitim yönetiminde liderlik: Teori araştırma ve uygulama. Ankara: Pegem Akademi.

Durmuş, M. (2015). Kamu Kurumu Yöneticilerinin Etik Liderlik Davranışı Gösterme Düzeylerinin Çalışan Algısı Yönüyle İncelenmesi: Kocaeli Üniversitesi Örneği. Kocaeli: T.C. Kocaeli Üniversitesi Sosyal Bilimler Enstütüsü.

Erçetin, Ş. (2000). Lider Sarmalında Vizyon. Ankara: Nobel Yayın Dağıtım.

Goleman, D. (2016). Duygusal Zekâ. İstanbul: Varlık Yayınları.

İşgüden, B., Çabuk, A. (2006). Meslek Etiği ve Meslek Etiğinin Meslek Yaşamı Üzerindeki Etkileri. Balıkesir Üniversitesi Sosyal Bilimler Enstitüsü Dergisi, 9(16), 32.

Kaplan, Ç. (2009). Kamu Yönetiminde Etik ve Kamu Çalışanlarının Etik Kavramını Algılayışları. Süleyman Demirel Üniversitesi İİBF Dergisi, 14(3), 244.

Kesimli, İ. (2013). Liderlik Davranış Türleri. Kırklareli Üniversitesi İktisadi ve İdari Bilimler Fakültesi Dergisi, 2(1), 1–10.

Kıngır, S., Şahin, M. (2005). Örgütsel Davranış Boyutlarından Seçmeler içinde: Yönetici ve Liderlik. Ankara: Nobel Yayın.

Koçel, T. (2015). İşletme Yöneticiliği. İstanbul: Beta Yayım A.Ş.

Sakarya, Ş., Kara, S. (2010). Türkiye'de Muhasebe Meslek Etiğine Yönelik Düzenlemeler ve Meslek Mensupları Tarafından Algılanması Üzerine Bir Alan Araştırması. KMÜ Sosyal ve Ekonomik Araştırmalar Dergisi, 12(18), 57.

Sertoğlu, R. (2010). Stratejik Liderlik. İstanbul: Etap Yayınevi.

Tabak, A., Sığrı, Ü., Eroğlu, A., Hazır, K. (2009). Örgütlerde Yöneticilerin Dönüştürücü Liderlik Algılamalarının Problem Çözme Becerilerine Etkisi: Kamu Sektöründe Bir Uygulama. Ç.Ü. Sosyal Bilimler Enstitüsü Dergisi, 18(2), 387–397.

Yatkın, A. (2013). Kamu Yönetimi Etiği ve Üst Düzey Yöneticilerin Çalışanlara Karşı Etik Yükümlülükleri. Akademik Bakış Dergisi, 1(38), 1–17.

Yıldırım, A. (2010). Etik Liderlik ve Örgütsel Adalet İlişkisi Üzerine Bir Uygulama. Karaman: T.C. Karamanoğlu Mehmetbey Üniversitesi Sosyal Bilimler Enstitüsü.

Yılmaz, E. (2006). Okullardaki Örgütsel Güven Düzeyinin Okul Yöneticilerinin Etik Liderlik Özellikleri ve Bazı Değişkenler Açısından İncelenmesi. Konya: Selçuk Üniversitesi Sosyal Bilimler Enstitüsü.

Yüksel, C. (2005). Devlette Etikten Etik Devlete: Kamu Yönetiminde Etik. Tüsiad Devlette Etik Altyapı Dizisi No: 2, İstanbul.

Buket Akdöl

Leaders as Ethical Role Models for 21st-Century Business Environment: Aspects from Humane-Oriented Contemporary Leadership Paradigms

1 Introduction

The organization of the new millennium puts the spotlight on the needs of the employees and the role of leadership to build intellectual capital and foster innovation. In addition, there has also been a growing need for leadership styles that put the interests of all society and ethical concerns above securing short-term profits. Also, humane orientation, which is defined as the degree of encouragements to people for being altruistic generous and kind to others, is becoming important in today's organizations. Servant leadership and ethical leadership theories consider these ethical concerns and humane orientation of today's leadership paradigm. These two paradigms have many differences as well as similarities. In this chapter, I compare and contrast these two theories in terms of their core concepts, dimensions, and the role of leaders and followers.

2 Current leadership paradigm

The demographic, social, and technological changes, increasing employee diversity, and corporate scandals of the recent decades shifted the focus of the contemporary management practices toward a more ethical and sustainable leadership approach that emphasizes the ethical decision-making, the attitudes of the employees, and social responsibility of the organization.

Previous researches suggested transformational and charismatic leadership could be unethical (Bass, 1985) if the main motivation is more selfish than altruistic (Howell and Avolio, 1992), and if the use of power is inappropriate (House and Aditya, 1997). Some scholars also differentiate between socialized and personalized charismatic leaders; socialized leaders being more ethical and personalized leaders potentially becoming unethical charismatic leaders over time (Howell and Avolio, 1992; Brown, Trevino and Harrison, 2005). With its focus on values, followers, and ethical behavior, servant leadership and ethical leadership are part of these emerging theories following the previous academic focus on transformational and charismatic leadership.

3 The importance of humane orientation in leadership

Humane orientation is defined as "the degree to which an organization or society encourages and rewards individuals for being fair, altruistic, friendly, generous, caring, and kind to others" (House et al., 2004: 569). In a humane-oriented society, people are generally sensitive toward others' concerns, differences, and well-being. Belonging and acceptance can be seen as the main motivators of people in the societies with high humane orientation. There are some characteristics of high humane-oriented societies and organizations. People feel responsibility to promote others' well-being and are against any kind of discrimination. There is a prioritization of the interests of shareholders rather than short-term profits. Managers show mentoring rather than supervising, use small span of control and face-to-face communication, and by showing compassion, care, and altruism, develop a sense of belonging and acceptance within the organization. On the other hand, people at the societies with low humane orientation can exalt power, self-interest, and material possession. People expect a social and economic system from governors and institutions to protect and promote others' well-being. There are formal relations, bureaucracy, and larger span of control at the organizations (House et al., 2004).

There is a greater need for motivation and empowerment in order to establish a positive work environment that enables employees to do their bests. Such an environment requires leaders that put employees in the center and pay attention to the people who are connected in business processes.

4 The importance of ethics in leadership

The values of the leader provide a reference point in making decisions, solving problems, managing interpersonal relationships between leaders and others in the company, and accepting or rejecting organizational goals and pressures. In addition, the values play an important role in the way a leader acts in an organization (England and Lee, 1974: 411; Washington, Sutton and Field, 2006: 702). Therefore, leaders can affect employees' perception of ethics and ethical levels of the organizations by formally defining norms for right and wrong, acting as a role model for ethical behavior, and setting appropriate reward systems for ethical behavior in the organization (Jaramillo et al., 2009: 352–353).

The unethical decisions and business practices may also have adverse effect on all stakeholders of an organization, including the society in general. The scale of the effects may range from low job satisfaction of an employee due to unfair promotion practices to colossal harm done to the society by the collapse of Enron Corporation.

New leadership theories have focused more on values and ethical behavior of leaders to consider the harmful effect of the previous leadership practices (Wong, 2002; Wong and Davey, 2007; Sendjaya, Sarros and Santora, 2008: 402–403).

5 Servant leadership theory

Servant leadership is a theoretical framework that defines a leader's primary motivation and role as service to others. It introduces a holistic approach to work, advocates a sense of community, and promotes sharing of power in decision-making by showing humility, authenticity, and stewardship. Servant leader also develops and empowers employees by standing back, encouraging them to be autonomous, forgiving mistakes, and accepting them for who they are (Spears, 1996: 33; Dierendonck, 2011: 1232).

Within the context of Greenleaf's servant leader, "service to others" is an ethical obligation (Greenleaf, 1977; Ehrhart, 2004; Jaramillo et al., 2009: 352). They prioritize the needs of the followers ahead of their own individual interests, or the short-term profit concerns of the company (Laub, 1999; Page and Wong, 2000; Laub, 2004; Washington, Sutton and Field, 2006: 700; Dierendonck and Nuijten, 2011: 250). Servant leaders use their power and status to serve others. While serving others, servant leader uses his/her power to convince, pursue, and develop followers instead of trying to accomplish the tasks by himself/herself. In other words, serving others means bringing out the best in every follower and developing their skills (Liden et al., 2008: 162).

Servant leaders help the organizations move toward higher ethical levels, which reflect the firm's ethical practices and commitment to ethics. As an example to this positive effect, Jaramillo et al. (2009: 358) find that servant leadership is positively related to salesperson's perceptions of the ethical level of the organization. It is also asserted that servant leadership has a positive effect on social responsibility of the organization. Servant leaders don't disregard the organizational goals while serving followers and are always accountable for the results of their leadership to others such as other leaders, shareholders, customers, and society in general (Page and Wong, 2000).

6 Ethical leadership theory

Ethic, which can be defined as moral principles that determine one's behavior, is one of the core principles in business management. Ethical codes, activities, and examples establish a base for building trust, credibility, fairness, and equity at any organization.

Ethical leader sets standards for ethical behavior and helps followers embrace these standards by supporting behaviors that follow these standards (Bass and Steidlmeier, 1999). Brown, Trevino, and Harrison defined ethical leadership as "the demonstration of normatively appropriate conduct through personal actions and interpersonal relationships, and the promotion of such conduct to followers through two-way communication, reinforcement, and decision-making" (2005: 120).

Ethical leadership is about a leader's ability to teach ethical behavior to the followers by being a role model to them and does not necessarily flow only from personal traits such as honesty and integrity. Ability to hold followers for ethical conduct and to communicate a sustained ethics message to followers is a good example for such teaching ability of the ethical leader. The ethical leadership can be discussed through a social learning perspective where the leaders influence the ethical conduct of followers by being role models for ethical behavior (Brown, Trevino and Harrison, 2005: 119).

Honesty (truth-telling), trustworthiness (can be trusted), integrity (principled behavior), altruism (serving the greater good), modeling, collective motivation, and encouragement are important dimensions of ethical leadership (Brown, Trevino and Harrison, 2005: 118–119; Martin et al., 2009: 131). Just like the servant leaders, ethical leaders also put effort into developing and empowering followers (Bass and Steidlmeier, 1999; Zhu, May and Avolio, 2004: 20; Kalshoven, Denhartog and De Hoogh, 2011: 53–54).

7 Comparison of servant and ethical leadership styles

The servant leadership's emphasis is on the development of the followers, and the ethical leadership is mostly about the directive and normative behavior. The servant leader is more concerned about how to enable the follower to want to do things themselves and the ability of the follower to carry out those things, and not so much about the norms of the organization. In contrast, the ethical leader's focus is on the compliance with the rules and the norms of the organization (Dierendonck, 2011: 1237).

Ethical leadership and servant leadership share similar dimensions such as honesty, integrity, trustworthiness, modeling, altruism, and empowerment. Items of ethical leadership scale (Brown, Trevino and Harrison, 2005) mostly focus on measuring ethical level of organization such as taking fair decisions, showing ethical behavior, listening, and having the best interest of employees in mind. While servant leadership scale contains all these items, ethical leadership scale lacks dimensions such as authenticity, sharing leadership, and interpersonal acceptance. In this view, one can consider servant leadership as more wide concept that includes ethical leader's behavior as well (Dierendonck, 2011: 1236–1237). Table 1 below provides comprasion of servant and ethical leadership styles.

Table 1: Comparison of Servant and Ethical Leadership Styles

Style of Leader	Focus of Leader	Role of Leader	Role of Follower	Expected Outcomes
Servant	Needs of followers	Serving the follower	Becoming more capable, wiser, freer, and autonomous	Satisfaction, development, empowerment, organizational citizenship behavior (OCB) commitment to service and societal betterment
Ethical	Ethical standards and norms	Being a role model to the followers	Exhibiting behavior in line with standards and norms	Ethical behavior, engagement, OCB

The servant leadership and ethical leadership styles differ in terms of role of the leader, focus of the leader, and role of the follower. Whereas the servant leader serves the follower by focusing on the followers needs, the ethical leader focuses on the ethical norms and standards and acts as a role model to the followers. The followers in the servant leadership are expected to become more capable and autonomous, and the followers in the ethical leadership are expected to become more compliant with the ethical norms and standards.

The common expectation from both leadership styles is positive employee attitudes such as job satisfaction, engagement, and organizational citizenship behavior. Also empowerment is an important outcome of both theories. But ethical leadership more specifically focuses on ethical behaviors and decisions in entire company (Brown, Trevino and Harrison, 2005), whereas servant leadership theories focus more on accountability, social responsibility, and common well-being of entire society (Laub, 1999, 2004; Page and Wong, 2000).

8 Conclusion

As the demographic, social, and technological changes after mid of the 1900s shifted the focus of the leadership paradigm toward more ethical and humane-oriented practices, many contemporary leadership approaches have emerged. While two of these approaches, servant leadership and ethical leadership theories, have so much similarities such as honesty, integrity, fairness, trustworthiness, listening, modeling, altruistic behavior, empowerment, and creating positive job attitudes, there are also some differences as well. First of all, these two theories differ in terms of leader focus and role. As servant leaders focus the needs of followers and display services to followers, ethical leaders with their focus on ethical norms and standards are seen as role models by their followers. There are also differences in terms of expected role of followers. As servant leaders expect more capable, wise, and autonomous followers, ethical leaders expect ethical decisions and behaviors from followers.

References

Bass, B. M. (1985). Leadership and Performance beyond Expectations, Free Press, New York.

Bass, B. M. and Steidlmeier, P. (1999). "Ethics, Character, and Authentic Transformational Leadership Behavior", The Leadership Quarterly, 10(2), 181–217 (online on 9 August 2014), https://pdfs.semanticscholar.org/e918/e7fd7ff62b-6fb086067f07503c756744758d.pdf

Brown, M. E., Trevino, L. K. and Harrison, D. A. (2005). "Ethical Leadership: A Social Learning Perspective for Construct Development and Testing", Organizational Behavior and Human Decision Process, 97(2), 117–134.

Dierendonck, V. D. (2011). "Servant Leadership: A Review and Synthesis", Journal of Management, 37(4), 1228–1261.

Dierendonck, V. D. and Nuijten, I. (2011). "The Servant Leadership Survey (SLS): Development and Validation of a Multidimensional Measure", Journal of Business Psychology, 26(3), 249–267.

Ehrhart, M. G. (2004). "Leadership and Procedural Justice Climate as Antecedents of Unit-Level Organizational Citizenship Behavior", Personnel Psychology, 57(1), March, 61–94.

England, G. W. and Lee, R. (1974). "The Relationship between Managerial Values and Managerial Success in the United States, Japan, India, and Australia", Journal of Applied Psychology, 59(4), 411–419.

Greenleaf, R. K. (1977). Servant Leadership: A Journey into the Nature of Legitimate Power and Greatness, Paulist Press, New York.

House, R. J. and Aditya, R. N. (1997). "The Social Scientific Study of Leadership", Journal of Management, 23(3), 409–473.

House, R. J., Hanges, P. J., Javidan, M., Dorfman P. W. and Gupta, V. (2004). Culture, Leadership and Organization: The GLOBE Study of 62 Societies, Thousand Oaks, Sage.

Howell, J. M. and Avolio, B. J. (1992). "The Ethics of Charismatic Leadership: Submission or Liberation", Academy of Management Executive, 6(2), 43–54.

Jaramillo, F., Grisaffe, D. B., Chonko, L. B. and Roberts, J. A. (2009). "Examining the Impact of Servant Leadership on Salesperson's Turnover Intention", Journal of Personal Selling & Sales Management, 29(4), 351–365.

Kalshoven, K., Denhartog, D. N. and De Hoogh, A. H. (2011). "Ethical Leadership at Work Questionnaire (ELW): Development and Validation of a Multidimensional Measure", The Leadership Quarterly, 22(1), 52–69.

Laub, J. (1999). "Assessing the servant organization: development of the Organizational Leadership Assessment (OLA) instrument", Unpublished Dissertation, Florida Atlantic University, Boca Raton (online on 18 April 2014), http://www.olagroup.com/Images/mmDocument/Laub%20Dissertation%20Brief.pdf

Laub, J. (2004). "Defining Servant Leadership: A Recommended Typology for Servant Leadership Studies", Servant Leadership Research Roundtable, August (online on 13 June 2014) http://www.regent.edu/acad/global/publications/sl_proceedings/2004/laub_defining_servant.pdf.

Liden, R. C., Wayne S. J., Zhao H. and Henderson, D. (2008). "Servant Leadership: Development of a Multidimensional Measure and Multilevel Assessment", The Leadership Quarterly, 19(2), 161–177.

Martin, G. S., Resick, C. J., Keating, A. M. and Dickson, M. W. (2009). "Ethical Leadership across Cultures: A Comparative Analysis of German and US Perspective", Business Ethics: A European Review, 18(2), 127–144.

Page, D. and Wong, P. T. P. (2000). "A Conceptual Framework for Measuring Servant-Leadership", In: S. Adjibolosoo (Ed.), The Human Factor Shaping the Course of History and Development, University Press of America, Boston (online on 18 April 2014) http://www.drpaulwong.com/wp-content/uploads/2013/09/Conceptual-Framework.pdf

Sendjaya, S., Sarros, J. C. and Santora, J. C. (2008). "Defining and Measuring Servant Leadership Behaviour in Organizations", Journal of Management Studies, 45(2), 402–424.

Spears, L. C. (1996). "Reflections on Robert K. Greenleaf and Servant Leadership", Leadership Organization Development Journal, 17(7), 33–35.

Washington, R. R., Sutton, C. D. and Feild, H. S. (2006). "Individual Differences in Servant Leadership: The Roles of Values and Personality", Leadership & Organizational Development Journal, 27(8), 700–716.

Wong, P. T. P. (2002). "Lessons from the Enron debacle: Corporate culture matters!", (online on 17 August 2014) http://www.meaning.ca/archives/archive/art_lessons-from-enron_P_Wong.htm

Wong, P. T. P. and Davey, D. (2007). "Best Practices in Servant Leadership", Servant Leadership Research Roundtable, July (online on 10 December 2013) http://www.regent.edu/acad/global/publications/sl_proceedings/2007/wong-davey.pdf

Zhu, W., May, D. R. and Avolio, B. J. (2004). "The Impact of Ethical Leadership Behavior on Employee Outcomes: The Roles of Psychological Empowerment and Authenticity", Journal of Leadership and Organizational Studies, 10(1), 16–26.

Esin Benhür Aktürk

Corporate Governance

1 Introduction

Although the concept of corporate governance has been used in the United States, Japan, and Europe since the 1900s, it has gained increased attention since the 1980s. The increase in the capital movements and globalization of technology and the following corporate scandals in European countries and the United States has led to the re-emergence of the concept of corporate governance. It has quickly become a recognized and accepted management philosophy in multinational companies, academia, and business world. Corporate governance is a business mentality that ensures fairness, accountability, transparency in a firm's relationships with its all partners and thus increases the productivity of the corporate.

Corporate governance can be defined as "blend of law, regulation, and appropriate voluntary private-sector practices which enables the corporation to attract financial and human capital, perform efficiently, and thereby perpetuate itself by generating long-term economic value for its shareholders, while respecting the interests of stakeholders and society as a whole" (Gregory, 2002: 1). Corporate governance is expressed in the most comprehensive sense as the arrangement of any business management to reach a goal. In the narrow sense, it is the rules and practices that ensure effective and prudent management and hence the success of the company in the long run. The basic principles of corporate governance are fairness, accountability, transparency, and responsibility. With these basic principles, corporate governance aims to ensure that the corporate performs optimally and becomes successful, competitive, and most profitable.

2 Corporate governance

The rapid development and change in business process happened in recent years have led to new ideas and approaches in business management. Corporate governance is one of the approaches that have come to life in business management. Factors such as the development of national and international economies, the progress of commercial relations, the increase of international and national capital flows, the decrease of shareholder's activities in management, and the increase in importance of the decisions of firms' boards of directors have influenced the birth of the concept of corporate governance. The failure of shared managements, the crisis, the misappropriation, the interlinking of commercial activities of the countries, and the change in the competitive conditions of partnerships have caused the concept corporate governance to gain importance. In light of these developments, corporate governance has begun to be discussed in international and national corporations and has become popular all over the world (Dinç and Abdioğlu, 2009: 159).

In recent years, a growing number of firms have been negatively impacted by the ongoing bankruptcy of firms. As a result of these negative situations, corporate governance has become very important. Corporate governance has become a type of management style that has been debated over time. Corporate governance is a concept that regulates relationships among all interest groups that seek to benefit from business operations while retaining all the rights of stakeholders and staff (Cengiz, 2013: 404). A common definition of corporate governance is not yet available. Different authorities and institutions make definitions according to their own interests and duties. These definitions of corporate governance indicate that firms and organizations also express their thoughts on this issue by their definitions. Corporate governance definitions of some organizations are given in Table 1.

Table 1: Corporate Governance Definitions and Approaches

Organization/Country	Issuing Body	Definition
OECD	OECD Principles/ Millstein Report	Corporate governance relates to the internal means by which corporations are operated and controlled
Belgium	Recommendations of Federation of Companies	The organization of the administration and management of companies, which is better known under the term "corporate governance," has to meet the expectations of the shareholders and the requirements of the economic process
	Dual Code of the Brussels Stock Exchange and the Belgian Banking and Finance Commission	"Corporate governance" refers to the set of rules applicable to the management and control of a company. It is the duty of the board of directors to manage the company's affairs exclusively in the interests of the company and all its shareholders, within the framework of the laws, regulations, and contentions under which the company operates

Organization/Country	Issuing Body	Definition
Denmark	Nørby Report and Recommendations	The goals, according to which a company is managed, and the major principles and frameworks that regulate the interaction between the company's managerial bodies, the owners, as well as other parties, who are directly influenced by the company's dispositions and business
United Kingdom	Cadbury Report	Corporate governance is the system by which businesses are directed and controlled.
The Netherlands	SCGOP (Stichting Corporate Governance Onderzoek voor Pensioenfondsen/ Foundation for Corporate Governance Research for Pension Funds) Handbook and Guidelines	Corporate governance concerns the way companies are managed and how management is supervised

Source: Gregory (2002: 11–20).

Corporate governance actually has effect on every kind of economic factor. It is seen that corporate governance is an important element in the development of economic activity, investor's confidence, and economic growth. This definition, which is related to the relationship with the shareholders, the board of directors, and other interest groups, makes it possible to determine the aims of the firm and to achieve these objectives. Managers are well aware of the benefits of good corporate governance to investment, stability, and growth. Firms are now well aware of the benefits of effective corporate governance to competitive strength (Kula, 2006: 49).

3 The history of corporate governance

Managerial weaknesses in the financial intermediary institutions such as Baring in 1996 and Sumitoma in 1996; financial corporate scandals in Parmalat, Enron, and WorldCom; and the systematic crises arising from the activities of the derivative markets re-emerged the importance of corporate governance in 2000s (Esen and Yılmaz, 2015: 223).

The initial studies about legal framework of corporate governance were carried out in the United States and the United Kingdom. The first definition of corporate governance was made in the Millstein Report of the Organisation for Economic Co-operation and Development (OECD) in 1998. The OECD Corporate Governance Principles, which are used as references for investors, beneficiaries, and decision-makers in every relevant business, were approved by the OECD Ministerial Council in 1999 (Güçlü, 2010: 1–2).

The concept of corporate governance was started to be used in Turkey in the early years of the 2000s. The business scandals and the negligence of the independent auditing firms in 2000s have seriously shaken the confidence of public to international firms. Accordingly, attempts have been made to act in the framework of corporate governance principles to prevent such events from happening again. The first legal arrangements related to corporate governance came with the Sarbanes–Oxley Act of 2002, issued in the United States. In November 2002, the report entitled "A Modern Regulatory Framework for Company Law in Europe" was presented to the European Commission and various steps for institutional governance were taken in many countries such as Japan, England, and France. In Turkey, corporate governance principles were published by the Capital Markets Board (CMB) in 2003 and the Istanbul Stock Exchange (ISE) decided in 2005 to establish the ISE Corporate Governance Index, which will subject to the companies that implement the corporate governance principles of the CMB (Esen and Yılmaz, 2015: 223).

The current and widely accepted studies on corporate governance are chronologically as follows:

- The Cadbury Committee Report in 1991
- The Greenbury Committee Report in 1995
- The Hampel Report in 1998
- The OECD Corporate Governance Principles in 1999
- The Sarbanes–Oxley Act in 2002

3.1 Cadbury Committee Report

The Cadbury Committee was set up in England in May 1991 with the aim of establishing the financial side of corporate governance. The creation of the committee is initiated by concerns about weak standards of financial reporting and accountability, a lack of clear enforcement framework for duties and working conditions of managers, failure of the independent auditing firms to reveal the expected quality of service due to their competition, and sudden failures in large enterprises. Especially the failure of the Maxwell publishing group at the end of the 1980s is one of the most important reasons for influencing the formation of the committee (Pekin, 2011: 12).

No obligation has been imposed on the implementation of the proposals presented in this report. Companies listed on the London Stock Exchange are required to announce to the public only whether the proposals contained herein have been fulfilled. Report includes a total of 19 proposals regarding reporting and supervision on the members of the board of directors, the executives, and the non-executive members. The Cadbury Report is regarded as a turning point in terms of corporate governance and forms the basis of the "Corporate Governance Principles" issued by the OECD in 1999 (Atamer, 2006).

The Cadbury Report not only helped to improve corporate governance in England but also affected other countries. The principle of "comply or explain" started to be implemented by corporate governance (Atamer, 2006). The first part of the Cadbury Report summarizes the responsibilities and duties of the supervisory board and the board of directors and defines the corporate governance as the system by which businesses are directed and controlled. It was stated that the report was prepared based on the principles of openness, integrity, and accountability (Doğan, 2007).

3.2 Greenbury Committee Report

In the 1990s, public and shareholders had concerns about the level of salaries and bonuses paid to senior executives in England. While the remuneration of senior executives, especially in the privatized industries, kept increasing, the public had an opinion that the managers of these companies did not have any effect on the optimum performance of companies (Karayel, 2006: 41).

Upon complaints about overpayments, a committee was established to respond to the concerns of shareholders and the public about the remuneration of managers (Kanbur, 2010: 34). The Study Group on Directors' Remuneration under the chairmanship of Sir Richard Greenbury met in council in January 1995 to make arrangements for the salaries and benefits of the managers in the UK companies. The report of the committee was issued as "Directors' Remuneration" in July 1995 (Doğan, 2007: 60).

The key themes of the report are transparency, accountability, full disclosure, alignment of director and shareholder interests, responsibility, and improved company performance. The report states that acceptance of report's findings will lead to improved corporate remuneration policies (Greenbury Report, 1995:7).

3.3 Hampel Report

The most recent committee report on corporate governance in England is the Hampel Report. The Hampel Report was issued in January 1998 by a committee under the chairmanship of Sir Ronald Hampel in England. Themes of the report are corporate governance, the role of directors, directors' remuneration, the role of shareholders, accountability, and audit (Committee on Corporate Governance, 1998).

The Hampel Report further reinforces the entire core framework of the Cadbury Report and the "Code of Best Practice" principles developed in this report. The corporate governance committee, led by Sir Ronald Hampel, was established to analyze what happened after the Cadbury and Greenbury reports and to assess whether further changes were needed. The committee reviewed the implementation of the Cadbury and Greenbury reports. The committee issued its preliminary report in August 1997 and final report in January 1998 (Kahraman, 2008: 28).

The Hampel Report emphasizes the need to improve the balance among stakeholders of the company. The report states that stakeholders such as employees, suppliers, customers, and lenders should also be taken into consideration for the success of the corporate. The report stresses that managers can carry out their legal duties against the shareholders only by developing and maintaining relationships with the stakeholders. Besides, the report points out the important role of institutional investors in the business they invest (Kanbur, 2010: 43).

3.4 Sarbanes–Oxley Act

This law was issued in July 2002 as the result of Enron accounting and corporate ethics scandals in the United States. The Sarbanes–Oxley Act contains a large number of provisions aimed at the complete independence of auditors and the independent auditing of financial statements of publicly traded companies (Pekin, 2011: 11).

This law is not only an accounting law but also a corporate law because it is a comprehensive reform of business practices. The act imposes provisions related to the managers of the enterprise and sanctions to those persons who do not fulfill their obligations. The provisions within the framework of this law concern most of the parties who are in a very important position in the process of the creation of the capital. For auditors, there is a new level of private supervision, public reporting, and a set of guidelines for the independence of audiences. For management, there are audited and internal reporting requirements for financial controls, reporting requirements, and the enhanced protection against conflicts of interest (Demircan, 2007).

4 Basic principles of corporate governance

4.1 Fairness-integrity principle

This principle describes how the business management behaves fairly to all shareholders and employees. Fairness also includes the protection of the rights of partners, including foreign partners and minority shareholders, and the implementation of existing contracts. The fairness principle covers the protection of rights to all stakeholders through equitable treatment. A fair and equitable management practice can be mentioned when the enterprise is on equal footing to all stakeholders (Öztürk, 2013: 24).

4.2 Transparency–openness–disclosure principle

Some of the business information is trade secret. Transparency is the disclosure of non-financial and financial information except trade secrets to the public in a timely, accurate, easy, understandable, interpretable, and easily accessible manner. The principle of transparency is a chain of approaches that encompasses both the pre-business activity and the ongoing and subsequent activities. It is a good corporate governance point of view to announce the performance of the company in the previous period as well as the targets and risks for the future time periods to investors. In this sense, management of performance, risk, and target issues are the basis for transparency and awareness for businesses and strengthen the "corporate" perception by stakeholders and investors (Acungüç, 2017: 21).

The recent financial crises and corporate scandals in the world have demonstrated the importance and application of the principle of transparency. In this context, the standards and methods used by the financial statements of the firms are also important. For example, the Sarbanes–Oxley Act enacted in response to Enron and WorldCom scandals make US corporations more transparent. After the law, corporations started to declare all their operations including off-balance sheet items in a more comprehensive and detailed manner. Thus, US corporations have become more accountable to the public (Çemberci, 2013: 8).

4.3 Accountability principle

Corporate governance is not just decisions made by managers. Businesses also need to be accountable. The transparency principle includes giving feedbacks about before, during, and after business activities. Contrary to the transparency principle, the accountability principle also covers the post-process whereby the management board is free to observe the performance of the senior management of the firm and to ensure accountability of the top managers to the stakeholders.

Responsibility must be shared between the board of directors and top management in order to achieve this achievement. Otherwise, it will be unclear who is the decision-maker and who is responsible for accountability on behalf of the decisions made. An effective and efficient task sharing between the top management and the board of directors is the most basic condition of accountability principle in corporate management. For this reason, reports related to corporate governance place emphasis on regulations related to the functioning and structure of the board of directors (TKYD and Delolitte, 2006: 5).

4.4 Responsibility principle

When making decisions to maintain their business life, firms should not act only for the purpose of creating added value or profit. In the context of corporate governance, the concept of responsibility awareness has become a subject of considerable interest. Firms should feel responsible not only for business partners or managers but also for shareholders, stakeholders, and the society. In the process of taking the decisions at the level of top managements or management boards, social ethical values and other moral factors should be considered. With this principle, it has become necessary for the business operator to secure social values and regulations in accordance with the law (Demirbaş and Uyar, 2006: 240).

5 Conclusion

In the globalizing world, the corporate governance appears as a form of management that is responsible for maximizing the profits of shareholders while focusing on the objectives of the enterprise. There is a constant conflict of interest between the shareholders and managers in publicly traded companies. These conflicts of interest are rooted in the fact that managers run the company according to their own interest, not the interests of shareholders. The lack of supervision in corporate governance also simplifies the duties of managers. The purpose of the corporate governance is to make sure that the corporate is run in the interests of the company and all its shareholders within the framework of the laws and regulations according to the principles of transparency and trust.

Corporate governance is basically the protection of interests of stakeholders of a company. It has been better understood recently and become a necessity to be competitive in the globalized world. Companies can achieve positive developments in the company's performance by reducing conflict of interests within the company through corporate governance. Internal and external audit and internal control facilitated by corporate governance have important role in fraud detection and prevention within the company. Corporate governance also provides great benefits to the country at the macroeconomic level. These benefits can be listed as foreign capital entry into the country, sustainability of stability, and increased investments.

References

Acungüç, A. Ç. (2017). *Kurumsal Yönetim Uygulamalarının Hisse Senetleri Borsada İşlem Gören Şirketler Üzerindeki Etkisi ve Değerlendirilmesi.* İstanbul: T.C. Okan Üniversitesi Sosyal Bilimler Enstitüsü.

Atamer, M. (2006). *Halka Açık Anonim Şirketlerde Kurumsal Yönetim ve Doğrudan Yabancı Yatırımlar Açısından Değerlendirilmesi.* Ankara: Hazine Müsteşarlığı.

Cengiz, S. (2013). "İşletmelerde Kurumsal Yönetin Kapsamında İç Denetimin Yeri ve Önemi: Borsa İstanbul'da Bir Araştırma." *Afyon Kocatepe Üniversitesi, İİBF Dergisi*, 15(2): 403–448.

Committee on Corporate Governance. (1998). *Final Report (Hampel Report).* United Kingdom.

Çemberci, M. (2013). "Kurumsal Yönetim İlkelerinin Türk Aile İşletmelerinin Yönetim İlkelerine Adaptasyonunun Değerlendirilmesi." *Akademik Bakış Dergisi*, 34: 1–14.

Demirbaş, M. and Uyar, S. (2006). *Kurumsal Yönetim İlkeleri ve Denetim Komitesi.* İstanbul: Güncel Yayıncılık.

Demircan, A. (2007). *Sarbanes Oxley (2002) Yasası ve Bağımsız Denetime Etkileri.* Edirne: Trakya Üniversitesi Sosyal Bilimler Enstitüsü.

Dinç, E. and Abdioğlu, H. (2009). "İşletmelerde Kırumsal Yönetim Anlayışı ve Muhasebe Bilgi Sistemi İlişkisi: İMKB-100 Şirketleri Üzerine Ampirik Bir Araştırma." *Balıkesir Üniversitesi Sosyal Bilimler Enstitüsü Dergisi*, 12(21): 157–184.

Doğan, M. (2007). *Kurumsal Yönetim.* Ankara: Siyasal Kitapevi.

Esen, S. and Yılmaz, N. N. (2015). "Borsa İstanbul 100 Endeksindeki Şirketlerin Kurumsal Yönetim Kriterleri Açısından İncelenmesi." *Research Journal of Business & Management*, 2(3): 220–237.

Güçlü, H. (2010). *Kurumsal Yönetim Uyum Derecelendirmesi.* İstanbul: İMKB Yayını.

Greenbury Report. (1995). *Directors' Remuneration: Report of a Study Group Chaired By Sir Richard Greenbury.* England: GEE Publishing.

Gregory, H.J. (2002). Comparative Matrix of Corporate Governance Codes Relevant to the Aruopean Union and Its Member States. Weil, Gotshal & Manges

LLP, Brussels. http://ec.europa.eu/internal_market/company/docs/corpgov/ corp-gov-codes-rpt-part3_en.pdf

Kahraman, C. (2008). *Kurumsal Yönetim Anlayışının Özel Sermayeli Bankaların Yapısı ve İşleyişi Üzerine Etkileri.* İstanbul: İstanbul Üniversitesi Sosyal Bilimler Enstitüsü.

Kanbur, A. (2010). *İşletmelerde Kurumsal Yönetim Uygulamalarının Örgütsel Değerler Üzerindeki Etkileri: İMKB Kurumsal Yönetim Endeksinde Yer Alan İşletmeler Üzerine Bir Araştırma.* Malatya: T.C. İnönü Üniversitesi Sosyal Bilimler Enstitüsü.

Karayel, M. (2006). *Türkiye'de İşletmelerde Kurumsal Yönetim Bilincinin Ölçülmesine İlişkin Batı Akdeniz Bölgesi'nde Bir Araştırma.* Isparta: Süleyman Demirel Üniversitesi, Sosyal Bilimler Enstitüsü.

Kula, V. (2006). *Kurumsal Yönetim Hissedarların Korunması Uygulamaları ve Türkiye Örneği.* İstanbul: Papatya Yayıncılık.

Öztürk, F. (2013). *Kurumsal Yönetim İlkeleri ve İç Denetimin Rolü.* İstanbul: T.C. Marmara Üniversitesi Sosyal Bilimler Enstitüsü.

Pekin, S. (2011). *Kurumsal Yönetim İle Finansal Tablo Manipülasyonu Arasındaki İlişki: İMKB Kurumsal Yönetim Endeksine Dahil İşletmelerde Bir Uygulama.* Burdur: Mehmet Akif Ersoy Üniversitesi Sosyal Bilimler Enstitüsü.

TKYD and Delolitte. (2006). *Nedir Bu Kurumsal Yönetim?* İstanbul: TKYD ve Deloitte Ortak Yayını.

Mehmet Sabri Topak

A Study on Sustainability Reporting of Chemical Industry Firms in Turkey

1 Introduction

After the late 1990s, the pressure on firms to be more transparent, accountable and responsible to their stakeholders has increased. This made firms to publish reports that cover a broad and diverse array of disclosures. Firms use these reports and information to fulfill their assumed responsibility to their stakeholders. In this context, sustainability concept has attracted popular attention and become a buzzword. A survey conducted by United Nations Global Compact (UNGC) and Accenture exhibited that 93% of the chief executive officers view sustainability as an "important" or "very important" factor for success (UNGC and Accenture, 2013). Likewise, sustainability reporting has become an important dimension of corporate governance and corporate voluntary disclosure practices.

In the years following the banking crisis of February 2001, laws and regulations concerning corporate governance and their enforcement have been drastically improved in Turkey. The new legal and regulatory framework includes Corporate Governance Guidelines issued in 2003 and directives related to audit and accounting standards and practices issued in and after 2003 by the Capital Markets Board of Turkey. Inevitably, all the corporate governance reforms that are implemented have profound effects on the disclosure and reporting standards of the publicly traded firms in Turkey (Macovei, 2009; Turan and Menteş, 2013). Although sustainability reporting is a voluntary practice in Turkey, like in most of the world, governments and international organizations promote and advocate for higher transparency and disclosure via voluntary reporting practices such as sustainability reporting.

The chemical industry in Turkey produces a wide variety of products, ranging from specialty polymers to personal care products that serve a diverse set of industrial sectors. About 70% of the chemicals produced in Turkey are used as intermediates or raw materials in other sectors, with the remaining 30% sold directly to end users. Turkey is the 14th largest importer of chemicals in the world and the 27th largest exporter of chemicals (Turkay, 2015: Ministry of Economy, 2016). Although chemical industry makes a significant contribution to Turkey's welfare and development, it is obvious that pollution from industrial activities negatively affects people and the environment. Thus, to explore and analyze the state of sustainability, reporting can help to understand and find ways to resolve negative externalities caused by the Turkish chemical industry.

There is limited research on sustainability and sustainability reporting practices in Turkey. Public and private firms have yet to discover the value of sustainability to improve organizational performance. This study intends to explore sustainability reporting practices of chemical industry firms in Turkey. The sample includes all the chemical firms that are listed on Borsa Istanbul (BIST) Chemical Index (XKMYA), which includes the 20 publicly traded chemical industry firms. Required data on sustainability reporting practices were manually gathered from annual reports and sustainability reports. The 3 dimensions (economic, environmental and social parameters) of Global Reporting Initiative (GRI) guidelines were employed (Mahmood and Orazalin, 2017) to provide a comprehensive overview of the sustainability activities of chemical industry firms listed on XKMYA. This study aims to contribute to our knowledge on current status of sustainability and sustainability reporting in the chemical industry in Turkey.

2 Development and state of chemical industry in Turkey

By the end of the 19th century, the production of chemicals was very limited within the boundaries of the Ottoman Empire. After the 1920s, the production of various chemicals such as medicine, agricultural chemicals, detergents, ink and dyes gained momentum. From the 1960s to 1980s, import substitution was the dominant economic policy, and public investments were concentrated on the fields that required high investments such as petrochemicals and fertilizers. On the other hand, private sector and foreign investments were mainly concentrated to high-profit-margin areas such as pharmaceuticals, soaps and detergents. By the 1980s, export-oriented economic policy was the dominant economic policy that led to a boom in production and exports of the chemicals (Ministry of Economy, 2016).

The production of the chemical industry in Turkey is generally aimed at the products required by the manufacturing industry and the directly consumable products. In the recent years, the Turkish chemical industry has improved significantly in terms of quality and productivity. The adoption of the European Union's technical standards has played an important role in the improvement of the chemical industry (TKSD, 2016). Turkey's chemical industry is expected to continue to grow. Increasing domestic market is one of the main drivers of this expected growth. As population and per-capita income in Turkey increase, the demand for the products of the chemical industry is expected to increase too. In addition, due to Turkey's proximity to and historical ties with emerging markets in Eastern Europe, Western Asia, the Caucasian region, the Middle East, and North Africa, trade with these regions is also steadily increasing (Turkay, 2015) (see Table 1).

Turkey exhibited an impressive economic performance following the 2000s. Major structural reforms were critical for this performance, allowing the economy to grow at an annual average real gross domestic product (GDP) growth rate of 5.6% from 2003 to 2016. The increased income made Turkey an upper-middle-income country. Turkey became one of the major recipients of foreign direct investment (World Bank, 2017; ISPAT, 2016).

Table 1: The Chemical Industry Export by Countries (Value: 1,000 USD)

Rank	Country	2013	2014	2015	2015 Share (%)
1	Iraq	1,272,079	1,124,201	972,424	5.9
2	Egypt	1,469,259	1,218,853	954,350	5.8
3	Germany	989,389	1,056,738	884,439	5.4
4	UAE	708,996	683,107	757,227	4.6
5	Italy	636,676	725,142	601,238	3.6
6	Saudi Arabia	216,203	413,375	510,601	3.1
7	Iran	646,033	630,646	502,830	3.0
8	United Kingdom	546,796	594,294	498,993	3.0
9	Spain	609,240	561,315	498,105	3.0
10	Russia	796,088	782,669	480,336	2.9

Source: Ministry of Economy (2016).

The chemical industry, together with the subindustries, employs nearly 200,000 people and has around 6,000 firms manufacturing various chemicals. A very small percentage of the chemical industry firms have more than 150 employees (Ministry of Economy, 2016).

3 Literature review

Sustainability reporting is a natural outcome of increased expectancies and demands of stakeholders from the firms. Stakeholders increasingly expect firms to disclose their business activities and the effects of these activities on society and environment, thus, pressuring firms to be more transparent by releasing reports that explain their activities. This approach where firms try to meet the transparency demands of their stakeholders is based on stakeholder theory. Stakeholder theory claims management of a firm should make decisions for the benefit of not only the financiers but also all stakeholders (Freeman, 1984; Freeman and McVea,

2001). Compared to Agency Theory, which assumes the priority of the firm is to maximize the benefit of its shareholders (La Porta et al., 1999), Stakeholder Theory has a more inclusive and broader approach (Feizizadeh, 2012), which makes stakeholder approach more suitable for the demands of various stakeholders regarding disclosure and transparency.

4 Data collection and methodology

The study includes all 20 firms listed on XKMYA. The data required for the research were gathered manually from the official websites, annual reports and sustainability reports' of the firms. The study analyzes 2015 sustainability reports of the XKMYA-listed firms. The 3 dimensions, economic (ECN), environmental (EN) and social (SOC) parameters of GRI guidelines were employed (Mahmood and Orazalin, 2017) to provide a comprehensive overview of the sustainability activities of XKMYA firms (see Table 2).

Table 2: GRI Dimensions and Indexing Methodology

GRI Dimension	Acronym	Indexing
Economic Index (%)	EC	Each of the 7 core indicators is valued "1" if the information on an item is disclosed, otherwise "0".
		Scores ranging between "0" and "7" are converted to percentages.
Environmental Index (%)	EN	Each of the 17 core indicators is valued "1" if the information on an item is disclosed, otherwise "0".
		Scores ranging between "0" and "17" are converted to percentages.
Labor Index (%)	LA	Each of the 10 core indicators is valued "1" if the information on an item is disclosed, otherwise "0".
		Scores ranging between "0" and "10" are converted to percentages.
Human Rights Index (%)	HR	Each of the 9 core indicators is valued "1" if the information on an item is disclosed, otherwise "0".
		Scores ranging between "0" and "9" are converted to percentages.

GRI Dimension	Acronym	Indexing
Society Index (%)	SO	Each of the 8 core indicators is valued "1" if the information on an item is disclosed, otherwise "0".
		Scores ranging between "0" and "8" are converted to percentages.
Product Reliability Index (%)	PR	Each of the 4 core indicators is valued "1" if the information on an item is disclosed, otherwise "0".
		Scores ranging between "0" and "4" are converted to percentages.

The EC dimension of sustainability is about the organization's impacts on the economic conditions of its stakeholders and on economic systems at local, national and global levels. The EN dimension of sustainability is related to organization's impacts on natural systems, including ecosystems, land, air and water. Environmental indicators cover performance related to inputs (e.g., material, energy, water) and outputs (e.g., emissions, effluents, waste). Environmental indicators also cover the performance related to biodiversity and environmental compliance. The SOC dimension of sustainability concerns the impacts an organization has on the social systems within which it operates. Social performance indicators identify 4 key performance aspects. These are labor practices, human rights, society and product responsibility (GRI, 2011):

1. **Labor Practices and Decent Work (LA):** Labor Practices are based on internationally recognized standards such as United Nations Universal Declaration of Human Rights; United Nations Convention: International Covenant on Civil and Political Rights and International Covenant on Economic, Social, and Cultural Rights; Convention on the Elimination of all Forms of Discrimination against Women (CEDAW); ILO Declaration on Fundamental Principles and Rights at Work and the Vienna Declaration and Program of Action.

2. **Human Rights (HR):** Human rights performance indicators demand organizations to report on the extent to which processes have been implemented, on incidents of human rights violations and on human rights issues such as nondiscrimination, gender equality, freedom of association, collective bargaining, child labor, and forced and compulsory labor.

3. **Society Performance (SO):** Indicators focus attention on the impacts organizations have on the local communities in which they operate, disclosing how the risks that may arise from interactions with other social institutions are managed and mediated. In particular, information is sought on the risks associated with bribery and corruption, undue influence in public policy making and monopoly practices.

4. **Product Responsibility (PR):** Performance indicators address the aspects of a reporting organization's products and services that directly affect customers such as health and safety, information and labeling, marketing and privacy.

5 Analysis and results

The most important finding of the study is the fact that only 5 of the 20 (25%) XKMYA-listed firms issue sustainability reports. Keeping in mind that XKMYA-listed firms are the biggest publicly traded chemical industry firms, 25% is a strikingly low rate. Table 3 displays the disclosure levels of the firms that issue sustainability reports for each dimension. One of the XKMYA-listed firms is excluded from the study because the firm is owned by a holding company, which released only one sustainability report that covers all the firms that are members of the holding group. This makes it almost impossible to distinguish the performance indicators for each individual firm.

Table 3: Disclosure Level of Sustainability Report Dimensions of XKMYA-Listed Firms for 2015

Firm	EC (%)	EN (%)	LA (%)	HR (%)	SO (%)	PR (%)
AKSA	86	53	60	56	25	25
AYGAZ	57	71	60	78	75	75
BRİSA	100	94	100	100	100	100
SODA SANAYİİ	71	41	50	44	38	50
TÜPRAŞ	86	59	60	56	50	50
Mean	80	64	66	67	58	60
Median	86	59	60	56	50	50

The lowest level of disclosure (transparency) is observed at SO dimension, with a mean of 58% and median of 50%. The second lowest level of disclosure is observed at P R dimension with a mean of 60% and median of 50%. SO and PR are the 2 dimensions that sustainability report–issuing firms shy away about the most. On the other hand, the highest level of disclosure is observed at EC dimension with a mean of 80% and median of 86%.

6 Conclusion

Chemical industry makes significant contributions to Turkey's welfare and development, but it is obvious that pollution from industrial activities negatively affects people and the environment. This makes it important for all stakeholders to be informed about the business decisions and actions of the chemical industry firms. Disclosure activities play a crucial role in this sense, and sustainability reporting is a useful tool to keep stakeholders informed.

The most important finding of this study is the fact that only 5 of the 20 (25%) firms publish sustainability reports, which means the level of disclosure is very limited in the chemical industry. Study results reveal that the least transparent dimensions of the sustainability reports are SO and PR. The most transparent dimension of the sustainability reports is the EC.

The reasons causing low transparency at the chemical industry is worth investigating. The relationship between sustainability reporting and firm-specific features such as ownership structures, board characteristics (size and diversity) are recommended topics for future research.

References

Capital Markets Board of Turkey, *Kurumsal Yönetim İlkelerinin Belirlenmesine ve Uygulanmasına İlişkin Tebliğde Değişiklik Yapılmasına Dair Tebliğ Hakkında Basın Duyurusu*, SPK, Ankara. http://www.spk.gov.tr/Duyuru/Goster/20120211/0

Feizizadeh, A. (2012). "Corporate Governance Frameworks", *Indian Journal of Science and Technology*, 5(9): 3353–3361.

Freeman, E. (1984). *Strategic Management: A Stakeholder Approach*, Pitman Press, Boston.

Freeman, E. and McVea, J. (2001). "A Stakeholder Approach to Strategic Management", Darden Business School Working Paper No. 01–02. https://ssrn.com/abstract=263511 Access date: 08.06.2015.

GRI – Global Reporting Initiative. (2011). "Sustainability Reporting Guidelines", https://www.globalreporting.org/resourcelibrary/G3.1-Guidelines-Incl-Technical-Protocol.pdf

ISPAT – Investment Support and Promotion Agency of Turkey (2016). Invest in Turkey, Ankara. http://www.invest.gov.tr/enUS/turkey/factsandfigures/Pages/Economy.aspx

La Porta, R., Lopez-de-Silanes, F., Shleifer, A. and Vishny, R. W. (1999). "Investor Protection: Origins, Consequences and Reform," NBER Working Paper No: 7428, National Bureau of Economic Research, Cambridge, MA.

Macovei, M. (2009). "Growth and Economic Crises in Turkey: Leaving Behind a Turbulent Past?", Economic Papers 386, European Commission, Economic and Financial Affairs, Brussels.

Mahmood, M. and Orazalin, N. (2017). "Green Governance and Sustainability Reporting in Kazakhstan's Oil, Gas, and Mining Sector: Evidence from a Former USSR Emerging Economy", *Journal of Cleaner Production*, 164: 389–397.

Ministry of Economy. (2016). "Chemical Industry", https://www.economy.gov.tr/portal/content/conn/UCM/uuid/dDocName:EK-232359 Access date: 08.06.2015

Türk Kimya Sanayicleri Derneği-TKSD (2016). "Turkish Chemical Industry 2015–2016", *Chemical News*, August, 34–39. http://tksd.org.tr/doc/2016_TKSD_Indian_Chemical_News.pdf

Turan, A. and Menteş, S. A. (2013) "Corporate Governance Practices: Dissemination on Turkish Web Sites", *Journal of Global Information Technology Management*, 16(1): 6–29.

Turkay, M. (2015) "Turkey's Chemicals Industry Expands into Global Markets", *American Institute of Chemical Engineers*, May, 50–54.

UNGC and Accenture (2013). The UN Global Compact—Accenture CEO Study on Sustainability 2013. United Nations, New York, NY.

World Bank (2017). The World Bank in Turkey, World Bank, Washington DC. http://www.worldbank.org/en/country/turkey/overview

Özer Özçelik and Ezgi Babayiğit Sunay

Ottoman Economic Crisis: Sabri F. Ülgener's Analysis Based on the Ottoman Economic Mentality

1 Introduction

When the history of economic fluctuations and crises is examined, it is observed that all the countries faced with these phenomena at certain periods at different times. In today's globalizing, world which is integrated in economic, political and sociocultural ways, the economic crisis that a country faces with is limited not only to that country but also to other countries in a short period of time. Sabri F. Ülgener, one of the most important personalities of the Turkish economic history, witnessed the turn of the Ottoman Empire to the New Turkish Republic. Thus, he gave thought to economic and social differences between the two societies. Ülgener investigated the causes of this profound difference between the Ottoman Empire and the Republic of Turkey whereby the Ottoman Empire protected itself from the capitalist world for many years but was destined to be destroyed and the Republic of Turkey tries to keep pace with the world and develops rapidly. Ülgener reasoned the causes of this profound diffidence to the Ottoman economic mentality. Hence, he searched the Ottoman economic mentality and crises that this mentality causes. This study focuses on the Sabri F. Ülgener's views on the Ottoman economic mentality and the relationship between the Ottoman economic mentality and the Ottoman economic crises.

2 Sabri Fehmi Ülgener (08.05.1911–01.01.1983): life, ideas and studies

Sabri Fehmi Ülgener is one of the most important representatives of the Turkish economic history, but he could not be appreciated enough when he was alive. The most healthy information about Sabri Ülgener can be learned from his student Ahmet Güner Sayar and Sayar's book named *Intellectual Portrait of An Economist*. Besides being an economist, Ülgener was a successful sociologist and lawyer. He lived both in the Ottoman Empire and in the Republican Period and thus witnessed socioeconomic conditions of both periods. Hence, he was able to successfully reflect the world of mentalities of both periods. Ülgener's mother belonged to the military class while his father belonged to the scientist class in the Ottoman Empire. Thus, his world of thought and personality was shaped with the help of these two sides (Sayar, 1998: 23).

Ülgener was an assistant at the law faculty of Istanbul University in 1933 when he met German professors who escaped from Hitler's pressure and taught economics at the Faculty of Economics in Istanbul University. He met representatives of the German Historical School such as Kessler, Rustow, Neumark and Isaac. Hence he caught the gates of a different world of thought. The "human focus" perspective of the German Historical School had a great impact on Ülgener's thoughts (Torun and Duran, 2010: 65). The fact that the German Historical School links religion with economics led him to think about the link between the economic mentality of the Ottoman Empire and the economic mentality of the Republic of Turkey. His thoughts were based on the idea that the past must be searched for to think about the future. Thus, the primary question to be asked is not where Turkey is going, but where it comes from (Sayar, 1998: 19). This question led Ülgener to investigate historical roots, the Middle Ages and the world order in the Ottoman State.

Sabri Ülgener is called the Weber of Turkey. He is influenced by the views of the German Historical School, especially those of Werner Sombart and Max Weber. He created his own research methodology based on his way of training and the views of the German Historical School on the relationship between religion and the mindset behind the social life.

In 1904, Weber emphasized in his book titled *The Spirit of Capitalism and the Protestant Ethics* that although capitalism had a long history, it completed its spiritual side with Protestantism. He called this spiritual side as the spirit of capitalism. Weber argued that Christianity was liberated from its chains after the emergence of Protestantism, which unveils the spirit of capitalism. Thus he argued that contrary to Marx, religion was not an obstacle to the development of social process but an incentive (Tatar, 2012: 152–153). Weber's causal connection between Protestant sectarianism and capitalism inspired Ülgener to question the reasons why Ottoman–Turkish society could not become capitalist and to reveal differences of perception between Islam and traditional Islam in Turkey in the 1930s, when Islamic religion was supposed to be the main cause of underdevelopment.

According to Weber, while Islam was a warlike society organization based on conquest and trophy in the early period, it turned into petty bourgeois monotheism by the effect of mysticism and so-called spirituality in the latter periods (Weber, 2011: 368). According to Weber, there are two reasons why capitalism cannot develop in Muslim countries: the first is the anti-capitalist formation of Islamic values, and the second is its traditional understanding of politics and economy (Canatan, 1993: 37). Weber argued that Muslims are bound to Islamic religion that focuses on conquest and trophy. That is why they are away from the rationality concept and elements of rationality (free market, rational legal system, bourgeois class, etc.) (Kurt, 2010: 7). In other words, Islam is a religion that fits the existing conditions, far from secularism (Özkiraz, 2003: 54). Islam's irrational, inward-looking and spiritual lifestyle could not be transferred to business life due to Sufis' viewpoint of Islam. Thus, Islam could not make connection between religion and economy as Protestantism did. Traditional politics' collection of power, on the one hand, and dependence of economic groups on the rulers, on the other hand, hampered the emergence of free souls and rational organizations that revives capitalism and maintained old traditions away from innovation (Canatan, 1993: 37).

According to Weber, the Protestant morality established an ideological infrastructure beyond the purely material aspect of economic systems. The Protestant spirit constitutes the capitalist spirit in this ideology (Torun, 2002: 96). Weber states that the concept of capitalism existed before Protestantism. He named this type of capitalism as "adventure capitalism". He argues that Protestantism is the cause of modern capitalism that focuses on profit and material success (Ortaköy, 2014: 46).

Although Ülgener analyzes Islamic societies using the Weberian method, he opposes Weber's one-sided approach to the Islamic religion and the thesis that capitalism will only be seen in Western societies. He argues that Weber's view is incompatible with the essence of Islam (Ülgener, 2006c: 57). Against Weber's subordination of Islam to a feudal base and seeing it as a religion of desert, Ülgener mentions that all of the cities where Islam is originated are trading centers and the verses of Quran about trade will support this fact. He also supports his counterstance with arguing that Islam rules working, good morals and work ethic.

Ülgener is the first scientist who applied Weberian method in Turkish–Islamic societies (Sayar, 2006: 29). Weber differentiates Eastern and Western societies based on rationality while Ülgener's analysis is based on mental world. According to Özkiraz (2008: 128), Ülgener's mental world analysis can be applied not only to the Turkish–Islamic world but also to the whole of the Eastern societies such as China, India and Iran.

Ülgener argues that the attitude of neoclassical economics to associate human with matter is a departure from the essence. He tries to reach the economic mind through the interaction of human with human (Sayar, 1998: 229). In other words, the human factor that positive economic analysis ignores is an element in Ülgener's method (Beriş, 2007: 325). His method starts from human and reaches human mentality. His method of analysis differentiates his studies from others and makes them original and interesting (Yılmaz, 2003: 492).

3 Studies of Ülgener

Ülgener's studies include many articles and translations in addition to eight basic books: *Tarihte Darlık Buhranları ve İktisadi Muvazenesizlik Meselesi* (1951), *İktisadi İnhitat Tarihimizin Ahlak ve Zihniyet Meseleleri* (1951), *İktisat Dersleri* (1952), *Milli Gelir, İstihdam ve Büyüme* (1962), *Zihniyet ve Din* (1981), *Zihniyet, Aydınlar ve İzmler* (1983), *Darlık Buhranları ve İslam Siyaseti* (1984) and *Makaleler* (2006).

4 The concept of mentality in Ülgener's studies

The perception of Islam as the reason for the economic backwardness that prevailed in the 1930s and Weber's view that Protestant Ethics of the 17th century contributed to the development of capitalism in Western Europe led Ülgener to search for the mentality that prevents Ottoman society to become capitalist (Sayar, 1998: 66).

According to Ülgener, the mentality is the norms, set of rules and behaviors adapted by economic agents. The mentality is an attitude toward the world and world relations. It is the sum of the values and beliefs adopted by someone in his/her life. In economic terms, moral and mentality do not always have to be parallel to each other, but sometimes they can even be completely opposite or even irrelevant (Ülgener, 2006a: 1; 2006b: 17). Ülgener believed that human beings and surrounding elements should be analyzed in order to examine the understanding of morality and mentality of an era. That is why he started to search for the literature and artworks of the Ottoman Empire when he was studying the world of morality and mentality of the Ottoman Empire (Sayar, 1998: 259). As a reflection of the human figure of the period, he looked at literature, poems, Quran, fables, laws, travel notes and so on of that period (Ülgener, 2006b: 12).

5 Economic depressions and crises in Ottoman society

Ülgener attempts to combine history and theories of conjuncture. One of his articles deals with the destabilization and price instability in Turkey as an aftermath of World War II while the other one is about depressions in the Ottoman Empire (Sayar, 1998: 351). His articles are motivated by the assumption that present problems can be found in the past. According to his way of analyzing, if we want to find solutions for present problems, we need to deeply analyze the problems and their reasons in the past (Ülgener, 2006d: 3).

Ülgener argued that present problems can be encountered in the past. In his argument, he was inspired by W. Sombart who associates the economic crisis that occurred in 1929 to depressions at the beginning of emergence of capitalism. Ülgener argued that in order to better understand economic instability and political instabilities and policies followed in the post-crisis era, we need to look at past economics including the medieval economics (Ülgener, 2006d: 4–5). This method of analysis led Ülgener to analyze depression and crisis in Ottoman Empire in order to analyze the stagnation and famine in Turkey after World War II. He confirms once more that history repeats itself.

In the Turkish economic literature, initially the word "depression" is used instead of the word "crisis". Depression indicates that the imbalance of supply and demand is strong after a certain level (Ülgener, 2006d: 7). The concept of depression in economic terms designates suddenly and unexpectedly emerging economic fluctuations in prices and quantities of goods and services and production factors in money markets. It is necessary to reach the damaging dimensions of the country's economy in order for these fluctuations to be called crisis (Kibritçioğlu, 2000: 5). The concept of depression in financial terms specifies that the deteriorations in the financial markets result from directing funds to the ineffective and inefficient economic agents due to exaggerations of moral hazard and adverse selection problems in the market (Mishkin, 1996: 17). The periodic movement of financial crises in the form of a vicious circle causes violent fluctuations, destroys the industrial sector, impoverishes the workers, and causes trade to fail (Jones, 1900: 1).

Ülgener examined the history of the crisis in terms of scarcity and based his analysis on the city economy of the Middle Ages. He pointed out that some historians who argue that pre-capitalist crises are the primitive antecedents of capitalism, and socialist and communist writers who accuse capitalism as the main reason of every negative event are full of prejudices and falsehoods (Ülgener, 2006d: 10).

Contrary to those who think that depressions in the Middle Ages were due to natural disasters such as famine and drought or political uncertainties before the overproduction depressions that capitalism created, Ülgener mentions that the crisis change their forms as a result of change in the economic, social, demographic and technical elements of the cities (Ülgener, 2006d: 17). In this context, it is the population increase that should be particularly emphasized. In the countries where population growth did not reach dangerous dimensions, the factors became natural and politically sourced and "from the outside". In countries where the increasing population began to distort the supply and demand balances, the factors became "inside to outside" (Ülgener, 2006d: 18).

The reasons of economic imbalances considered by people in the underdeveloped cities of the Middle Ages are simple and far from objective. This type of urban persons were inclined to connected event around themselves to mystical and metaphysical reasons and they were far from realism. That is why they are not the subject of economics. However, Ülgener insisted on the fact that there may be objective expressions within this type of subjective expressions (Ülgener, 2006d: 27). There was a cycle idea on the mentality of Ottoman people at the end of the 18th century. This idea was based on the Quranic verse of "After every difficulty there is convenience, after every difficulty there is ease" (Ülgener, 2006a: 47).

Ülgener thoroughly examined *Mukaddime*, written by a Turk-Islamic scholar Ibn Khaldun, and stated that the first realist ideas in the history of the crisis were from Ibn Khaldun, who lived in the 13th century. Ibn Khaldun is a philosopher who is expected to look at the issue of economic imbalance in terms of stagnation and scarcity as the environment in which he is in. In contrast, Ibn Khaldun, who lives very far away from industrial capitalism, is one of the theorists of depression because of his handling of the subject from the point of abundance (Ülgener, 2006d: 37–38). Ibn Khaldun assessed both aspects of economic imbalance in a market-oriented manner and dealt with how market actors are affected by these imbalances and how to solve them by both scarcity and abundance. Ibn Khaldun, as a medieval thinker, brought objective analyses and solutions to economic affairs.

Ülgener examines the recent periods of the Ottoman State and presents the most typical example of the narrowing crisis. Unlike the surrounding capitalist world, the Ottoman Empire followed the provisionism policy (consumer-oriented policy) in the economy for many years. The Ottoman Empire implemented policies aimed at achieving economic equilibrium opposite to the export-increasing policies implemented by the liberal states. However, these policies resulted in contrary to the aim and cost of living and shortages reached serious levels. The fact that mass consumption centers, especially Istanbul, cannot meet the needs of the increasing population, depreciation of the money and increase of financial burden are the main and long-term reasons of the crisis (Ülgener, 2006d: 75). Besides, distance to the production centers takes the costs to much worse levels. The economic and political turbulence in the Ottoman Empire caused migrations all over the Empire. On the other hand, the shortage of commodities as a result of migrations caused prices to increase, which led to the subsistence crises (Ülgener, 2006d: 70). Economic depressions were manifested in the form of price increases in the city centers while they were accompanied by hunger and death in rural areas (Ülgener, 2006d: 71). The Ottoman Empire was deprived of income sources with the end of conquests at the stagnation period of the Empire. The severe increase in expenses of the army and the palace caused devaluation, which led to the prices to increase several times. While these factors constantly disrupted the economic balance, two important factors supported this imbalance and acted as a driving force to transform it into a crisis: scarcity and hoarding. Ülgener describes these two factors as evasive and accelerating (Ülgener, 2006d: 84). Apart from natural causes of scarcity such as weather conditions and epidemics, there are political causes such as war, blockade and corruption, and financial reasons such as devaluation of the money and producers' dissatisfaction with profitability (Ülgener, 2006d: 85–92). Profiteering (hoarding) is more dangerous than scarcity for transforming the economic imbalance into a crisis (Ülgener, 2006d: 95). The reason why hoarding is more dangerous than scarcity is that it is subjective and involves human factor. Although crisis induced by external factors takes place once, hoarding is an extremely detrimental factor for the economy due to its multiple and long-term repetition capability (Ülgener, 2006d: 84).

The cumbersome mentality observed in feudal societies influenced the Ottoman society. Mentality of Sufis and the economic system of overexploitation worsened economic crises of the Ottoman Empire. Along with capitalism, the Western world has entered into a period of abundance and prosperity due to the increase in production level and the accumulation of capital. This welfare period caused something opposite to scarcity crises. It caused abundance crises due to decrease in prices as a result of mass production. Contrary to the scarcity crises, the abundance crises continue in short term and contribute to the development of the economy. Ülgener also noted that there are also similarities between the two. He stated that panic and excitement are the basis of the speculation experienced in the abundance crisis and hoarding experienced in the scarcity crisis. Underneath all of these is the greed for profit, which is difficult to be controlled. The greed for profit results in hoarding in the scarcity crises while the greed for profit results in speculation in the abundance crises (Ülgener, 2006d: 113–115).

6 Conclusion

Human is the most important factor that is both influencing and influenced during the capitalist period and pre-capitalist period. The human being shapes his/her life with his/her ambition and enthusiasm. The aim of wanting more and to legitimate every mean to reach this goal constitutes the mentality of human being not only in the past but also in the present-day world. Although the view that the globalizing and capitalizing world has exacerbated the exploitation of the world and created gaps in the standards of life is still a widespread opinion, Ülgener proves that capitalism is not the only reason by giving the example of the Ottoman Empire that was left out of the capitalist system but still faced with similar situations. Economic structural fluctuations and crises that change form, dimension, time, or place will never come to an end unless structural solutions to economic structure are provided and the moral concept is internalized by societies.

References

Beriş, H. E. (2007). *Zihniyet, Aydınlar ve İzmler, Sabri Ülgener: Küreselleşme ve Zihniyet Dünyamız*, ed. M. Yılmaz, Türkiye Kültür ve Turizm Bakanlığı, Ankara.

Canatan, K. (1993). "Kapitalizm, Protestanlık ve İslam", *Bilgi ve Hikmet Dergisi*, 2, 35–42.

Jones, E. D. (1900). *Economic Crises*, Kessinger Publishing, USA.

Kibritçioğlu, B. (2000). Finansal Krizler: Belirleyicileri, Öngörülebilirliği ve Yayılma Etkisi, Hazine Müsteşarlığı Uzmanlık Tezi, Yayın No: 6600, Ankara.

Kurt, A. (2010). "Weber' in İslam Görüşü Üzerine Bir Değerlendirme", *Uludağ Üniversitesi İlahiyat Fakültesi Dergisi*, 19(1):1–23.

Mishkin, F. S. (1996). "Understanding Financial Crises: A Developing Country Perspective", NBER Working Paper Series, No: 5600, May.

Ortaköy, S. (2014)."Sabri Ülgenerve Max Weber'de İktisadi Zihniyet", İstanbul Üniversitesi Sosyal Bilimler Enstitüsü, Yayımlanmamış Doktora Tezi.

Özkiraz, A. (2003). "Sabri Ülgener' in Max Weber Eleştirisi", *İstanbul Üniversitesi Siyasal Bilgiler Fakültesi Dergisi*, 28:49–61.

Özkiraz, A. (2008). "Prof. Dr. Sabri F. Ülgener Hayatı ve Eserlerine Dair Özet Bir Sergileme", *İş Ahlakı Dergisi*, 1(1):123–136.

Sayar, A. G. (1998). *Bir İktisatçının Entelektüel Portresi*, Ötüken Yayınları, İstanbul.

Sayar, A. G. (2006). *Ülgener Yazıları*, Derin Yayınları, İstanbul.

Tatar, C. (2012). "Din ve Kapitalizm", Sosyoloji Konferansları, *İstanbul Üniversitesi İktisat Fakültesi Yayınları*, 45:149–168.

Torun, İ. (2002) "Kapitalizmin Zorunlu Şartı Protestan Ahlak", *Cumhuriyet Üniversitesi, İktisadi ve İdari Bilimler Dergisi*, 3(2):89–98.

Torun, F. and Duran, H. (2010). "Sabri F. Ülgener ve İki Eseri Üzerine Bir Değerlendirme", *İstanbul Üniversitesi Sosyoloji Konferansları*, 42, 63–75.

Ülgener, S. F. (2006a). *Zihniyet, Aydınlar ve İzmler*, Derin Yayınları, İstanbul.

Ülgener, S. F. (2006b). *İktisadi Çözülmenin Ahlak ve Zihniyet Dünyası*, Derin Yayınları, İstanbul.

Ülgener, S. F. (2006c). *Zihniyet ve Din*, Derin Yayınları, İstanbul.

Ülgener, S. F. (2006d.) *Tarihte Darlık Buhranları*, Derin Yayınları, İstanbul.

Weber, M. (2011). *Sosyoloji Yazıları*, Parla, Taha, (çev.), Deniz Yayınları, 13. Baskı, İstanbul.

Yılmaz, M. (2003). *"Sabri Fehmi Ülgener"*, *Modern Dünyada Siyasi Düşünce: Muhafazakarlık*, ed. A. Çiğdem, Cilt: 5, İletişim Yayınları, İstanbul.

Hasan Boynukara and Cengiz Karagöz

The Basic Preoccupations of Postcolonial Literature and the Windrush Generation

1 Introduction

This chapter attempts to offer an insight into the primary assumptions and tendencies of postcolonial literature by centering on its preeminent scholars and their theoretical convictions as regards the impacts of colonialism on the colonized people. The legacy of colonialism has been discussed concerning to what extent an overall freedom and an anti-colonial system could be secured since the ex-colonies gained their political independence. The viewpoints that refer to similar points in postcolonial literature are among the highlighted issues in this research. Also, the members of the Windrush Generation such as V.S. Naipaul, George Lamming, Sam Selvon and C.L.R. James, who left the Caribbean and immigrated to England and who are marked with their unique thoughts on the postcolonial Caribbean nation, are briefly explored.

Focusing on the postcolonial literature means to draw attention to the latent power of literature in the colonial period as it can be traced from Viswanathan's claim that "the English literary text, functioning as a surrogate Englishman in his highest and most perfect state, becomes a mask for economic exploitation ... successfully camouflaging the material activities of the coloniser" (1998: 20). This implies that literature cannot detach itself from the intervention of a worldview, culture and ideology in literary texts through which the Western countries try to impose their perceptions on the colonized nations and convince them that the Western thinking and civilization mean development and humanism. In other words, the opening of courses and departments in which English literature is taught in the colonized lands exposes a landmark where "native populations came to internalise the ideological procedures of the colonial civilizing mission" (Gandhi, 1998: 145). On account of this discipline, it becomes highly easy for the colonial powers to colonize the native peoples without consulting to weapons, violence and wars. As a result, the colonized peoples unconsciously embrace the Western thoughts during their studies on English literature which implicitly praises the Eurocentric values as well as disregards the Eastern societies' contribution to the world history as Gandhi asserts that "Urged to memorise choice passages from English literary masters, the colonial child submits to the secret logic of spiritual and political indoctrination" (1998: 146). The use of literature in the school curriculums of the Oriental nations as a project of silencing and brainwashing the native citizens seems to have achieved in attaining the purposes of the Western countries to a great extent in the sense that it is by and large possible to observe that the students from the Third-World countries are of the opinion that the only path to development is to be in pursuit of the Eurocentric thinking.

Edward Said maintains that "imperialism and the novel fortified each other to such a degree that it is impossible ... to read one without in some way dealing with the other" (1994: 71). Said's idea appears as justifiable if it is observed that black characters in novels or other works in English literature, since the Renaissance in which the European colonialism began, have been reflected as the ones that need to be educated, civilized owing to their barbaric nature. *Heart of Darkness*, for instance, could be regarded as a masterpiece which illustrates the colonial attempts and the relationship between the white and the black societies in colonialism: "Marlow left for Africa in a French steamer. His first impression in response to the Dark Continent was that of awe and estrangement; feelings which reflect his geographical displacement and cultural alienation" (Acheraiou, 2008: 141). The fact that Congo is called a "dark land", which makes Marlow feel strange and anxious, points out a certain division of the world nations as those whose geographical features are outlandish and those whose geography is so enlightened as to spread it even to the dark ones. In the novel, Conrad on the surface gives the impression that he does not approve colonialism and discrimination; nevertheless, he criticizes not colonialism in reality but the colonial oppression and coercion of the Belgian empire and its failure in colonialism while exposing Britain as the perfect colonialist power in a shrouded manner (Acheraiou, 2008: 149). Therefore, literary works touching on the issues of colonialism and the colonial relationship between the Western and the Oriental nations need to be analysed by exploring the hidden ideas and what lies beneath the text instead of concentrating on merely the surface meanings.

2 Postcolonial literature

Like any other period in history, the postcolonial period also naturally possesses its literature and its literary tendencies that are mainly concerned with the consequences and impacts of colonialism on both the colonizers and the colonized nations. Postcolonial literature may be said to have emerged together with its conspicuous writers, literary products, themes, writing styles and characters which make it differ remarkably from the previous literary periods and texts. Among this period's literary texts and concerns, the questions of who have produced postcolonial literary products, for what purposes those products have been written, whether any significance of postcolonial literature has existed for the colonized peoples and their struggle, whether all of the texts have criticized the colonialist nations or have reflected any complicity with the colonial ambitions, and what the key features and inclinations of characters in the literary texts have displayed from the outlook of cultural identity and psychology are often the focal points of postcolonial literature.

Postcolonial literature seems to have evolved out of several phases in which the first literary works could be seen to have been produced by "a literate elite class", being both white and black individuals, who aimed to serve the purpose of justifying colonialism and whose works were not able to illustrate the real native values; instead, they handled the issues by approaching matters in terms of the Western powers, the metropolitan views of the centre, rather than the oppressed peoples and their viewpoints (Ashcroft et al., 2004). The first native writers of that literature were, most possibly, so alienated from and ashamed of their native culture that they sought to satisfy their white masters with their great efforts to praise the superiority of the Western civilization over the black and Oriental world while scorning their civilization and culture in direct or indirect ways.

Postcolonial literature, however, does not always signify the virtues and achievements of the Western nations by placing emphasis on their supremacy; instead, the reader may discern that the native writers of postcolonial literature in the latter stages predict the downfall of the British Empire and that the ways these writers try to argue attest to the existence of contesting views between the colonialist and anti-colonial ones (Gandhi, 1998). Anti-colonial voices in postcolonial literature arise as those that are plainly opposed to the colonialist arguments of those who support colonialism and become a sign of the attempts of the native peoples to purge their lands of the colonial legacy and maladies. Desiring to define their own culture and the Western societies rather than being defined by them, they have sought to reflect the subject matters of colonialism and postcolonialism from the perspective of the colonized peoples who were always overpowered and hushed by the colonizing nations. "To give expression to colonized experience, postcolonial writers sought to undercut thematically and formally the discourses which supported colonization – the myths of power, the race classifications, the imagery of subordination" (Boehmer, 2005: 3). While aiming to shed light upon the real face of colonialism with an exceptional emphasis on oppression and violence, these writings strive to strip the colonized peoples of their inferiority complex which surfaced on account of the colonial violence and domination caused by the

Western countries. In order to lay bare, the main preoccupation and ambition of the postcolonial writings of the native societies, Jameson insists that:

> Third-world texts, even those which are seemingly private and invested with a properly libidinal dynamic – necessarily project a political dimension in the form of national allegory: *the story of the private individual destiny is always an allegory of the embattled situation of the public third-world culture and society.* (1986: 69) (Emphasis is original)

Even if those writers' texts have been supposed to be inspired by their individual experiences and concerns, what lies behind the literary products of postcolonialism is the undertaking of postcolonial writers to call to mind the collective memories, historical facts, native values and the national legacy of their ancestors in order to encourage the native societies on the way to decolonization.

Language as the primary tool of communication in postcolonial literature gains incomparable connotations in terms of its potential influence that exceeds the lines of communication. To illustrate, Thiong'o makes a statement that "Language carries culture, and culture, particularly through orature and literature, the entire body of values by which we come to perceive ourselves and our place in the world" (1987: 16). For this reason, it is very much the case that using colonial languages has disrupted the ways the native peoples define themselves and have their awareness of which cultural framework they belong to. Postcolonial writers, most probably, tend to feel the need of initiating their anti-colonial struggle on the basis of linguistic terms even though they have written their products in English. In postcolonial texts, the role of language as an effective tool forces postcolonial writers to displace English as the colonial language by relocating it in the context of the colonized space in two ways: one of these ways requires English to be robbed of its privileged status provided by the powerful metropolitan centre whereas the second one imparts the message that English could be used in such a way that it is adapted to new uses that refuse to comply with the standard norms of the Western linguistic practices (Ashcroft et al., 2004: 37). Through deviating from the Western imperatives in such ways and not abiding by certain linguistic norms on purpose, the Third-World authors demonstrate that they can make use of the colonial language in its distorted and newly invented forms as a means of spreading their own cultural values and national sensitivities across the world. By inventing new varieties or dialects of English language, they believe that they can undermine the Western discourses and views because challenging the standard linguistic rules and uses of the Western nations in some sense amounts to subverting the semantic constructions and ways of thinking of the Western world. In addition, they introduce their native cultural elements and thinking into the Western countries by inserting their native concepts and phrases into English when they produce their literary works in that language. Unlike the colonial period in which English was imposed on the colonized societies with the aim of detaching their bonds from their indigenous values, collective memories and peculiarities, the postcolonial period has emerged as a process where the colonized nations attempt to impose their native conceptions and patterns on English by producing literary texts in which they reshape and reproduce English according to their needs and desires in a way that is very different from the one determined by the Western countries.

One of the most commonly observed themes and issues in postcolonial fiction is the concept of migration which includes the movement of the Third-World nations to the Western metropolises with a variety of expectations and ambitions. As Chambers discusses it, "Migrancy ... involves a movement in which neither the points of departure nor those of arrival are immutable or certain. It calls for a dwelling in language, in histories, in identities that are constantly subject to mutation" (2001: 5). This presents exhaustive evidence that draws attention to the fact that migration constitutes a process of renewal and fragmentation in which migrants' conceptions of language and culture are always destabilized and unsettled. "Movement and migration, and all the ideas that come with it of the human condition of restlessness and new mobile identity formations, has had a noticeable impact on literary production too" (Moslund, 2010: 3). It is no doubt that postcolonial literature for the most part involves writers such as George Lamming, Naipaul, Salman Rushdie and Hanif Kureishi who handle migration on the basis of its consequences for migrants' understanding of home, culture and identity. These writers seek to find answers to such matters; do the metropolitan centres provide what they desire and what they hope for themselves? Do the immigrants preserve their ties with their homeland and recall their former cultural values? Furthermore, these writers' texts examine the aspect of relation between the immigrants and the Western population and also whether or not the immigrants are embraced and valued by the Western citizens. Owing to their racial origins and skin colours, it has come to be seen that "The immigrants had, of course, been consigned to slum houses and forced into multi-occupation. Now there were fears that they would move further afield into the white residential areas" (Sivanandan, 2008: 101). In addition, postcolonial literary works have engaged themselves with whether these immigrants might be accepted as permanent visitors who never want to return back to their homeland or temporary visitors who achieve in leaving the metropolis and return back to their original regions.

The political outcome of decolonization has never been democratic regimes as it can be concluded from the first local leaders whose ruling system could be identified with "the military dictatorship and one-party regimes" (Birmingham,

2009: 4). Ahluwalia raises the issue of these local leaders' oppressive acts and policies when it comes to their personal profits by claiming that "even so-called legitimately elected rulers are prepared to resort to violence in order to maintain their sources of revenues, which are allocated through patrimonial relations" (2001: 65). Even though they did not admit that they oppressed their society under some excuses by imposing the Western notions on the native peoples, nearly each citizen of the society was dissatisfied with their leaders' ways of ruling and attitudes for those leaders lost their keen interest in the troubles and welfare of their citizens.

Pessimistic notions about overall freedom and decolonization may be claimed to run through the postcolonial period although a large number of colonized nations have gained their political independence. Doubts and assertions as regards the hardship of achieving real decolonization have often been raised and referred to the concept of neocolonialism as Nayar remarks that "Neocolonialism is furthered in the former colonies through the role of the elite. Whether in economics or academia, Westernized intellectuals, specialists and cultural intermediaries determine the debates, policies and actions of governments and institutions, and control the flow of ideas" (2015: 115). The gap between this class of elites and the masses has been widened to a great extent, which discloses a new phase of exploitation triggered by the native black colonizers. This group of local elites was sent to Europe for their education prepared by the colonialist ideology and rationale, which resulted in the fact that their living and thinking ways entirely imitated the Western fashion since they adopted the belief that the colonial thoughts and manners are superior to theirs and that they had to abandon their native culture (MacQueen, 2007). Therefore, this education generated new types of black people who began to think that their indigenous cultural features are essential to be modified or fully left on their route to the modern and civilized world. These leaders could "justify their political rule and claims of cultural superiority over their own countrymen in the name of their privileged access to the narratives of modernization" (Krishna, 2009: 4). The main factor in their alienation and contempt for their native population was being indoctrinated with the Western notions which forced them to believe that development can be achieved with the application of the white masters' methods.

As Birmingham puts it, "The new rulers not only preserved the frontiers of their colonial adversaries but also hitched their postcolonial fortunes to the former colonizers" (2009: 5). On the surface, anti-colonial uprisings seemed to grant the native society freedom and radical transformations that they had longed for ages; nevertheless, this process only gave rise to more political prospects for the native elites and carried on the same means of economic colonization as in the colonial age (Kohn and McBride, 2011: 106). The lack of nutritional, monetary and other vital sources for the masses in the ex-colonized lands has not been removed and bettered even after their local leaders' occupying the administrative position, often as a result of not being elected by their society in a democratic voting system. As a result, the new system came to produce nothing more than an economic drawback as well as political failure due to the fact that the local elites accomplished their assignment to keep on the flow of the goods and materials to the colonialist nations in reference to the commands of the colonizers.

Another subject matter regarding the emergence of neo-colonial tendencies in the ex-colonized lands that has been raised in postcolonial literary products has to do with the perception of absolute decolonization whose existence has often been suspicious owing to some developments in the once colonized countries. The literary texts which concentrate on real decolonization usually reveal the author's worries about the likelihood that the colonizing countries could find a way of maintaining their colonialist system in which they might exploit the native land without weapons. This system is put into action by means of the local elites that are very willing to colonize their native citizens in favour of the white colonizers. To what extent this system might be demolished has been disputed for ages, and two views on decolonization have been predominantly accepted. One of these views contends that a violent revolution must be carried out by all of the members of a colonized nation with sincerity, anti-colonialist sentiments and the sense of a collective soul. Through this revolution, it seems likely that the impacts of colonialism on the colonized peoples could be wiped out forever and that a new system could be established with the participation of the masses as Fanon asserts that the only way of devastating the colonialist system and its malady is to fall back on the same method utilized by the colonial powers and which comprised the violence of "searing bullets and bloodstained knives" (1963: 37). On the other hand, the second view asserts that the impacts of colonialism seem to have been so deep and persistent that it is nearly pointless to organize and put into effect anti-colonialist intentions in order to construct an order that is founded on the native values of the colonized nations, so these nations are doomed to live together with the colonial influences on the cultural, economic and political dimensions. In relation to this issue, Bhabha offers the Algerian revolution as an example of how impossible it became for the postcolonial nations to purge their cultural milieu of the Western bearings:

> In the moment of liberatory struggle, the Algerian people destroy the continuities and constancies of the nationalist tradition which provided a safeguard against colonial

cultural imposition. They are now free to negotiate and translate their cultural identities in a discontinuous intertextual temporality of cultural difference. The native intellectual who identifies the people with the true national culture will be disappointed. The people are now the very principle of "dialectical reorganization" and they construct their culture from the national text translated into modern Western forms of information technology, language, dress. (1994: 38)

Bhabha's argument gives an account of the interwoven structure which comes into being as a result of intermingling of the native elements with the Western norms; thus, revolution that is relied on as a means of achieving an anti-Western formation in the ex-colonized nations does not come to the expected conclusion in terms of the ones who desire to attain a totally native operation of the political and cultural system.

3 The Windrush generation

Those who immigrated to Britain in the post-war period from the Caribbean consisted of not only workers who were escaping from their homeland and who were struggling to overcome the colonial problems. "Ex-servicemen, teachers, students, writers and intellectuals" were also among them who have been called the "Windrush generation" as a result of immigration "before the 1968 Act" (MacPhee, 2011: 43). This generation became the source of inspiration for the following ones who were hearing that the leading citizens of the Caribbean were leaving the islands one by one with the aim of benefiting from the promising circumstances of the British metropolis which they imagined was equipped with any means and opportunities necessary for their development.

Among the immigrants who left their homeland with the purpose of having a more prosperous life and a higher career, there were some intellectuals "who had fled their home towns and villages with one driving purpose in mind: to become a writer" (Schwarz, 2003: 9). The post-war Britain was thought to possess a shining and engaging metropolis like London in which the Caribbean intellectuals and literary figures would find scholarly sources and libraries while producing many theoretical and literary writings owing to the presence of well-known publishing houses and fitting conditions for their careers. The Windrush generation involved the Caribbean writers such as "C.L.R. James, George Lamming, Wilson Harris and V.S. Naipaul and Sam Selvon" (Weedon, 2004: 68). They produced literary works making up the fundamental part of the postcolonial literary tendencies and aimed to propose their individual postcolonial discourses regarding the outcomes of colonialism in the once colonized nations as well as the possible solution methods for these nations that were just trying to recuperate from the colonial wounds in economic, political and cultural terms.

Believing that it is not impossible for the colonized black nations and particularly the Caribbean peoples to restore the natural gifts and capacities hidden under the racist pressure, C. L. R. James draws upon "the dangers of a nationalism predicated solely on race, fearing with typical prescience that racialist nationalism could obscure the aspirations of mass participation and creativity, exchanging white oppressors for Black" (Harney, 2006: 182). Thus, James, most probably considering the structure of the Caribbean islands which consist of a variety of races and ethnic societies and being worried about the tendency of this structure to be easily divided through racial conflicts, envisages that basing nationalism solely on racial notions would give rise to political regimes where native rulers do not regard the valuable potential of the lower class citizens and their involvement in the ruling process of the country. Instead of relying on literary products like the novel as one of the most appropriate means of generating national sentiments for the unity of the islands, he makes it clear that cricket carries the capability of keeping the native citizens' national and collective sensitivities at higher levels because of being played commonly all over the islands as the favourite game and as a carrier of cultural values, which can be noticed in one of his novels, *Beyond A Boundary*, which deals with the idea that the federation attempts in the Caribbean islands turned out to be mere failure even though James desired the islands to be ruled by means of a federation until that disappointment and that literature cannot create enough space to establish a national solidarity as can be understood from that experience (Szeman, 2003). James must have observed that sport events could be more successful in gathering native people around the concept of nation and brotherhood given that these events are held in front of many people and watched across the world, particularly when they took place in international organizations, but literary texts are consumed not with crowds simultaneously but individually, which provides them with less capacity to make readers concentrate on national enthusiasm and national unity.

Rather than attempting to refute the claims of the colonialist nations concerning the inferiority of the colonized nations and to encourage the colonized ones to fight the colonial oppression, Naipaul does not suppose himself as a Caribbean citizen who belongs to the cultural and political peculiarities of those islands, but prefers to situate himself in a transnational position where he can occupy and enjoy the advantages of a "universal civilization" (Thomas, 2003). He is of the opinion that the cultural and political structure of once colonized nations was so overwhelmingly destroyed and the imperialist nations' impact on those nations was so unshakable that the Third-World nations are under the obligation of getting accustomed to living with that impact and damage, so their attempts to rebuild an anti-colonialist order in terms of all aspects are futile. As for his notions on the Caribbean islands, it can be observed that in his novels "The Caribbean was a place in which people were divided by race, filled with resentments and lacked shared myths. They had no history of cooperation, or the wealth to provide comfort to losers of office" (King, 2003: 194). On account of such inner conflicts that have been inherent in the Caribbean population, the islands will not be able to settle down and construct a new tranquil system where not any chaotic event and upheaval exist. Because each racial and ethnic population has its own historical facts and distinctive social experience despite being destructed by the colonialist powers, each of them possesses different tendencies and needs, especially in social, cultural and political aspects, which enlarge the gap between the societies in the Caribbean and which make them very pertinent to being exploited by any powers. Moreover, his views on colonialism can be said to be ambiguous in that he frequently stresses the point that European powers enslaved and plundered the sources of the colonized nations while introduced civilization and modern thinking to those nations that lagged behind the civilized world with inner struggles and constant attacks caused by other Eastern nations (King, 2003). Therefore, Naipaul can be accepted neither as an intellectual who ardently criticizes and rejects the colonialist ambitions nor as an enthusiastic supporter of the colonized nations as he finds deficient sides in both European powers and the colonized nations.

George Lamming does not seem to display any pessimistic feelings about the possibility of constructing a system that is based on an anti-colonialist grounding despite the fact that the Caribbean islands experienced oppressive and destructive effects of colonialism for long years. Exile is often touched upon in his works as Thiong'o emphasizes that "In his novels he seems to go further, to suggest that exile – a physical removal or withdrawal from one's immediate society – is an active process, and almost necessary" (1978: 127). Consequently, experiencing exile in the imperial metropolises such as London does not generate alienated individuals for the colonized nations, functioning as an essential part of gaining their real consciousness and the sense of unity among themselves. If members of the colonized nations want to subvert the colonial process and its impacts for their overall decolonization, they have to leave their homeland in order to observe and experience oppressive manners that emerge owing to their black colours in the metropolitan centres of the Western countries, which prompt them to return back to their native lands as transformed and new individuals who enthusiastically desire an order in which solidarity, brotherhood, peace and nationalist feelings are dominant constituents instead of the imperialist policies. Imagining that "the new West Indian nation is to be produced through the production of an essential West Indian identity that transcends the particularities of discrete islands", Lamming does not hesitate to claim that immigrating to the Western metropolises paves the way for founding a federation system in the Caribbean which could arise from a durable recovery and restoration after immigrants' psychological damage that they had while in the imperial centre (Szeman, 2003: 96). Therefore, he supposes that it is necessary for the Caribbean society to put aside their racial and cultural distinctions if they want to establish an anti-colonial political regime and that it is highly possible for the Caribbean peoples to achieve such an end after living away from the islands for a while and thus comprehending their common sufferings in the colonial processes and coming closer to each other more intimately.

As opposed to the notion that the population of the Caribbean islands possesses certain cultural borders isolated from each other, Sam Selvon supposes the Caribbean islands, not least Trinidad, as a territory in which a variety of cultures exist by lending and borrowing from each other, sometimes from the European culture, and thus presenting a cultural richness or a creolized cultural atmosphere, instead of a gloomy and poor blending, which the native people enjoy experiencing instead of a gloomy blending (Harney, 2006). He evaluates the existence of such various cultures and races in the Caribbean islands from an optimistic viewpoint, suggesting that the cultural distinctions among the native societies should not be seen as a means of causing antagonistic divisions among each other because their original cultural values could not retail their essential characteristics in isolated frontiers in the face of a profound interaction of different cultures in the islands. Playing with language by using the non-standard form and context, Selvon, who has left an enormous impact on his next generations with his approach to London and linguistic forms, draws attention to the "mongrel" nature of the London city which takes in an intricate world of black immigrants and reflects these immigrants by deconstructing their stereotyped position (Nasta, 2004). Through a variety of experiences and the use of non-standard English, his characters exemplify the perception that sharp generalizations cannot be reached easily in spite of their collective problems and that even their linguistic features confirm the impossibility of their overall adaption to the British culture and overall dissociation from the Caribbean past.

4 Conclusion

As a conclusion, which may be drawn from the discussions above, it could be said that postcolonial literature makes reference to the lasting influence of colonialism on the ex-colonized peoples in many respects and seeks to offer credible solutions if possible. Postcolonial scholars seem to be in disagreement with regard to any solution which could dispel the colonial plague from the native land in a permanent way. As for the Caribbean writers of the Windrush generation, it might be claimed that each of them lays out his distinctive suggestion which bears on the resonance of migration on the basis of either its healing or fragmenting impression.

References

Acheraiou, A. (2008). *Rethinking Postcolonialism*. New York: Palgrave Macmillan.

Ahluwalia, P. (2001). *Politics and Post-colonial Theory*. London: Taylor & Francis.

Ashcroft, B., Griffiths, G., and Tiffin, H. (2004). *The Empire Writes Back*. New York and London: Taylor & Francis.

Bhabha, H. (1994). *The Location of Culture*. New York: Routledge.

Birmingham, D. (2009). *The Decolonization of Africa*. London: Taylor & Francis.

Boehmer, E. (2005). *Colonial and Postcolonial Literature*, 2nd Edition. Oxford: Oxford University Press.

Chambers, I. (2001). *Migrancy, Culture, Identity*. London and New York: Taylor & Francis.

Fanon, F. (1963). *The Wretched of the Earth*, Trans. Constance Farrington. New York: Grove Press.

Gandhi, L. (1998). *Postcolonial Theory*. Australia: Allen & Unwin.

Harney, S. (2006). *Nationalism and Identity*. Jamaica: University of the West Indies Press.

Jameson, F. (1986). "Third-world literature in the era of multinational capitalism." *Social Text*, 5(3): 65–88. Retrieved 02.05.2016 from https://www.jstor.org/stable/pdf/466493.pdf

King, B. (2003). *V. S. Naipaul*, 2nd Edition. New York: Palgrave Macmillan.

Kohn, M., and McBride, K. (2011). *Political Theories of Decolonization*. New York: Oxford University Press.

Krishna, S. (2009). *Globalization and Postcolonialism*. USA: Rowman and Littlefield.

MacPhee, G. (2011). *Postwar British Literature and Postcolonial Studies*. Edinburgh: Edinburgh University Press.

MacQueen, N. (2007). *Colonialism*. UK: Pearson Education Limited.

Moslund, S. P. (2010). *Migration Literature and Hybridity*. USA and UK: Palgrave Macmillan.

Nasta, S. (Ed.) (2004). *Writing across Worlds*. New York and London: Taylor & Francis.

Nayar, P. K. (2015). *The Postcolonial Studies Dictionary*. UK: Wiley.

Said, E. (1994). *Culture and Imperialism*. New York: Vintage.

Schwarz, B. (2003). "Introduction: Crossing the seas", In *West Indian Intellectuals in Britain*, edited by Bill Schwarz. UK: Manchester University Press, 1–31.

Sivanandan, A. (2008). *Catching History on the Wing: Race, Culture and Globalization*. Pluto Press, London.

Szeman, I. (2003). *Zones of Instability: Literature, Postcolonialism and the Nation*. London: The Johns Hopkins University Press.

Thiong'o, N. (1978). *Homecoming*. London: Heinemann Educational Books.

(1987). *Decolonizing the Mind*. Zimbabwe: Zimbabwe Publishing House.

Thomas, S. (2003). "V. S. Naipaul", In *West Indian Intellectuals in Britain*, edited by Bill Schwarz. UK: Manchester University Press, 228–248.

Viswanathan, G. (1998). *Masks of Conquest: Literary Study and English Rule in India*. Oxford: Oxford University Press.

Weedon, C. (2004). *Identity and Culture: Narratives of Difference and Belonging*. England: Open University Press.

Gonca Uncu and Gülsüm Çalışır

Gender of Color: When Did Girls and Boys Start to Wear Pink and Blue?

1 Introduction

Every generation develops new definitions of femininity and masculinity during their era. These definitions begin with the birth of the person and continue throughout the life of the person. Our behaviors, attitudes, and looks are largely determined by society/community. Sex discrimination begins with the birth of the child and reflects itself out with baby clothes. The colors of baby clothes are also determined by the society. Every color has different meanings in different cultures. However, some colors were proposed for baby boys and girls worldwide. Thus, the meaning of these specific colors is also used in sex discrimination from the beginning of very first days in someone's life. Because the names given to children are not considered enough to distinguish gender, the most important factor that plays a decisive role in the child's physical appearance is the clothes and the colors of these clothes. Common wisdom is pink for girls and blue for boys. The history of this belief is very old. The use of pink and blue in baby clothing first appeared in the mid-19th century. However, the use of colors for gender discrimination precedes World War I.

Today, pink and blue are turned into consumer goods and popular culture symbols. Especially pink, which is a symbol of femininity, is symbolized by the popular color of girls and women. The identification of women and men with color has a direct effect on consumption habits as well as gender roles. It is not common to see a man dressed in a pink sweater. Comparing to pink, blue is less restrictive color. According to the researchers, blue might be preferred for both genders but blue is still a dominating color for males.

Discriminating gender by these specific colors is strongly criticized for being a component of marketing from fashion to consumer goods. It is discussed by researchers whether it is necessary to have gender color and this separation is a real need for the community. This study focuses on the history of color representation of gender, its evaluation in time, and why gender needs color distinction.

2 Gender and color

The origin of the word "gender" goes to the 1970s. Gender refers to social behaviors, roles, and activities based on the sex of a person. Men and women who make up the society are exposed to gender discrimination (Ökten, 2009: 303). The gender roles of women and men are shaped by the society's expectations about their behaviors and duties. These expectations are taught by the cultural norms of the society during the socialization process of women and men. In these cultural codes, woman is always the weak one who needs protection by man. She is obedient and tenderhearted. Her physical look makes her a needy and dependent personal. On the contrary to woman, man is always strong, brave, and warier. His main role is being powerful and protecting his women and his land. These gender roles abide by men and women from the beginning of humankind (Oglesby and Hill, 1993: 720). These roles are determined by social and cultural habits and traditions, not by biological differences. The society expects to exhibit these behaviors from men and women by setting specific archetypes for the people. These expectations make man and woman passive in the society. Each gender lives with the roles imposed on and exhibits learned behaviors. In particular, women are the most damaged one about gender equality. How she is going to act, walk, dress, and speak are all determined by invisible rules in the community (Çalışır and Çakıcı, 2015: 7). When individuals act different from the gender roles determined by the society, they can face with exclusion from the society. Breaking down these stereotyped beliefs and roles is difficult and often impossible (Henslin, 2003: 289). Those who act outside these roles are called "marginal." They have to live in abstraction from the society and face many elements of social repression.

Each society redefines masculinity and femininity identities with its cultural criteria according to time they live in. The individual whose gender roles and choices are determined by the society is a passive entity whose looks and behaviors are determined from the moment of birth. It is a matter of curiosity about how the gender segregation phenomenon, which is physically made visible through color separation in accordance with the birth of the child, is born and spread. The first use of blue and pink to distinguish girls and boys was just before the World War I. However, the identification of girls with pink first started in the mid-19th century (Maglaty, 2011). It is seen that both girls and boys were worn white lace dresses without regarding any separation in the 1800s. The reason for this is that the purity of white color represents cleanliness and innocence. Another reason to prefer white is that its cleaning is easy. Another view considers that gender is the regulator of social relations and the behavior of individuals and is therefore necessary and useful within the social order. The social roles produced for women and men are also cultural constructs at the same time. Whereas describing a woman and a man by their gender roles is to imprison them in a certain area. Women and men are intellectually free individuals. Therefore, it is inadequate to identify them with cultural variables determined by the society (Scott, 2007: 11).

Cultural norms and beliefs have also changed and transformed people's color preferences. Today, many different cultures have identified the pink with the girls and the blue with the boys. Therefore, the child sees these colors and is surrounded by these distinctive colors from the time of birth. However, the child is not aware of this distinction until the age of one. According to a research, a boy can reach the distinction that the pink is not his own color at the age of two. Girls and boys are aware of the sex difference from the age of two and they can understand the definition of girl–boy distinction through what they see around them. The color choices that children are exposed to determine children's behavior as well as parents' behavior toward children (Hammond, 2014).

Photo 1 and 2: 32ⁿᵈ President of the United States: Franklin Delano Roosevelt, New York, 1884 (Bentman, Corbis)

(https://www.buzzfeed.com/bennyjohnson/fdr-had-the-greatest-childhood-ever?utm_term=.amDqqoLMP#.we0JJEwQG)

Until the end of the 1800s, the gender difference was not considered and all children were dressed in elegant white-collared dresses and skirts. In Photo 1, the white dress and the skirt that the American President Franklin Delano Roosevelt wears tell us how clothing habits were in 1884 in the United States. Sex discrimination is not recognized in children's haircuts as well. In his book *Pink and Blue: Telling the Boys from the Girls in America*, historian Paoletti (2013) investigated the stages of this dramatic change and searched when children were given up wearing these natural white clothes and they were forced to pink and blue distinction. The author mentions that children have been dressed in white clothes until the age of six over the centuries. Parents are afraid that the wrong colors will lead the child to heresy after certain age (Maglaty, 2011).

The concept of gender of colors belongs to the 20th century, and it is specific to the Western world. The fashion and textile industry rapidly developed along with the Industrial Revolution. In this period, the colors have been diversified and colors specific to girls and boys have begun to be proposed. Until the 1800s, pink was a color used especially by boys, while blue was a color that girls wear too. In 1918, a magazine called *Ladies' Home Journal* claimed that pink is more suitable for men because of its stable and strong color, and that the blue is the most suitable color for girls because it looks more delicate and elegant (Frevele, 2011). Until the 1950s, pink and blue were not united with girls and boys. In Nazi Germany, the pink was identified with femininity. Nazis labeled homosexuals by using a pink triangle form. In the Christian belief, blue was a feminine color since Holy Virgin was depicted by blue in the tradition. Due to this religious belief, the ritual of blue dressing for girls was widespread. However, this view changed permanently in the 1950s by thinking that pink is the best color for girls and blue is the color most suitable for boys. It is argued that the identification of pink with the woman started with a movie named "Funny Face" in the 1950s. The pink clothes of Audrey Hepburn in the movie led to the identification of pink with the woman (Frassanito and Pettorini, 2008: 881–882). As can be seen, the identification of girls with pink is a concept that belongs to the 20th century and has spread uncontrollably by capitalism. The 1970s was the beginning of the era when the pink enfolded the girls. Increasing mass production and growing chain of stores along with rising capitalism have fostered consumption society and gender discrimination has been used as a tool of consumption. The pink has become one of the means of making this distinction and increasing consumption. Today, this color creates a uniform image of women, imprisoning girls within the borders of the pink. In the girl children's department of toy stores, pink is a dominant and also very eye tiring color. There is a more diversity in boys' departments. For boys, there is a more liberal choice of clothes, colors, and toys. Almost all toys belonging to girls are designed for their appearance, not their mental development, and all the toys and clothes are in pink tones. "Pink" is not just a name of color, it is the name of a label that is affixed on the woman since childhood, and it has been turned into a popular culture icon (Arıcan, 2012). Arıcan (2012) criticized this issue in the following way and argued that girls were intentionally prevented from mental development since childhood:

> In the pink painted department store for girls, there was not one toy to introduce science to the girls and make them to think among Disney's princess toys, princess clothes, makeup and manicure sets, and even toy credit cards with Disney's princess picture on it. All of the toys seemed to teach girls to dress up, blush, and wait for the prince on white horse without thinking about science and real life issues.

The sex discrimination by color is shaped in American culture. In 1927, the *Times* magazine published a list of American stores where color-coded clothes were sold. In most of the shops in this period, pink clothes for boys were offered and sold. Until the 1940s, certain color patterns were not dictated to boys and girls. With increasing mass production, the child's style has been redefined and clothing preferences have been permanently determined by sex discrimination. Girls are expected to wear like their mothers and boys like their fathers at the school. But the breakup of this taboo by women has started with feminism and women's freedom movements in the 1960s. In this era, women who opposed the definition of masculinity and demanded equal rights had come up with a so-called phrase: "Tomgirl." The phrase of Tomgirl emphasizes the place and importance of the woman in the society, and at the same time, it starts a period in which the woman can also be seen as more masculine as man and be able to wear unlimited clothes and colors (Paoletti, 2013).

Sex discrimination by color is popularized by popular culture and pink has been turned into a symbolic color for girls with a conscious perception. American culture has made an important contribution for pink to be the icon of popular culture. One of the most concrete examples of this is the Barbie doll culture. The Barbie doll, which has an important role in the life of girls and their socialization, defines female and gender roles for girls since it has been created in the 1940s. Exposed to intense criticism of gender discrimination, every tone of pink is used in the logos, packaging, and clothes of Barbie dolls (Uncu, 2015). A Barbie doll is sold every three seconds around the world, and this doll touches almost every child's life in the world. So the perfect life that Barbie has is causing girls to admire the pink from their early ages. Girls want to look like Barbie (Rogers, 1999: 15–20). This is a desire for something unrealistic and it has a rather devastating effect in the life of girls. Every kind of textile and beauty product known as Barbie pink is a cultural bombardment carried out on women. This pink bombardment, where girls are exposed from a young age, supports consumptionism. This intentional color pressure over the girls restricts girls and makes them unqualified personals in the society.

3 Conclusion

In this study, girls' and boys' attitudes toward colors have been analyzed in order to understand whether they are making an instinctive preference or they prefer them because the majority of textile products are in pink for girls and in blue for boys. It is concluded that the identification of colors by gender is a phenomenon belonging to the last century. This phenomenon became popular and is supported by the consumption society. This is a necessity for the consumption. The consumption society offers new habits and new forms of life to the consumers through advertising for its own continuity. Beginning from the 1950s, advertisements have imposed new forms of life and behaviors on people. Color is one of the elements of gender division. With this distinction, women are reminded of their femininity. With such a distinction, the woman has become an active demographic group at the socioeconomic scale. This is a distinction of modernism. Indeed, in the medieval period, bright colors such as pink, red, and purple represent the magnificence, and the kings and aristocrat class preferred these colors. Today, it can be said that the construction of masculinity and womanhood is a reflection of the consumption society. The preference of pink and blue is actually an imposition of popular culture on girls and boys. The choice of gift and clothing according to sex is the reflection of this imposition. However, such a distinction didn't exist in the 19th century. The children were dressed in white clothes and lace dresses without any gender discrimination. Other colors began to be used beside white over the years. However, this situation did not directly lead to a gender division at that time. The 1900s were a time when colors were reflected more on children's clothes. Unlike today, pink colors were recommended for boys and blue colors were recommended for girls in this period. Proposition of different colors for different sex is a necessity for the growth of capitalism and industrialism. When it came to the 1920s, the dress became a proper outfit only for girls and the boys started wearing pants. This new color distinction reflected in all the clothes. In the 1940s, the distinction between pink for girls and blue for boys was accepted by textile companies. Until the 1980s, despite the rise of anti-separation voices and campaigns, the textile industry flaunted production with color and dominated the market for clothing style fashions by sex. So that a man dressed in pink is found strange, it is thought to in a gay style or a "girl-like" clothing. Color is a concept that exists in nature, and nature has not imposed such a distinction on people. This distinction is a created phenomenon by human effort. The cause is closely related to capitalism and is a pattern created to produce and consume more. In order to raise free and independent women, there is a need for generations that cannot comprehend these patterns, think multifaceted, and make their own choices. Children must be freely dressed to stop this distinction. Parents have a significant role in this change.

References

Arıcan, I. (2012). Kızlar Pembe Giyer, Erkekler Mavi. http://www.acikbilim. com/2012/04/dosyalar/kizlar-pembe-giyer-erkekler-mavi.html Access date: 03.04.2017

Çalışır, G. and Çakıcı, O. F. (2015). Toplumsal Cinsiyet Bağlamında Sosyal Medyada Kurulan Benlik İnşasının Temsili. *Turkish Studies – International Periodical for the Languages, Literature and History of Turkish or Turkic*, Vol. 10 (10): 267–290.

Frassanito, P. and Pettorini, B. (2008). Pink and blue: the color of gender. *Children's Nervous System*, Vol. 24 (8): 881–882.

Frevele, J. (2011). Tracing the Origins of Gender-Specific Clothing for Children. https://www.themarysue.com/gender-specific-clothing-for-children/ Access date: 14.05.2016

Hammond, C. (2014). The 'Pink Vs. Blue' Gender Myth. *BBC Future*. http://www. bbc.com/future/story/20141117-the-pink-vs-blue-gender-myth Access date: 03.05.2017

Henslin, J. M. (2003). Social Problems. New Jersey: Prentice Hall.

Maglaty, J. (2011). When Did Girls Start Wearing Pink? http://www.smithsonia nmag.com/arts-culture/when-did-girls-start-wearing-pink-1370097/ Access date: 03.04.2017

Oglesby, C. A. and Hill, K. L. (1993). Gender and Sport, Handbook of Research on Sport Psychology. New York: Macmillan Publishing Company.

Ökten, Ş. (2009). "Toplumsal Cinsiyet ve İktidar: Güneydoğu Anadolu Bölgesinin Toplumsal Cinsiyet Düzeni". *Uluslararası Sosyal Araştırmalar Dergisi*, 2/8 Summer, 303–312.

Paoletti, J. B. (2013). Pink and Blue: Telling the Boys from the Girls in America. Indiana: Indiana University Press.

Rogers, M. (1999). Barbie Culture. London: SAGE Publications.

Scott, J. W. (2007). Toplumsal Cinsiyet: Faydalı Bir Analiz Kategorisi, Çeviren: Aykut Tunç Kılıç. İstanbul: Agora Kitaplığı.

Uncu, G. (2015). Popüler Kültür İkonu Olarak 'Barbie' Bebek; Toplumsal Cinsiyet Bağlamında Yaratılan Yeni Kadın İmgesi. 1. Uluslararası Oyun ve Oyuncak Konfersansı, 6–8 Mayıs, Erzurum.